Contemporary Russia
as a Feudal Society

Contemporary Russia as a Feudal Society

A New Perspective on the Post-Soviet Era

Vladimir Shlapentokh

In Collaboration with Joshua Woods

palgrave
macmillan

CONTEMPORARY RUSSIA AS A FEUDAL SOCIETY
Copyright © Vladimir Shlapentokh 2007.

First published in 2007 by
PALGRAVE MACMILLAN™
175 Fifth Avenue, New York, N.Y. 10010 and
Houndmills, Basingstoke, Hampshire, England RG21 6XS.
Companies and representatives throughout the world.

PALGRAVE MACMILLAN is the global academic imprint of the Palgrave Macmillan division of St. Martin's Press, LLC and of Palgrave Macmillan Ltd. Macmillan® is a registered trademark in the United States, United Kingdom and other countries. Palgrave is a registered trademark in the European Union and other countries.

ISBN-13: 978-0-230-60096-6
ISBN-10: 0-230-60096-4

Library of Congress Cataloging-in-Publication Data

Shlapentokh, Vladimir.
   Contemporary Russia as a feudal society : a new perspective on the post-Soviet era / Vladimir Shlapentokh ; in collaboration with Joshua Woods.
      p. cm.
   Includes bibliographical references and index.
   ISBN 0-230-60096-4 (alk. paper)
   1. Russia (Federation)—Social conditions—1991– 2. Russia (Federation)—Politics and government—1991– 3. Russia (Federation)—Economic conditions—1991– I. Woods, Joshua. II. Title.

HN530.2.A8S547 2008
947.086—dc22   2007017988

A catalogue record of the book is available from the British Library.

Design by Westchester Book Group

First edition: December 2007

10 9 8 7 6 5 4 3 2 1

Printed in the United States of America.

To my dear Russian sociologists Boris Firsov, Boris Grushin, Elena Petrenko, Vladimir Shubkin, and Vladimir Yadov, whom I love and highly respect.

"EACH TIME HAS ITS OWN MIDDLE AGES."

Iosif Trachtenberg

CONTENTS

Acknowledgments ix

Introduction 1

1 The Failure of the Integrative-System Approach
in Post-Soviet Russian Studies 7

2 The Segmented Approach and Feudal Model
for the Study of Post-Soviet Russia 19

3 Weakness of the State 35

4 Oligarchs and Corrupt Bureaucrats 55
The Purchase of Political Power

5 The Oligarchic Ideology and Its Opposition
to the Liberal and Totalitarian Ideologies 75

6 The Royal Domain 85
*The Thin Line between the Nation's Assets
and the President's Private Wealth*

7 The Local Barons after the Soviet Collapse 95
Ideology and Practice (1989–1996)

8 The Local Barons under Putin's Moderate Feudalism
(2000–2006) 117

9 The Precariousness of Property in Contemporary
Russia and the Middle Ages 133

10 Personal Relations as a Core Feature of Feudalism 151

11 Private Security 173
A Typical Feudal Phenomenon

Conclusion	183
Notes	191
Bibliography	237
Name Index	255
Subject Index	263

ACKNOWLEDGMENTS

First of all I would like to thank my collaborator Joshua Woods, with whom I worked jointly on literally each sentence and each idea in this book. Next, my sincere thanks goes to Arunas Juska, Larry Busch, Robert Solo, Peter Manning, Roger Kanet, and Eugene Huskey for their intellectual and emotional support of this project, as well as for their thoughtful comments. I am grateful to Dmitrii Shlapentokh and Vladimir Kontorovich, as well as Andrea Hamor and Vera Nikolskaia, with whom I discussed, for my great benefit, issues related to this text. My special thanks to Vera Bondartsova, who was a permanent and creative member of our small research group. Without this group I would not have realized many of the issues of contemporary Russia. I would also like to thank Vera for her editorial contributions to this text.

Introduction

In September 2006, the famous Russian journalist Aleksandr Minkin made a clever reference to Jonathan Swift's novel *Gulliver's Travels* to denounce the rampant corruption in Putin's regime. The journalist cited Swift's narration in the book of the statements made by high officials from three countries, Lilliput among them, who claimed to have never appointed a decent man to any position, because only wicked, mendacious, and hypocritical people made suitable leaders. As a matter of fact, Swift's classic tale has many inroads into contemporary Russia. It might also be used, for instance, to explain the hot public discussions in Moscow over the labeling of the country's political system.

Throughout the summer of 2006, the Russians watched with amazement as two of Putin's leading aides—Vladislav Surkov, a key Kremlin ideologue, and Dmitrii Medvedev, the first deputy chairman of the government and a possible heir to the Russian throne— vehemently debated the character of Russian society. The bickering between the two dignitaries, which began in June 2006, was similar to the famous struggle in the land of Lilliput between those who insisted on breaking eggs at the big end and their opponents who ardently preferred breaking eggs at the small end. While Surkov described Russian society as a "sovereign democracy," his opponent, responding a few months later, insisted that the adjective "sovereign" was redundant. He regarded the term as absurd if applied to the economy, which, in the global world, with the deep interdependence of all countries, cannot be sovereign.

In the process of their terminological wrangling, the participants of the debate, like the citizens of Mildendo, the Lilliputian capital, tried to distinguish between "sovereign democracy" and "managed democracy," between "sovereign democracy" and "democracy," and between "sovereign democracy" and "independent democracy." A similar debate emerged over whether the term "sovereign democracy" could be applied to Russia alone, or to any country that challenged the

United States, such as China or some Latin American countries, as suggested by the leading political scientist Andranik Migranian.

In Lilliput, the battle between the supporters of the different ways of breaking eggs led to 11,000 deaths. In Russia, the dispute between Surkov and Medvedev did not bring such a disaster, but passions in the summer of 2006 in Moscow ran high, and several dozen top politicians, scholars, and journalists joined the battle. The terminological squabble extended to the headquarters of the ruling party, "United Russia," where its leaders Oleg Morozov and Viacheslav Volodin were split in their fealty to the two Kremlin politicians. Valerii Zorkin, the chairman of the Constitutional Court, joined the discussion, taking Surkov's side and contending that his position was supported by the Russian constitution. Minister of Defense Sergei Ivanov also took Surkov's side and described "sovereign democracy," a "strong economy," and "military might" as the triad of Russia's "national values." The opposition finally joined in, mostly supporting Medvedev. They suggested that the use of any adjective for democracy implies that Russian democracy is not normal, a view that justifies Putin's authoritarian regime.

While the position of the Lilliputian emperor was understood by his subjects (he resolutely supported "Small Endians"), the Moscow elites had to guess which camp Putin favored, so as to be ready to "adjust their views immediately." Maxim Sokolov, a journalist with brilliant satirical talent, suggested that the victory or defeat of the adjective "sovereign" may predict which of the Kremlin clans will win in the 2008 presidential election. However, Putin sent out a blurry signal on his stance in the terminology war, refusing to take a clear public position and only acknowledging in his September 2006 meeting in Valday the importance of the debate over the adjective.

The argument over terminology in Russia only looks ridiculous on the surface. In his time, Swift disregarded the conflict's deep political, religious, and social roots. In the Russian case, the scuffle over terms reflected a serious problem that has faced the country since the collapse of Communism: the lack of consensus about the nature of society. The debate also revealed the country's animosity toward the West and the emphasis placed on "the Russian project of democracy." Those who defended the term "democracy" enrolled themselves in the anti-Western camp. They were particularly hostile, as the pro-Kremlin political scientist Sergei Markov noted, toward the countries that initiated the "color revolutions" (Ukraine and Georgia in the first place), claiming that their brand of democracy was weak and heavily influenced by the United States. These countries were regarded as "not sovereign."

The conflict over the term "sovereign democracy" represented only a small part of a much larger debate over the characterization of contemporary Russian society. Not only ordinary Russians but also experts inside and outside the country were at odds regarding almost all elements of society. As discussed in detail later, Russia was labeled in a number of different ways, from a "normal" Western-type country to a "criminal" society.

One of the basic assumptions of this book is that most of these labels accurately describe certain aspects of Russian society. Without denying the importance of the country's liberal, authoritarian, criminal, and other characteristics, this book introduces the "feudal model" for studying post-Soviet Russia. The weakness of the central administration is the most important element of the feudal model. This weakness is the cause of other feudal elements, including the emergence of multiple power centers, a heightened level of lawlessness and corruption in society, an increased need for private security, and the growing importance of personal relations in politics and the economy. While defining and stressing these feudal elements in the case of contemporary Russia, this book also utilizes a comparative approach. It draws specific parallels between post-Soviet Russia and several other societies, including contemporary Western democratic nations, the Soviet Union, and, most notably, Middle Ages Europe. The general goal of this book is to elucidate many otherwise strange and seemingly incompatible developments in contemporary Russia, a country that continues to play a crucial role in the world.

In the first two chapters of the book, I offer a review of the literature on contemporary Russia, a theoretical discussion of the feudal model, and a preliminary application of the model to post-Soviet Russia. In addition to a review of the feudal model as an ideal type, I explain the analytical benefits of drawing comparisons between countries and across historical contexts. The remainder of the book is devoted to illuminating the most important political, social, and economic characteristics of contemporary Russian society. Chapter 3 examines the weakness of the central administration (a key element of the feudal model) and its primary social consequences: crime, corruption, and political instability. The level of lawlessness in post-Soviet Russia demonstrates a clear break with the Soviet past, as well as a strong resemblance to Western European societies of the Middle Ages.

The next five chapters analyze the role of three major social actors in contemporary Russia: oligarchs, the president, and governors. Chapter 4 looks at the impact of oligarchs (given their enormous financial resources) on political outcomes—a phenomenon that was practically absent during the Soviet period. In Chapter 5, I analyze the feudal (or oligarchic) ideology, which justifies the feudal elements in society and legitimizes the roles of those who challenge the central administration. This chapter examines how the oligarchic ideology, "the ideology of the few," was directed against democratic institutions, "the rule of many," as well as against authoritarianism, "the rule of one." The oligarchic ideology suggests that only the leaders of big corporations, like the feudal lords of the Middle Ages, are equipped to run society. From this perspective, almost all of their activities, including crimes and acts of corruption, are beneficial to society.

Chapter 6 describes the Russian presidents' "domain" (that is, their personal control over state resources). As notoriously demonstrated by the Yeltsin regime, and to a lesser extent by Putin, the use of presidential power for the accumulation of personal wealth, while impossible during Soviet times, was commonplace in post-Soviet Russia. In the Middle Ages, kings and other leaders were also motivated by private wealth. In both cases, the leaders' personal riches were used to retain and expand their political power. Placing the focus on governors (or local barons), Chapters 7 and 8 describe the often tenuous relations between the center (Moscow) and the provinces. Disputes between local power centers and the central administration were common in both Middle Ages Europe and contemporary Russia. The intensity of these disputes fluctuated during the post-Soviet period, in line with the country's changing political and economic circumstances. As in the Middle Ages, the central administration was usually unable or unwilling to interfere in regional politics. The local barons were allowed to dominate life in the regions, while amassing vast fortunes for themselves, their families, and their close-knit social and political circles, which again links the Middle Ages to contemporary Russia.

The final three chapters of the book are centered on specific characteristics of contemporary Russia, all of which have close parallels in Middle Ages Europe. Chapter 9 focuses on the precariousness of private property in post-Soviet Russia. Chapter 10 treats the topic of personal relations—in contrast to the rationalized bureaucratic relations of ideal-type democracies—in Russian politics and economic matters. When it comes to the selection of cadres, "connections" mean everything in contemporary Russia, just as kinship ties represented key social patterns in the Middle Ages. The last chapter of the book describes private protection agencies (known as *krysha* or roof) as important aspects of Russian society. With the weakness of the state in the post-Soviet period, the role of protecting big businesses and powerful individuals was left in the hands of private organizations (some legal, some criminal).

In the Conclusion, I offer a succinct summary of the book's major points. I also develop a general argument that the feudal model, as demonstrated by the case of Russia, can be used as a fruitful analytical tool, in combination with other models, for understanding many contemporary societies.

CHAPTER 1

THE FAILURE OF THE INTEGRATIVE-SYSTEM APPROACH IN POST-SOVIET RUSSIAN STUDIES

INTRODUCTION

Although Americans are divided on many social and political issues, the majority of the population generally accepts the idea that private property, a market economy, and democratic institutions represent some of the fundamentals of American society. In Russia, at the beginning of the twenty-first century, there was not only intense polarization in people's attitudes toward specific political and economic issues, but also major differences in the way they characterized the society's political and economic systems.

The list of labels that experts use to characterize contemporary Russia is quite long. The first group of terms consists of general definitions of the society, such as "normal society," "transitional society," "transformational society," "Orthodox civilization," and "Euro-Asian civilization." The second group refers to political characteristics: "monarchism," "elected monarchy," "paternalistic society," "directed democracy," "sovereign democracy," "managed democracy," "super-presidential republic," "criminal-syndicalist state," "authoritarianism," "totalitarianism," "Putinism," "a democratic form of Caesar's rule," "feudalism," "a split society," and "Russian-style democracy." The third group of terms describes the society's economic structure: "oligarchic capitalism," "violent capitalism," "criminal capitalism," "kleptomaniac capitalism," "gangster capitalism," "predatory capitalism," "market bolshevism," "crony capitalism," "raw capitalism," "jungle capitalism," "corporate society," "shopkeeper's feudalism," "bureau-cratic-oligarchic capitalism," "nomenklatura capitalism," and "man-aged business." The fourth group stresses the issue of national identity, using terms such as "a society of ethnic Russians," "Eurasian nation," "international empire," "a country for all people who live in it," "a part of Western civilization," and "European nation." Finally, some authors focus on definitions related to the country's status in the world, includ-ing "superpower," "energetic superpower," and "raw materials attach-ment to developed countries."

As a matter of fact, the debates over the nature of twentieth-century Soviet society were also quite intense, both inside and outside the country. The official propaganda insisted that the Soviet Union was a true socialist society, while some Soviet intellectuals saw the so-ciety as having a "distorted socialism," and some Western Sovietolo-gists saw it as a totalitarian society that had nothing to do with socialism. However, the absolute majority of the Soviet people, in-cluding most of the intelligentsia, had no access to this debate and ac-cepted the official version. Therefore, the labeling of Soviet society, unlike post-Soviet Russia, carried no serious public importance.[1]

RUSSIA IS ALREADY A NORMAL SOCIETY OF THE WESTERN TYPE

Several admirers of the post-Soviet developments have been eager to declare that the reforms have been successful and that the transforma-tion of Russia is complete. In their opinion, Russia is a "normal soci-ety." Inside the country, this view has been advanced by Kremlin representatives. For instance, Vladislav Surkov, one of Putin's ideo-logues, declared in June 2006 that Russia was a "sovereign democ-racy."[2] Surkov's statement was accepted by the ruling party, "United Russia," as its ideological platform.[3] This view implies that Russia en-joys not only a normal democracy, as any Western country, but also a political order that takes Russian history into account and does not tolerate lessons from the West on the definition of democracy. Pro-Kremlin politicians and experts such as Andranik Migranian, Kirill Privalov, and Gleb Pavlovskii assume that "sovereign democracy" is already a "fait accompli,"[4] while others maintain that Russia is still in the processes of building it.[5]

Among Western experts, a similar premise about the normalcy of Russia was developed by Andrei Shleifer and Daniel Treisman, who substantiated their stance with economic analyses. In their view, a country's average income per head can be used as the major determinant of the social and political structure of society. They contend that it shapes the country's political organization, the level of development of the market economy, the level of corruption and crime, the role of big business in society, the level of democracy, the division of powers, the honesty of elections, media freedom, and violence against journalists. This peculiar form of economic determinism implies the universality of economic, social, and political processes in the world. Using this approach, they label Russia a "middle income democracy."[6]

Russia Will Eventually Become a Normal Society

Most universalists (who are usually optimists) recognize some problems with Russian democracy, but believe that the challenges will gradually disappear through the "process of bargaining and negotiation" between various actors. Yegor Gaidar, the director of the Institute of Transitional Economy, is among the most noted Russian "transitionalists," even if his publications after 2000 were less optimistic than those during the 1990s. In any case, as late as 2007, the name of his institute had not changed.[7] The term "transition," however, was so discredited in the late 1990s that several transitionalists adopted the vaguer term "transformation" to represent their school of thought. Among those who use this concept are two famous Russian sociologists: Tatiana Zaslavskaia, who sees the transformation process (even if "weakly managed") as the most important feature of society,[8] and Vladimir Yadov, who explicitly rejects the term "transition" and, citing Anthony Giddens, talks about "the incessant process of the transformation of social structures."[9] This view is supported by several social scientists, including L. Beliaeva[10] and L. A. Khakhulina.[11]

It is remarkable that, at an annual meeting held by the Moscow School of Social and Economic Sciences in 2007, the concepts of "transition" and "transformation," and even the term "dynamics," which had been dominant at the previous sessions in 2005–2006, almost disappeared and were replaced by vague terms such as "continuity" and "intermittence." What is more, in their flight from the terms that had prevailed only a few years before, the participants of the meeting resorted to the relatively narrow term "path dependency," which was mostly used to describe the dependence of technological progress on its previous level, as well as to a few other terms (to use only the titles from the papers given at the meeting), such as "evolution," "institutional heritage," "repetition of the past," "traditionalism," "restoration," and "reanimation."[12]

Several Western authors, even if they do not use the terms "transition" or "transformation," belong to the optimistic camp when it comes to describing Russia. In spite of the problem of corruption, Archie Brown is confident in "the building of capitalism in Russia"; he sees creating a "law-governed market economy" and "democracy" as Putin's major challenges.[13] David Lane holds a similar view. He accepts the liberal capitalist model for Russia and claims that the economy is "set in a mould of capitalism." In the 1990s, as he contends, the command economy was eliminated, market rules were established, and prices were determined by the market.[14] James Millar, an economist, is no less optimistic about the final victory of the market economy, because "the alternative, autarky, failed miserably."[15] Other universalists include political scientists Tom Remington,[16] Luke March,[17] R. W. Davies,[18] and William Cocherham.[19]

Some members of this group believe that Russia has no choice but to move toward a full-fledged liberal model, focusing, however, on the obstacles to achieving this goal. Such is the vision offered by Timothy Colton and Michael McFaul, who suggest that, "flawed though it may be, democracy is still a superior system to the alternative."[20]

These scholars do not suggest any other model for understanding Russian developments. While assessing the chances for "the infliction of full-blown dictatorship" as not very high, they still believe in the ultimate victory of the liberal model, particularly because of the growth of the economy and the middle class. When they reveal their apprehensions about an acceleration of antidemocratic trends in Russia, they do not consider what type of society Russia would become if such trends took hold.[21] Seeing the liberal model as the goal of Russian evolution, Cameron Ross wrote that "by reasserting the rule of law and due process, Putin's reforms are positive steps in creating equal rights for all citizens across the federation."[22] Eugene Huskey sees Putin as a leader whose actions may unintentionally push the country toward liberal society.[23]

AUTHORITARIANISM: CONTINUITY WITH THE USSR

A considerable number of analysts operate with the Soviet model as the best explanation of post-Soviet Russia. Those who belong to this group use labels such as "authoritarian" or "directed democracy." Liliia Shevtsova's definition of contemporary Russia oscillates between the "oligarchic authoritarianism" of the Yeltsin period and the "bureaucratic authoritarianism" of Putin's time.[24] Such is also the view of the famous sociologist Yurii Levada[25] and Russian historians V. Shelokhaev,[26] V. V. Zhuravlev,[27] V. N. Dakhin,[28] and N. G. Shcherbinina,[29] and the philosopher L. Poliakov.[30]

Among Western authors, Stephen White supports the "authoritarian" model and rejects the "transition" model outright: "Russia's post-communist experience cautions against some of these early mechanistic approaches (i.e., transition to democracy). Authoritarian forms of politics did not automatically give way to pluralism, and new constitutions did not automatically mean new politics."[31]

Nikolai Petrov and Darrell Slider belong to this group, even if they do not deny some liberal elements in post-Soviet Russia. They wrote: "When looking for parallels from Russian and Soviet history to understand Putin and his policy, the figure who most readily comes to mind is Yurii Andropov who started by emphasizing discipline and order." They also referred to Stalin, who, like Putin, came to power through intricate bureaucratic maneuvers. Stalin arranged for the regions to be led by his "loyal followers" and created a complicated system of power verticals that strengthened control over the regions.[32] Authors who see Russia as an authoritarian state use several surrogate terms, such as "Caesar's democratic rule"[33] or "directed democracy." Stephen Hedlund also gravitates toward the view that, with the failure of the economic reforms and the emergence of "predatory capitalism," Russia is returning to the old-style, autocratic rule.[34]

MONARCHISM AND EMPIRE: CONTINUITY IN RUSSIAN HISTORY (OR PATH DEPENDENCY)

Many scholars have characterized the country as a monarchy, which rejects the division of power, as in prerevolutionary Russia. The clearest defender of this view is Viktor Danilov, a famous Russian historian who talks about the restoration in Russia of "samoderzhavia" (or self-autocracy).[35] Another historian, A. I. Shcherbinin, insists that "in our country state power is understood exactly as Hobbes and Yurii Krizhnich (an apologist of the Russian absolutism of the seventeenth century) understood it, not as simply 'the property' of the tsar, but a sacral thing which can be transferred to the heir."[36] The same view is held by the prominent philosopher Vadim Mezhuev[37] and the sociologist Andrei Zdravomyslov.[38] Authors who use the names of Russian leaders to characterize the society ("Yeltsinism" or "Putinism") usually belong to the same "authoritarian" group.[39]

A number of authors, particularly those with nationalist orienta-
tions, focus on the concept of empire in their descriptions of Russia.[40]
The historian Aleksei Miller contends that "the empire is the oldest
form of social life" and is more viable than the "nation state."[41] These
authors glorify the tsarist and Soviet empires and insist that even now
Russia is in the process of forming "the Fifth Empire."[42] Followers of
the Eurasian ideology such as Aleksandr Dugin, the ideology's leading figure, also support the empire perspective and talk about Russia's
special mission in the world.[43]

Even liberals have shown interest in the concept of empire. For instance, Anatolii Chubais introduced the term "liberal empire."[44]
Chubais borrowed the idea from Piotr Struve, a Russian politician
who, before the revolution, also wanted to combine liberalism with
an imperial policy.[45] Chubais is followed by Leonid Gozman, an ideologue from the party "The Alliance of Right Forces," who contends
that "Russia is a natural empire."[46]

A Unique Civilization

A number of authors have proposed the idea that Russia represents a
special, unprecedented case in history. Andrei Konchalovskii, a prominent Russian intellectual, in his discussion on the crisis of Western liberalism, contends that the country, as in the past, represents a sort
of Byzantine civilization that glorifies its leader.[47] The philosopher
V. Fedotova calls Russia the "other Europe," explaining that even if
Russia is geographically close to Europe, it is clearly different from
the traditional European civilization.[48] Vladimir Yadov supports Fedotova's view,[49] while Aleksandr Akhiezer labels Russia a "split society,"
divided since the time of Peter the Great between two irreconcilable
parts, one pro-Western and one pro-Eastern.[50]

Distorted Economic Structure

Oligarchic Society as a System and a Model

A large group of authors describe Russia as an oligarchic society. Let
me begin with the authors who label Russia "oligarchic" (or corporate) but do not link it to feudalism. The term was particularly popular during Yeltsin's time. Many analysts, and not only journalists, used
the term "seven bankers' regime" (*semibankirshchina*) to describe the
country. It referred to a group of bankers who supported the Yeltsin
regime in exchange for major assets and influenced all major political

decisions in the Kremlin, particularly the selection of people for major state positions. The historian O. V. Gaman-Golutvina wrote about the dominance of "the political financial oligarchy that was fighting with the bureaucracy in 2000."[51] Another historian, S. Peregudov, noted the dominance of "corporate capital."[52] The same view was shared by his colleague V. I. Il'in.[53] Economist E. Maiminas talked about "the system of bureaucratic or bureaucratic-oligarchic capitalism."[54]

Several Western authors also describe Russia as an oligarchic society. The oligarchic model is used by William Tompson, who argues that corporate consolidation in Russia is extremely high. "Ownership was hardly dispersed in the late 1990s, but the post-devaluation recovery triggered a wave of mergers and acquisitions, largely driven by cash-rich exporters who began acquiring under-priced industrial assets at home."[55] The Russian authorities have not attempted to stop this trend.

Andrew Jack argues that the oligarchs have defined the economic system in Russia. "They symbolized a very curious, Russian-style form of capitalism. They were forces for growth and progress, but also meddled in politics and tried to impose a highly centralized form of development." At the same time, he talks about "managed business," pointing to the growing economic role of the state.[56] Peter Rutland sees post-Soviet Russia as an oligarchic society.[57] The advocates of "oligarchic capitalism" were close to a group that labeled contemporary Russia as "criminal capitalism" or a "criminal society."[58]

Bureaucratic Capitalism

The idea that Russia is ruled by bureaucrats began to spread in the late 1990s and particularly in Putin's time. Some authors talked about the continuity of the Soviet regime when bureaucracy ran society.[59] In late 2006, Aleksandr Sevast'ianov, a leftist political analyst, described Russia as a weak state with a deeply corrupt and irresponsible bureaucracy.[60] The term "crony capitalism" was close to "bureaucratic capitalism" and some authors, including Rutland, used the terms as synonyms.[61] Other authors talked about "Kremlin capitalism."[62]

Criminal (or Violent) Capitalism

The characterization of Russia as a criminal society was also quite common. For instance, Stanislav Govorukhin wrote a book about Russia called *Criminal Society*. Several others described the country in similar terms, including Grigorii Yavlinsky, who used the term "cor-porate-criminal system."[63] Vadim Volkov attempted to justify this concept with empirical data.[64] William Webster talked about a "crim-inal syndicalist" society.[65]

Antitheorists

A considerable number of scholars simply avoid even mentioning the-oretical constructions. Virginie Coulloudon describes the flourishing of corruption in post-Soviet Russia and the refusal of both presidents to fight it. She does not, however, say anything about the implications for the liberal model.[66] Some authors operate with dozens of concepts to describe Russia, and it is almost impossible to figure out which of them represents their ultimate vision.

FLAWS IN THE CURRENT DESCRIPTIONS OF RUSSIAN SOCIETY

Practically all definitions of Russian society are mutually exclusive, and it is not surprising that each of the proposals discussed above has met with strong resistance from other participants in the debate. Take, for instance, the idea that Russia is already a "normal society," which has been advanced by Shleifer and others. In order to substan-tiate their thesis that Russia is a "middle income democracy," Shleifer and his coauthor analyze the political order and economy of the country. The confrontational tone in their description of "the democ-racy of a middle income country" could be tolerated if the process of democratization had just begun, but not at a time when the vector of the political process has already moved in the opposite direction. It makes sense that they did not even mention the shelling of the Parlia-ment in 1993 when the trend toward the restoration of authoritarian-ism began. Against common sense, they describe the new constitution as "not undemocratic." They pretend, along with Surkov, that the State Duma is indeed an independent democratic body. They suggest that the Duma can overrule presidential decrees. This idea would only provoke laughter in Russia, from Kaliningrad to Kamchatka. Con-trary to the Russian people and analysts, they describe the elections as "free and fair," while totally ignoring the Russian data. The transition of power from Yeltsin to Putin did not arouse any suspicions about the country's democratic character.

The concept of "sovereign democracy," which, in fact, is intended to justify the departure of Russian society from the principles of democracy, has even been critiqued by some people close to the Kremlin.[67] Dmitrii Medvedev, the deputy chairman of the government, notes that the use of the adjective suggests that the authors of the term "have in mind something different than traditional democracy."[68]

The descriptions of Russian society in negative terms have flaws as well. The assertion that Russia is an authoritarian or even a totalitarian society is only partially true. Many developments in Russia are incompatible with the authoritarian model. Russian governors, for instance, enjoyed a great deal of autonomy within their regions. Despite the strong antidemocratic measures of the Kremlin, there are still some relatively free elections that influence the country's political processes.

The oligarchic model also falls short of explaining the major developments in Russia. It ignores or underestimates the role of the powerful central administration and the functioning of some liberal institutions. Several Russian authors rejected the oligarchic model, suggesting that it had been invented by bureaucrats who wanted to shift the blame for the country's problems onto greedy businesses. As described by Evgenii Chernov, a writer for the prestigious journal *Novoie Vremia,* in 2006, "It cannot be seriously asserted that oligarchs ruled Russia in the 1990s. After all, the influence of all the 'oligarchs' taken together was still incomparably less than the influence of the Chernomyrdin-Viakhirev group. And what about the Railroad Ministry? What about the Nuclear Energy Ministry and the RAO Unified Energy Systems? It was they, not the likes of Berezovskii or Friedman, who always had a grip on Russia's vital arteries." The author went on to insist that when certain ambitious "oligarchs" tried to control state officials, rather than the other way around, they rapidly found themselves elsewhere—some in London, some in Israel, and others in far less comfortable locations. The author argues that the oligarchs and big businesses in general were created by the bureaucracy and never played any independent role in Russian politics. Certain individuals and companies attempted to play politics, but they lost the game, instantly and hopelessly, as in the cases of Konstantin Borovoi, who created the first stock market in post-Soviet Russia, as well as the well-known entrepreneurs Artem Tarasov and the Chernyi brothers.[69]

A CRITIQUE OF THE INTEGRATIVE-SYSTEM APPROACH

The case of post-Soviet Russia shows that the attempts to define Russian society in terms of one "integrative system" (liberal, authoritarian, or any other) have not been productive. As a matter of fact, this problem can be seen in the analysis of many societies, including the United States, Mexico, and Japan. The most popular definition of the integrative system is "a whole that cannot be divided into independent parts without losing its essential properties or functions."[70] This concept can be a useful tool of analysis. Since the 1960s, when system analysis emerged as a special discipline, the concept has been successfully applied in several different areas of research, biology, linguistics, economics, and sociology, among others. The inclination to use one system for the analysis of any phenomenon in the world is deeply embedded in the scholarly mind. As noted by John Horgan, author of several books on the philosophy of science, "The pursuers of this 'theory of everything' have wandered in fantasy realms of higher dimensions with little or no connection with reality."[71]

However, the uncritical use of the concept in social analysis has led to problems, because neither the social nor the economic realms of life can be described in terms of one system. Those who used this approach tended to explain any element that did not fit the system as "residual," "marginal," or "temporary," even if these elements played a very important role in society. The Soviet ideologues, for instance, described the illegal markets and criminality as "the heritage of the past" or "the deleterious impact of the West." The analysts of the new African states that emerged after World War II described them as "normal democratic nations" and attributed the high levels of corruption and regular military coups to the abuses of the colonial past and the continued interference of imperialists in Africa. In a similar vein, American conservative thinkers who praise the country's democracy and free market usually describe the problems of corruption as "marginal" and "temporary."

Parsons' Holistic Vision of the World

The use of "one system" for the analysis of society follows the integrative-system approach developed by Parsons, whose "grand theory of society" adhered to a universalistic and holistic vision of the world.[72] The integrative-system approach was used by many scholars in Parsons' time and after it. Ruth Benedict, in her *Patterns of Culture,* supposed that it was possible to identify one key factor that could describe a whole society.[73] She offered a concept that explains American culture as dominated by feelings of guilt and Japanese culture as dominated by feelings of shame. Those who support this view, however, are forced to note that both mechanisms can be found in

any culture, though in different proportions.[74] Scholars have identi-
fied other key factors, such as Harry Triandis' notion of collectivism
versus individualism, self-enhancement versus self-transcendence, and
Shalom Schwartz's concept of "openness to change."[75]

The Political and Economic Dichotomy of the Integrative-System Approach

In the spirit of the holistic approach, there is a strong tendency among
social scientists to assume that any given society can be politically clas-
sified as either democratic or authoritarian. During the second half of
the twentieth century, this dichotomous approach became entrenched
in the minds of most politicians and intellectuals around the globe (in
the West as well as in Russia, China, and other countries) due to the
confrontation among Nazism, Communism, and democracy.[76] The
holistic paradigm also influenced the economic literature, which often
operated only with two types of economy: market and command.[77]
The advocates of the neoclassical model shared, to use Robert Solo's
expression, the same "singular approach," describing the Western
economy as a system based on perfect competition with prices as the
only regulator.[78]

Mainstream economists support the neoclassical model as a good
approximation for the description of the market economy, just as sociologists believe in the "cultural model," in which social values are
generated, like prices, through the spontaneous activities of the public. The economists who use perfect competition as the point of reference describe their object of study in a rather elegant and seemingly
consistent way using mathematical models. With this approach, they
tend to ignore the role of various economic organizations that have
their own patterns of economic behavior. For instance, corporations
negotiate with each other over prices and use the privileges that come
from rent-seeking activities. They often underestimate the impact of
bureaucracy and the state on economic processes. They also mostly
disregard the important role of the underground economy and organized crime. As Robert Solo stated, "[E]very actual economy is composed of a number of different forms of economic organizations."[79]

The Dichotomy in Transitional Studies

In the 1980s, the spirit of holism inspired the belief that mankind was
moving toward a complete triumph of liberal capitalism, as suggested
by Francis Fukuyama in *The End of History*.[80] Many authors who

wrote about the economic processes in post-Communist countries assumed that a command economy can only move toward a market economy.[81] The same belief underpinned the ideology of the international financial organizations that were certain in the 1980s and 1990s that universal privatization and globalization would unify economic changes for the better in all countries of the world.

The integrative-system approach led some scholars to conclude that totalitarianism, as it existed in the USSR, can only be replaced by democratic order, as though this transition is the only conceivable prognostication of change. They assume that the starting and ending points of a state's transition are well defined and easy to identify. As a result, several authors who continue to hold fast to the concept of transition have had difficulty explaining what really happened in Russia, because, evidently, the transition to Western capitalism failed. Apparently, they do not know how to treat the societies that emerged after the collapse of Communism.[82]

CONCLUSION

The disarray in the literature on contemporary Russia reflects a deep fragmentation in all dimensions—ideological, political, social, economic, ethnic, and cultural. It stands as a reminder that no one social-political system has been able to dominate Russian society. The descriptions of Russia as a "criminal," "oligarchic," or "bureaucratic" society are as problematic as the claim that Russia is a "normal democratic society" or a society steadily moving in that direction. The dominance of the integrative-system approach explains in part why numerous theories have failed to fully explain the social, political, and economic changes in post-Soviet countries. An alternative approach to the study of post-Soviet Russia will be offered in the next chapter. By rejecting the integrative approach and adopting a segmented analysis, society will not be treated as a single system, with various "deviations" from a given model, but as a conglomeration of social segments—liberal, authoritarian/totalitarian, and feudal—that enjoy a significant degree of power and independence, which changes over time and under different social conditions.

CHAPTER 2

THE SEGMENTED APPROACH
AND FEUDAL MODEL FOR THE STUDY
OF POST-SOVIET RUSSIA

INTRODUCTION

As discussed in Chapter 1, the major flaw in many analyses of contemporary Russia is the tendency to use a single model for describing the nature of this society, while ignoring other analytical tools. Those who focus on the liberal and market elements of post-Soviet Russia usually disregard the characteristics of this society that are best explained by the authoritarian (or in some cases totalitarian) model. At the same time, those who see Russia as an authoritarian society often overlook the elements of the liberal model. The two sides, however, are united in their disregard for the developments that can be explained only with the feudal model. This neglect is especially problematic because, as argued in this book, the feudal model, in many respects, is a better tool for understanding Russia than the other two models. This book advocates a segmented approach that recognizes the importance of using multiple models for analyzing any society. At the same time, given the literature's emphasis on either the authoritarian or the liberal models, this book focuses on the feudal model. I suppose that only the format of a textbook would allow for a full-scale description of a society using several models at once. In the context of this book, I am forced to pay most of my attention to the feudal model.

THE SEGMENTED APPROACH IN SOCIAL ANALYSIS

The segmented approach developed in this book supposes that almost all societies in history comprise different types of social organization. My first articles on the segmented (or multilayered) approach were published in the 1990s.[1] This approach also assumes that most types of social organization that existed in the past still exist today, just as many primitive biological organisms still exist and interact with much more complex organisms. The number of different social organization types in history is quite limited. Certainly the number is also far fewer than the limited number of DNA types that nature uses to create the organic world. The most important forms of political organization include authoritarian (or hierarchical), democratic, and feudal. These three types are close to the famous Aristotelian typology of societies, which is based on how many people run them: one person (authoritarian), a few (feudal or oligarchic), and many (democratic). There are other types of political organization, including communal or anarchistic, but their relative roles in history are minimal. We can also speak about criminal organizations as a special form of social life.

The segmented approach supposes the coexistence and interaction of various social structures in each concrete society in the past and present. The specifics of each society are determined by the relative role of each social organization and their interaction with each other. Similar patterns of behavior can be found in any society, in the past or present. The patterns of behavior that Georg Simmel wrote about include conflict and solidarity, superiority and subordination, and loyalty and treason. Essentially, these patterns do not change over time, even if the specific historical context changes. Otherwise, the reading of Thucydides' *History of the Peloponnesian War,* about the major events of the fifth century B.C., or Machiavelli's *The Prince,* about developments in Italian politics in the early sixteenth century, would not interest contemporary readers. Several authors insist that there are many commonalities in the patterns of international behavior between the Middle Ages and the contemporary world. Fernando Cardoso, a Brazilian sociologist who also served as the country's president, wrote about the similarity between the political disintegration in the Middle Ages and that in the contemporary world, in which, by 2000, the number of states had tripled.[2]

This view is directed against an exaggerated historical approach, as described by many social scientists, particularly those with Marxist backgrounds, who believe in the incessant change of social structures under the impact of technological and economic progress. They revere Heraclites of Ephesus, who became famous as the "flux and fire" philosopher for his proverbial utterance, "All things are flowing." These scholars conduct historical studies aimed mostly at explaining the origin of "new" contemporary institutions and the cause of several current phenomena, such as racism in contemporary America, xenophobia in Germany, class structure in France and England, or the backwardness of African countries.

While in no way denying the importance of historical studies for this purpose, I in fact argue that the study of the past will also help us better understand the present because of the strong similarities in social organizations and patterns of behavior over the centuries. At the same time, the view developed here is even more opposed to the approach of social scientists who simply ignore the past or treat it as irrelevant to contemporary society. With pleasure, they cite Walter Benjamin's now famous phrase that history is only "a flash of memory."[3] Textbooks in sociology, political science, and economics contain very little material on what happened only 50 years ago, without even speaking about such remote epochs as ancient Rome or the Middle Ages.

To explore this idea, I analyzed nine American textbooks on sociology.[4] This analysis showed that most major events of the eighteenth and nineteenth centuries were almost totally ignored. The Industrial Revolution was mentioned in the nine books only eight times (slavery received six mentions; European colonization, six mentions; the American Revolution, five mentions; the French Revolution, four mentions; the American Civil War, four mentions; ancient Rome, three mentions; and the Enlightenment, three mentions).

From this perspective, only the segmented approach, which is based on the idea of coexistence of various types of social organization and patterns of interaction, makes it possible to understand the variance of societies across the world. This approach is close to Weber's perspective on social research, particularly his concept of "ideal types." According to Weber, an ideal type "is formed by the one-sided accentuation of one or more points of view and by the synthesis of a great many diffuse, discrete, more or less present and occasionally absent concrete individual phenomena, which are arranged according to those one-sidedly emphasized viewpoints into a unified analytical construct." Weber wrote that "the same historical phenomenon may be in one aspect feudal, in another patrimonial, in another bureaucratic, and in still another charismatic."[5] He also talked about capitalism as existing in "China, India, Babylon, in the classic world, and in the Middle Ages."[6]

No less important to the segmented approach are the ideas of Georg Simmel. The concept of "forms" was central to Simmel's sociology. He saw society as a constellation of forms. He defined "forms" as the mental structures or models that researchers isolate in social reality in order to make this reality intelligible. Simmel's "ideal forms" are close to Weber's "ideal types," both of which represent intellectual constructions that allow researchers to analyze and understand some aspect of social reality.[7]

Simmel saw the history of mankind as an assortment of abstract types of organization and patterns of behavior that are distributed among different epochs in a very specific way. His analysis of contemporary society was systematically interspersed with examples from ancient Greece, and of feudalism and capitalism. Of course, in each historical context, the relative role of each type of social organization varies and the patterns of behavior change; their specific combination defines the specific character of each society.

Durkheim was, in many respects, in a different camp from Simmel and his followers. However, even he was prone to discuss "absolutism" as a form of government that can be found not only in France in the seventeenth century, but also among "the most diverse social types," such as those existing toward the close of the Roman Empire, or in a multitude of uncivilized monarchies. He treated the family and several other institutions with the same line of thinking.[8]

Along with these outstanding scholars, several others have studied various social institutions from the perspective of universalism. Some authors analyzed individual universal institutions including "gift-giving," as in the case of Marcel Mauss; "reciprocity and complementarity," Robert Merton; "social hierarchy," Roland Mousnier; and "international coalitions," Ole Holsti. Among my allies are those historians who, through the logic of their studies and under the impact of new historical developments, found it necessary to apply the same types of social relations to different epochs. Market relations in the ancient world drew the attention of historians of the eighteenth and nineteenth centuries, when capitalism made its great encroachment into European life. Equipped with the new capitalist paradigm, scholars such as Karl Kautsky, the famous Austrian Marxist of the early twentieth century, or Michael Rostovtzeff, an American historian of the same century, found similar forms of social organization in Greece and Rome. In the second half of the twentieth century, François Furet, under the influence of Soviet totalitarianism, revised the history of the French Revolution, trying to prove that it was not a necessary stage in French history. He suggested that the Jacobins were

"Bolsheviks," who, like Russian Communists, were unconcerned about the welfare of their country.

The segmented approach is close to the dimension of Marxist theory that emphasized the split of society into antagonistic classes. It supposes, as Marxists and left radicals developed it later, that these classes have different cultures, ideologies, and styles of life.[9] In this respect, special attention should be directed to the ideas of Perry Anderson. Using Marxist terminology he developed a view similar to the segmented approach. He suggested that each society represents a combination of different modes of production, and not only one mode, as orthodox Marxists insist.[10] Several non-Marxist authors were also critical of the integrative-system approach and considered various societies as consisting of different, mutually hostile parts.[11]

Other allies of the segmented approach focus on the multicultural character of most societies, both today and in the past. Scholars who support this view include Michael Mann,[12] Charles Taylor,[13] Stephen Brooks,[14] Mark Orbe,[15] and several others.[16] There are, of course, radical differences between multiculturalism and the segmented approach of Simmel's tradition, which is developed in this book. While the former concentrates its attention on the coexistence of different cultural and ethnic groups, the latter focuses on the coexistence in a given society of different forms of social organization. Still, both approaches are critical of holism and systemic analysis.

Among those who view social reality as a combination of many new and old patterns of behavior are several experts on international relations. One of them, Kenneth Waltz, who represents the neorealist school, insists that the texture of international politics remains highly constant; patterns recur and events repeat themselves endlessly.[17] Marcus Fischer, who also supports the neorealist approach, suggested that "feudal politics were not fundamentally different from modern politics."[18]

As strange as it may seem, it is reasonable to enroll Vladimir Lenin as an advocate of the segmented approach, though he was clearly drawn to this concept not on theoretical grounds, but by common sense, as he observed Russian reality after the civil war. Indeed, in 1921, he talked about the coexistence in Soviet Russia of five "social structures" (*uklad*): patriarchy, small commodity production, private capitalism, state capitalism, and socialism.[19]

Of course, Lenin's description of Russia in the 1920s, after the introduction of the new economic policy, with the surge of small and midsize businesses, was accepted by the official Soviet ideology.[20] It was Stalin who, having declared in 1936 that the Soviet Union built socialism, started treating many elements of society (for instance, vegetable and fruit markets) as remnants of the past.[21]

The perception of Russia as a fragmented society started to spread by the end of the 1990s, when it became evident to several observers that the transformation of Russia into a "normal liberal society" had failed. These observers realized that several forms of capitalist and even democratic relations coexisted in Russia, from traditional authoritarian ways of running the country to feudal tendencies in the provinces. Authors such as A. Martynov went so far as to assert that "the multiple layers of society are not at all a specific feature of Russia, but are typical for any developing society."[22] Martynov supported the concept of "mixed society" and talked about various types of economic activity in Russia.[23] Some researchers focused on the multilayered vision of society as it was revealed in the Russian countryside, where various types of farms coexisted, from "subsistence" farms that only provided food for their owners to large industrial agricultural companies.[24]

The segmented approach to defining Russian society was accepted objectively (even if it was not named in this way) by some Western scholars. In some ways, Richard Sakwa's book *Putin: Russia's Choice* (2004) uses an approach close to my theoretical framework. The author suggests that in the post-Communist period, Russia developed as if three different "orders" had been superimposed upon each other. These included the statist, patrimonial, and liberal democratic orders, all of which are important to keep in mind when analyzing post-Soviet Russia.[25]

The Feudal Model as an "Ideal Type"

Each ideal model has its own advantages in describing certain societies. For instance, the totalitarian model is particularly important for the analysis of the Soviet or Nazi societies, even if all social phenomena in the Soviet Union or in Hitler's Germany cannot be explained with this model. The liberal model is best for analyzing Western societies, but again it is necessary to consider other models, including the authoritarian and feudal models, for the analysis of particular elements of these societies. The feudal model, of course, can be best applied to the European societies of the Middle Ages.[26] Some authors have also considered the applicability of this model in the analysis of societies outside Europe—for instance, societies such as Tokugawa's Japan.[27]

A few revisionist historians have attacked the concept of feudalism, arguing that the differences between the so-called feudal societies

(French, British, or German) were so great that the concept itself is dubious.[28] In a more contemporary work, Clifford Backman suggested that not only is the term feudalism confusing and ineffective, but also feudalism never existed, because an ideal model of feudal relations never existed.[29]

In fact, these authors agree with the Middle Ages nominalists and their neopositivist followers, such as Willard Quine, who focused on the differences between particular phenomena and denied the significance of "universals" as an empty concept. On the same grounds, it is possible to reject such concepts as capitalism, liberal capitalism, democracy, and socialism as inapplicable to the United States and Japan or the Soviet Union and Cuba.

There are various definitions of feudalism, as an ideal model, that are useful for understanding Middle Ages Europe, Japan, and some other countries, as well as various developments in contemporary societies. There are two major schools that use the feudal model. One school, the economic or agrarian one, is represented by Marx and Weber, who saw the major features of feudal society in the dominance of landlords and the agrarian character of society. Another school, the political one, with Fustel de Coulanges (the famous French historian of the second half of the nineteenth century) as its most famous mouthpiece, saw in feudalism a society with a weak central state and high autonomy of several political actors. I join the position of the political school in feudal historiography and focus on the weakness of the central administration, the high level of disorder, and the existence of pluralism of power. This school placed at the center of the feudal model a thesis that stressed the advantages of relatively small social units over big ones in maintaining order and enhancing prosperity within regions or corporations.[30] This model also supposed that societies governed by "the powerful few" have an advantage. Societies led by small political units ("small" in comparison to the state), as was the case in the Middle Ages, or by the local population, as is the case in contemporary democratic societies, were better off than societies governed by a single leader, the head of the central administration, or the representatives of federal democratic institutions, who are far removed from their local constituencies.

These are the major features of the feudal model. It implies that the central administration must cooperate with various powerful actors, including regional leaders, corporations, and wealthy individuals, as well as churches and other major social actors. In exchange for legitimacy—and this commodity can be provided only by the central administration—various social actors supply the supreme leader with troops, money, and support in the election process.

In concluding his monumental work *Histoire des Institutions Politique de La Ancienne France,* Fustel Coulanges wrote: "From the Roman Empire up to the tenth century two facts were developed without break: the gradual weakening of political authorities, the second, the progress of big estates and patronage." He underscored that big estates and patronage became the most powerful institutions. They assumed the function that public power had accomplished in previous centuries. It was, in essence, a feudal regime.[31] European society at the close of the Dark Ages was characterized by extreme military insecurity, which was caused, on the one hand, by the wars among the successors of Charlemagne and, on the other, by the incursions of Vikings, Magyars, and Muslims. Of course, the degree of insecurity differed in different places and times, but it nevertheless not only contributed to high transaction costs, especially information costs, but also gave rise to an extremely high demand for military protection that formed the basis for the political relationships emerging in medieval Europe.[32]

The concept of vassal relations as the basis of feudalism was developed by Marc Bloch and other members of the famous Annales School.[33] These relations can be treated as a direct consequence of the weakness of the central state and the dependence of the king on feudal lords and other "big actors." It is remarkable that a few contemporary authors (for instance, Barbara Rosenwine) have treated vassalage as "voluntary and public," disregarding the fact that it was a form of protection against disorder in the absence of a strong central state.[34]

At the same time, many other historians of the twentieth century were rather close to the vision of de Coulanges. Pierre Dubuis wrote that "the major characteristic of feudalism is the decomposition of the monarchic power."[35] This definition of feudalism was accepted by several contemporary scholars, such as American historian Marjorie Chinball[36] and French historians Jacques Le Goff[37] and Laurent Théis.[38]

The prominent historian François-Lois Ganshof also supported this view. He focused on the military and legal aspects of feudalism, as well as manorialism. For him, feudalism was a society in which people's dependence on others was extremely high. It was a society with a specialized military class, which occupied the highest levels of the social hierarchy. In this society, according to Ganshof, there was a wide dispersal of political authority among different political actors who acted in their own interests using power that was usually monopolized by the state.[39] The English writer Paul Vinogradoff was close to this vision of feudal society. He too focused on the political fragmentation of society. In Russia, the same concept of feudalism was applied by the historian Nikolai Pavlov-Sylvanskii.[40]

Elements of feudalism in Russia emerged in the Kiev State in the ninth century, when the king was only seen as a senior among other warriors, as described by Russian chroniclers of the twelfth century.[41] In the Russian-Byzantine negotiations, the prince and the members of his team were equal partners. Later, it was the Russian boyars (feudal lords) who became the major figures of the Russian political structure until the period of absolutism under Ivan the Terrible.

Feudalism and Related Concepts

As a mode of organizing a big territory, feudalism should not be confused with federalism or with the decentralization of society. Federalism supposes that all territorial units, whatever their level of autonomy, are obliged by law to participate in the maximization of the utility function, or welfare, of the whole society, while feudalism means that each unit tries to maximize its own utility function and considers the interests of the whole, whether an empire or a nation, as a constraint that is taken into account as little as possible.[42] At the same time, feudalization of society is almost synonymous with regionalization, which supposes the tendency of the regions to focus only on their own utility function.[43] Another concept that overlaps with feudalism and regionalization is the self-determination of ethnic, religious, or cultural entities. To separate the feudal tendency from separatism, which aims at the independence of a territory, is always a difficult task for politicians as well as social scientists. The case of Chechnya is a good example. Should Chechen separatism be considered a manifestation of feudal tendencies in post-Soviet Russia, or should it be treated as a movement toward independence, as proclaimed by Chechen leaders in 1990–1991? The answer to this question depends on the ideological position of those who make these judgments.[44]

Is Feudalism Relevant to Contemporary Society?

For several authors, feudalism, as a social system, seemed irrelevant to modern society, particularly for social scientists who insisted on the ideographic perception of history. In the seventeenth century, still close to the time of classic feudalism, Montesquieu declared that the feudal laws in Europe represented a unique phenomenon that emerged once in the world and would never be repeated. Voltaire protested against this view, declaring that feudalism was an old form of social organization that existed everywhere. Most contemporary scholars follow Montesquieu, not Voltaire. They seemingly share the view that the feudal model is irrelevant to contemporary society. To begin, the term feudalism is rarely mentioned in sociological text-books.[45] A great exception is Neil Smelser's *Sociology*, in which the concept of feudalism is mentioned six times, even if the phenomenon is treated as belonging to the past.[46] When Smelser talked about America as a "pluralistic society" with many centers of power, which he opposed to the "individualistic democracy" model, he was refer-ring to a society with feudal elements.[47] At the same time, Smelser talked about disintegrative processes in several states, which were deter-mined by the destatification of international relations, a spawning of for-mal and informal networks (sometimes Mafia-like), terrorism, guerrilla actions, uncontrolled ethnic conflicts, and the weakening distinction be-tween public and private violence. He compared these developments with those of medieval times.[48]

Some authors recognize the feudal traits in contemporary society without labeling them as such. Stein Rokkan, for instance, drew a dis-tinction between numerical and corporate pluralistic democracies. While the first type is evidently related to mass or inclusive democracy, the second, which Rokkan describes as a society in which government creates policies by bargaining with pressure groups, is a sort of feudal, oligarchic society.[49] What is more, the whole concept of polyarchy in-troduced by Robert Dahl evidently recognizes the role of feudal ele-ments in contemporary Western society. Dahl operates with the concept of competitive oligarchies, which assumes a limited role for the public in political processes, but the absence of total hegemonism, which is a clear sign of feudalism.[50]

Between the two models of feudalism—economic/agrarian versus political—the former was generally more reluctant to see feudalism beyond Europe and the Middle Ages. However, some advocates of the economic model extended feudalism beyond Western Europe. Weber, for instance, saw feudalism as a worldwide phenomenon exist-ing across all epochs. It could be found not only in Middle Ages Eu-rope, but also in the preclassical period of Greece, in the last period of the Roman Republic, and even in Ptolemaic Egypt. Citing no less than a dozen forms of feudalism and evidently treating it too broadly,

Weber saw it, however, as belonging to the past. As one exception, Weber did not exclude the compatibility of some capitalist phenomena, such as wholesale trade, with partrimonialism, which, however, can only indirectly be equated with feudalism.[51]

The members of the second camp, the political group, saw feudalism as a general type of social relations. Marc Bloch, even if he did not focus on the weakness of the central administration as the major generic feature of feudalism, nevertheless departed from the land paradigm and placed vassal relations at the center of feudalism, which allowed him to see feudalism as a universal phenomenon.[52] Susanne Karstedt was among the contemporary scholars who were close to Bloch's view. For Karstedt, feudalism did not relate to a particular historical period nor imply a specific stage of economic development.[53] She rejected the view that the patrimonial and feudal structural patterns disappeared with modernization. Instead, as Karstedt insisted, these patterns were successful in the world.[54] A few other scholars were close to her ideas, including John Hall[55] and Peter Duus.[56]

However, the most consistent advocates of the universalism of feudalism were those for whom feudalism meant a weak central administration and a type of society that was ruled by the few. It can be labeled, following Aristotle, as an "oligarchic" society. Carolyn Webber and Aaron Wyldavsky focused on the characterization of European feudalism based on the absence of a central coercive capacity and the independence of participants. They said that noncentralized governments existed in different times and places (in Mesopotamia during the Kassite period, in Egypt during the Middle Kingdom, in Japan between the ninth and eighteenth centuries).[57] Other scholars also saw feudalism as a type of society that overlapped with the contemporary world. They deviated from the land school of feudalism, which focused on the hierarchical social structure in contemporary society.[58] The intellectual John Dewey, for instance, talked about "industrial feudalism" when he described the role of big corporations in modern America.

THE TASKS OF THE FEUDAL MODEL IN CONTEMPORARY SOCIAL ANALYSIS

There have been several developments in the contemporary world that are at odds with the dominant neoclassical model in economics and the pluralistic model of democratic society as developed by political scientists. Among these developments are the noneconomic, often illegal, activities of corporations, the non-merit-based "selection of cadres" by government, and the inability of the central and local administration to guarantee the security of people and institutions. There is a great deal of data and thousands of books and articles available on each of these issues. My task is to organize these data within a theoretical framework. There are two approaches to these issues: one used by mainstream economists and political scientists who believe in the absolute dominance of liberal and democratic values in Western society, and the other based on Marxist class theory.

The mainstream in economics and political science either marginalizes these developments or treats them as deviations from the normal state of affairs. Marxists and neo-Marxists tend to explain all these developments as a consequence of class structure and the dominance of capitalists. I challenge both of these approaches.

As an illustration of this idea I discuss criminal protection in contemporary Russia as well in other countries, including the United States. It is well known that rackets, or the criminal protection of private businesses, are a universal phenomenon in the contemporary world. Criminal protection expanded tremendously in post-Soviet Russia, while it was almost unknown in the Soviet Union. Several authors who write about private protection in the contemporary world see it only through the prism of the capitalist model, describing the criminal organizations that protect private businesses as capitalist enterprises that sell their services. Even authors who focus on the differences between mafias and "normal capitalist firms" use capitalist firms as the point of reference. They talk about the clients of mafias as "normal" market agents who want to reduce the cost of their goods with the help of criminal organizations, whose major "market activity" consists of violence. They mostly ignore the fact that "the help" was often imposed on them. (I discuss this issue in detail later.)

Almost none of these authors thought about the Middle Ages when they described private protection as an omnipresent phenomenon. The feudal model, with its focus on the weakness of the state, describes private protection as a necessary element of life in the Middle Ages. Behind private protection was violence, even if a voluntary search for "roof" in the Middle Ages—the famous "commendation" (a person's exchange of personal freedom for protection given by a feudal lord)—was a frequent development. Criminal private protection in contemporary society should be analyzed using at least two models of "ideal society": feudal and capitalist. This point of view was strongly defended by the famous Russian historian Aron Gurevich, which made him a target of sharp critiques by orthodox Marxists, who insisted that the peasants had been coerced into serfdom.[59]

FEUDALISM AND RUSSIA

I first advanced the feudal model for analyzing Russian society in an article published in 1996.[60] The article was widely discussed in the literature. Anatolii Lieven, citing my article, suggested that "bastard feudalism" was a good description of Spain and Latin America in the nineteenth century and early twentieth century.[61] Also referring favorably to my article, Richard Ericson proposed the idea of naming Russian society as "industrial feudalism." The author singled out such features as the weak state, decentralization of power, personalized authority, and strength of personal networks.[62] The same view was advanced by Peter Stavrakis, who also accepted my proposal to consider the feudal elements of post-Soviet Russia, particularly those related to the interaction between the central and local authorities.[63] Taking a similar position, Stephen Blank focused on the codetermination of power and wealth in post-Soviet Russia.[64]

Several Russian authors have discussed the commonality between Russia after 1991 and the feudalism of the Middle Ages. Between January 2000 and May 2006, the term feudalism was used in 50 national Russian newspapers 532 times. Andrei Konchalovskii, who is engaged intensively in the country's intellectual debates, has often cited feudalism as a good description of contemporary Russia.[65] Ruslan Grinberg, the director of the Institute of Economics, a leading academic institution in Moscow, declared that "Russia has all the features of feudal society."[66] The economist Petr Orekhovskii suggested that the Russians have "the luck to live in feudal society."[67]

Some Russian authors talked about Russia's movement from authoritarianism to the Middle Ages.[68] One of them was Yuliia Latynina, a prominent journalist with a strong historical background. She justified the applicability of the feudal model ("industrial feudalism") to Russia using several arguments, such as the conflict between the center and regions,[69] the corporation as an "industrial feudal empire,"[70] the permanent war between corporations—which has nothing to do with normal competition, because the major means in this war were various illegal actions including direct violence[71]—the lack of respect for private property, and the dominance of feudal culture with war representing "the cheapest way to increase wealth."[72] Latynina's vision of Russia was supported by Sergei Guriev.[73] In addition, the philosopher Eric Soloviev talked about "the shopkeepers' feudalism."[74]

THE IMPORTANCE OF THE AUTHORITARIAN AND LIBERAL MODELS IN THE ANALYSIS OF RUSSIA

In no way do I underestimate the importance of the authoritarian (and in some cases totalitarian) and liberal models in the analysis of contemporary Russia or any other society. In fact, even in the Middle Ages, when the feudal order was dominant, there were many elements of society that had an authoritarian or liberal character. There is no doubt that the rule of feudal lords within their estates and the regime inside the Catholic Church were consistently authoritarian or even totalitarian. The feudal hierarchy did not suppose any freedom of action for people at the bottom. Yet, within this society, which was not homogeneous, there were democratic-like institutions, whose members (all from the ruling elite) made decisions and voted after deliberations.[75]

The authoritarian (or totalitarian in its harsher forms) model is understood here as an analytical construction that describes the organization of strict hierarchical controls held by a leader. The "ideal" totalitarian society supposes that the state has a total monopoly on information, education, and the arts. The omnipresent political police and a network of informers are indispensable elements of such a society. The total control of the state over the economy and means of production is an organic part of the totalitarian society, even if its milder version, the authoritarian model, supposes the existence of private property, though under the control of the state. The totalitarian model also supposes the state's total hostility toward any form of democracy or political freedom.[76]

As a matter of fact, many elements of post-Soviet Russia, particularly those during Putin's regime, can be interpreted only in terms of the authoritarian model. By the end of his second term in 2007, Putin concentrated more power than any other Soviet leader after 1953. In only three years, he eliminated all traces of the division of power. He turned the Parliament into a puppet institution, not unlike the Soviet Supreme Council of the past. The judicial system became as obeisant to Putin as it was to the Soviet masters of the Kremlin. Putin also reduced the independence of the media. Russian TV became a direct instrument of the Kremlin. Putin would appear no less than five to seven times during a typical 30-minute news program. In fact, he made more television appearances than comrade Brezhnev did in Soviet times. In most cases, the president was portrayed as a great leader who takes care of everything in the country.[77]

At the same time, whatever the authoritarian and feudal tendencies in Putin's Russia, it is important not to overlook the country's many liberal elements. Private property and competition, even with their many limitations, are deeply embedded in the fabric of Russian society, along with the freedom of economic activity. People move freely inside the country and travel outside its borders for business and vacations as well as to emigrate. National and local elections, even if they are mostly unfair, are still an important part of the political order, and the authorities spend a lot of time and resources to control the outcomes.

CONCLUSION

In this book, I attempt to show that there have been major developments in contemporary Russian society that can be explained adequately only if the analysis is based on the segmented approach, which supposes that various "ideal models" should be used as tools of research. The study of Russia demonstrates how important it is not to confound social reality with the models that are necessary for its analysis. An examination of post-Soviet Russia from the segmented perspective, with a special focus on the elements of feudalism, may be quite productive. Joining the political school's definition of feudalism, this chapter focused on the weakness of the state and the lack of law and order. As a matter of fact, the feudal model promises to be a useful tool for understanding not only Russia, but also any society in which the central administration cannot perform its duties.

CHAPTER 3

WEAKNESS OF THE STATE

INTRODUCTION

The weakness of the state represents the central feature of the feudal model. As central authority in any society weakens, disorder increases and the feudal elements of the society flourish. Central authority was weak in both the Middle Ages and post-Soviet Russia. Until the establishment of absolute monarchies in the seventeenth century, disorder was a permanent part of life in the Middle Ages, even if the pattern of relations between various power structures fluctuated over time. Given the country's serious problems with crime and corruption, disorder was a typical feature in post-Soviet Russia as well.

As in the Middle Ages, relations between the center and other powerful actors in Russia changed over time. Under Yeltsin, for instance, the governors and oligarchs were able to challenge the central administration; under Putin, their political influence was limited to their respective fiefs.

This chapter considers the effects of a weak state in the context of both the Middle Ages and post-Soviet Russia with an emphasis on the prevalence of crime and corruption. Who were the main targets of criminals in these societies? How did the fear of crime affect ordinary people and elites? What were the characteristics of corruption in the two societies? How did corruption impact bureaucracy, law enforcement agencies, the judicial system, and other state agencies? How was the level and character of corruption linked to fluctuations in central power?

TYPES OF STATE WEAKNESS

My approach to the issue of the strength of the state differs from that of many contemporary social scientists. Scholars have proposed characteristics of the state's strength, such as the relative size of the public sector and the autonomy of the federal government from other social actors.[1]

There are two dimensions of state weakness. The first arises from the inability of the ruler, or the ruling class, to protect the regime against political rivals. The second type of weakness is seen in the ruler's inability to implement laws and directives in his territory. The first feudal kings in the post-Roman period were deficient in both respects. They found it difficult to protect their thrones and were generally unable to govern the country as a whole. However, the situation changed when the Merovingians came to power. Louis IX was confident in his rule over Paris, though he lacked the necessary resources for controlling the countryside.

The rule of Boris Yeltsin (1991–1999) was very similar to the rule of the French kings immediately after the collapse of the empire of Charles the Great in the early ninth century. During Yeltsin's tenure, the two major actors in post-Soviet Russia—oligarchs and governors— openly challenged the central administration. They were not only completely autonomous within their own fiefs, but also influenced national politics.

With Putin's rise to power, many things changed and Putin gained the power to protect himself against any rival in the country. However, the regime remained inefficient in many ways and was unable to control all the regions and major social actors. It was also highly susceptible to crises involving security and the economy. The public perceived the Kremlin as unable to coordinate relations between the center and regions. By the end of 2005, as political analyst Aleksandr Sevast'ianov noted, the Russian state was weak and deeply corrupt. Numerous Russian observers have made similar arguments, perhaps to the point where the observation itself has become trivial.[2]

CAUSES OF STATE WEAKNESS

There are at least two causes of state weakness. Weakness may derive from a lack of unity among elites or from an increase of corruption. In the first case, the leader and the ruling elite, torn by internal struggle, prove unable to run the country efficiently. This was the case following the collapse of the Carolingian Empire, when the descendants of Charles the Great waged a protracted war that fragmented the empire.

In a similar case, the central administration simply lacks the resources to subjugate or convince the regional power holders to obey commands from above and establish order in their sectors. Such was the situation in the late 1980s and early 1990s in Russian society. During perestroika, the central administration became weaker as a result of the reforms that undermined the dominant role of the Communist Party and the state.

One of the most obvious examples of disunity among elites was seen in the rise of Boris Yeltsin. In 1990–1991, Yeltsin, a former member of the politburo, created an alternative power center outside Gorbachev's Kremlin using the Russian Federation as his social and political basis. In his fight against the central administration, Yeltsin looked for allies and encouraged each region "to take as much sovereignty as possible," a suggestion he came to regret one year later. Feeling insecure as the master of the Kremlin after the collapse of the Soviet Union in 1991, Yeltsin continued to look for support among local elites.

The second cause of weakness lies in the processes of corruption. As the role of corruption increases in the center, the ruler and other leading politicians become more dependent on power holders outside the central authority. In this way, a contemporary society with a corrupt government may look like a society from the Middle Ages. Corruption was certainly a leading cause of the weakness of Yeltsin's regime. He acted like a king whose main goal was to stay in power by all means necessary while enriching himself and his family. George Breslauer aptly noted that a leader should be judged by his or her goals and not by some normative standard. However, even with this realistic approach, one could not find on Yeltsin's "scale of values," as described by Breslauer, such crucial values as "personal power" and "family wealth."[3] The impact of personal interest on post-Soviet leaders and the political processes in Russia was mostly ignored in the publications of Michael McFaul[4] and Donald Barry.[5] These and other authors evaluated the efficacy of Yeltsin's and Putin's leadership based on their own standards.[6]

Meanwhile, to achieve both goals, power and wealth, Yeltsin preoccupied himself with the creation of his own "domain." The situation did not change when Putin came to power. Hence the state remained weak and inefficient. The subject of the ruler's domain will be discussed in detail in a later chapter.

THE DISRESPECT FOR LAW

Scholars generally follow one of two different perspectives on the Middle Ages. Some focus on the feudal order that was finally installed after the period of turmoil in early medieval society. These authors include Georges Duby, who wrote *Féodalités*,[7] David Douglas, with his focus on contractual military service as the major feature of feudalism (at least in its Norman version),[8] and to some degree also François Ganshof, with his emphasis on the legalistic elements of feudalism.[9] They saw feudal order as a well-developed hierarchical network of actors with elaborated codes of behavior. Each stratum of the population, from warriors and priests to peasants, was said to have its own function.

These authors give the impression that Middle Ages France, around the year 1000, was an orderly society. In a large volume by Duby, very little is said about the banditry and violence in France during this period. The extensive table of contents (12 pages) lists sections about numerous religious and intellectual phenomena of the time, but never mentions one section about the level of social order in society.

Another perspective supported by many leading medievalists, which seems more realistic to me, portrays the level of order in society as precarious. While the monarchy issued laws, established a judiciary system, and tried to encourage order, the central authority often remained weak and ineffective. Feudal codes of honor existed, and the church attempted at times to preserve peace in society, but the most important characteristic of the Middle Ages was the deep disrespect for law. Several historians—from Fustel de Coulanges and Marc Bloch to contemporary researchers such as Hunt Janin,[10] Barbara Hanawalt,[11] and Claude Gauvard[12]—describe societies in the Middle Ages as chaotic, disorderly, and dangerous. Natalie Zemon Davis contended that from the sixteenth century onward, and perhaps as early as the mid-fifteenth century, everyone could recount a crime story that they had heard or experienced.[13]

The situation in post-Soviet Russia, particularly in the first years after the collapse of the Soviet Union, was quite similar. Take, for example, a description of the society made by James Finckenauer and Yuri Voronin in their book *The Threat of Russian Organized Crime* (2001). They wrote that in the decade after the collapse of the Soviet Union the world became the target of a new global crime threat from criminal organizations, and criminal activities poured over the borders of Russia and other former Soviet republics such as Ukraine. They pointed out that the nature and variety of the crimes being committed seemed to be unlimited—drug and arms trafficking, steeling automobiles, trafficking of women and children, and money laundering were among the most prevalent.[14]

According to Vladimir Pleshakov, an expert from the Ministry of Internal Affairs, "the number of crimes perpetrated in the USSR per year was several times lower than the number of crimes committed in post-Soviet Russia."[15] In the 1990s, the level of many different crimes was very high, including street crimes, burglary, and the murder of businesspeople. The number of murders and robberies increased between 1992 and 2004 by roughly 50 percent (from 23,000 to 32,000 and from 185,000 to 251,000, respectively). The number of assaults almost doubled as well (from 30,000 to 55,000). Moreover, the number of recidivists among those sentenced by the courts declined from 39 percent to 26 percent during the same period (1992–2004), which suggests that the number of people who committed crimes increased.[16]

ORGANIZED CRIME IN RUSSIA

The level of organized crime in Soviet society was relatively low. However, the weakening of the state, party, and official ideologies, along with the legalization of private property and the lack of control over privatization, led to an eruption of crime and corruption.

The major elements of criminal society emerged during perestroika. The people's lack of trust in official bodies further stimulated the criminal expansion. Between 1985 and 1990, the number of registered crimes increased by 30 percent, while the relative number of crimes whose perpetrators were not found increased drastically, from 18 percent in 1985 to 49 percent in 1988 and 63 percent in 1989.[17]

After 1991, criminal organizations began to mushroom in the county. Already by the mid-1990s several criminal groups became as well known in the country as the new banks and corporations. By 1995, there were 14,000 criminal groups operating in Russia; in 1988, there had been only 50.[18] In the 15 years after the anti-Communist revolution, criminal organizations seized companies in almost every region of the country. In 2006, according to the minister of internal affairs Rashid Nurgaliev, criminal groups controlled the "fuel, metallurgy, lumber and fish industries." These organizations included the Liubertsy Group in Moscow; Tambov in Leningrad; 29 Complex in Naberezhnye Chelny; and the Uralmash Group, the Central Criminal Group, and the Blues in Ekaterinburg and Nizhnii Tagil.[19]

Dangerous Roads

Travel during the Middle Ages was often a dangerous enterprise.[20] Travelers, merchants, and pilgrims faced various dangers from robbers and thieves, as well as from the arbitrariness of "petty kings" who used tolls as lucrative businesses.[21] The sermon that the Bishop of Beauvais gave in the year 1023 to King Robert le Pious described the crimes committed along the roadside as the most frightening and heinous crimes in France.[22]

As in the Middle Ages, the roads in post-Soviet Russia were also quite dangerous. The fear of being stopped and forced to relinquish cash became a normal part of life for Russian drivers. If in the Middle Ages customs guards and soldiers extorted money from travelers, in post-Soviet Russia it was the job of police officers, traffic cops in particular, and, of course, criminals. In Russia, passenger and freight trains were often targeted as well.[23] In 2006, the Chinese minister of foreign affairs issued an official advisory, suggesting that his compatriots in Russia should avoid using trains altogether. The official noted that Russian planes were much safer.[24]

The Fear of Crime in the Middle Ages and Contemporary Russia

People in the Middle Ages and contemporary Russia experienced the fear of crime differently, depending on their place in society. Peasants and artisans in feudal times feared their neighbors and small-time bandits. Feudal lords and bishops feared their powerful rivals, but were less concerned about ordinary criminals. The fear of crime in France in the aftermath of the Hundred Years' War was not far removed from the same problem in Russia in the 1990s. A French historian wrote that the fear of crime permeated French society in the late Middle Ages, and the population believed that crimes such as murder, arson, rape, highway robbery, incest, and sodomy struck at the very heart of society and threatened to tear apart the social fabric. He also noted that the clergy saw these stereotypical crimes as God's punishment for the sins of his people, but blamed the king for not doing more to protect his subjects. Humanists joined in the discussion of crime and urged judicial reform on the king. The fear of crime, therefore, played a major role in the emergence of the French state at the end of the Middle Ages.[25]

Fears of Ordinary People

In many respects, the fears of ordinary people in post-Soviet Russia were the same as in the Middle Ages. With the collapse of the Soviet Union, the people watched as centralized fears were replaced by decentralized ones. In other words, the fear of the powerful state was replaced by the fear of a multitude of criminals, gangs, corporations, and rich people who took over the job of repressing ordinary people. Street criminals, burglars, and small criminal organizations were the main threats to ordinary Russians (no less than two-thirds of the population were "afraid" of these threats, according to polls conducted between 1992 and 2006; among them one-half were "very afraid").[26] The fear of criminals became part of everyday life in Russia. Any aggressive-looking individual on the street appeared as a serious threat.

In the past, the Soviets had often bickered with each other on buses, in restaurants, or on the streets. Riffraff were abundant in Russian cities and often pestered people. However, in Soviet times, as opposed to now, an assailant usually only represented himself or a few friends. Those who dared to respond to the assailant—either verbally or physically—safely assumed that no major power stood behind the offender. After 1991, the situation changed. People had to think twice before defending themselves, as the perpetrator could be backed by a powerful criminal organization. Even in the case of a simple car accident, people feared the reaction of the other driver. In the blink of an eye, the victim could demand compensation equal to the value of a new car, with bodily injury or death as the only alternative. Landlords in Russia were also affected by the criminal world. They grew to expect anything and everything from their tenants. Some landlords were known to lower the rent for criminally involved individuals so as to ensure their own safety. Those who were interested in selling their apartments feared that during the transaction they would lose their property or be killed. This was a special concern for retired or elderly people.[27]

By the end of the decade, according to a survey conducted by me, the fear of crime held second place on a list of a dozen fears. It yielded only to the fear of economic disaster. Seventy percent of the Russians mentioned the fear of criminals.[28] According to another survey administered in 1997, 27 percent of Russians were afraid of being severely injured or killed by criminals, and 26 percent feared becoming victims of thieves and thugs.[29] The same survey showed that the overall crime level in the country caused concern among 38 percent of survey respondents; 50 percent said they were very concerned and only 12 percent did not worry about crime at all.[30]

In the first decade of the twenty-first century, the fear of crime continued to dominate the Russian mind. In surveys conducted in 2002 and 2005, the fear of crime was placed second among ten fears, close behind the fear of inflation and pauperization.[31] The fear of crime diminished the quality of life of ordinary Russians who, with their full distrust of the police, felt helpless against criminals.

Though they lived in permanent fear, the public accepted crime and corruption as "normal" parts of everyday life. By the mid-1990s, the Russians were no longer surprised about the nearly routine murders of businesspeople, politicians, and journalists. In the not-so-distant past, murders had produced huge waves of headlines throughout the media. By the mid-1990s, the same event was usually only briefly mentioned in the press.[32]

THE RELATIONSHIP BETWEEN CRIME AND BUSINESS

In post-Soviet Russia, businesspeople maintained ambivalent relations with criminals. On one hand, since the beginning of privatization, they were terribly afraid of criminals. On the other hand, businesspeople often relied on criminals to solve their problems.

Criminals in Service to Businesspeople

Criminal organizations often worked as agents for businesspeople. They aided the security apparatus of corporations and terrorized the firms' rivals.[33] Vladimir Gusinskii, who became an icon of Russian democracy in a strange twist of events in 1999, publicly blackmailed people. According to Yeltsin's security chief Aleksandr Korzhakov, Berezovskii asked him to "eliminate" Gusinskii, his rival in business and politics. The deep connections between the managers of Avtovaz, a major car manufacturer based in Tolliatti, and a powerful organized-crime syndicate were widely discussed by several Russian and foreign journalists.[34] The cooperation between business and criminals was particularly prevalent at the local level.[35] Various sources suggested that collaboration among criminals, officials, and businesspeople had become a serious problem in Krasnoiarsk, Kursk, Ekaterinburg, Petersburg, Cheliabinsk, Sochi, and several other cities.[36]

Though corporations were ambivalent toward organized crime, like the major social actors of the Middle Ages, they held negative attitudes toward petty criminals. In 2000–2002, big corporations, particularly in metallurgy and the oil trade, declared a war on the local criminal gangs. They also procured the services of the local police to successfully squeeze out crime in their areas.[37]

The Coalescence of Criminal Organizations and Businesses

Criminal organizations not only served businesses as "violence managing agencies," to use Vadim Volkov's terminology, but also became deeply enmeshed in the business itself.[38] The most widely cited data were provided by the Ministry of Internal Affairs in January 1994, based on estimates by the Russian government's Analytical Center for Social and Economic Policies. It claimed that criminal gangs controlled or owned (the study was not specific in its terminology) 40,000 businesses, including 2,000 in the state sector. The majority of businesses in Russia (up to three-quarters) paid illegal protection money. The center provided even more alarming data, stating that 55 percent of the capital and 80 percent of the voting shares of private enterprises had been transferred into the hands of criminals. These and similar estimates inspired the authors of the U.S. Center for Strategic Studies report (edited by William Webster) on Russian organized crime to claim that "roughly two-thirds of Russia's economy is under the sway of the crime syndicates."[39]

CORRUPTION AS AN INDICATOR OF STATE WEAKNESS

"Corruption" in the Middle Ages

Along with violent crime, Middle Ages Europe and contemporary Russia also suffered from the effects of corruption, even if the term was not used in the Middle Ages. In the Middle Ages, particularly in periods of intense political fragmentation, people suffered a great deal from various arbitrary charges imposed by feudal lords, the church, royal emissaries, and the courts. Some of these charges were considered "gifts," which did not, however, make them less costly to the "giver."

Interest in corruption among medieval historians, as Trevor Dean noted, has a relatively recent origin.[40] J. C. Waquet suggested that "corruption has been treated anecdotally rather than systematically by historians" and that "nobody takes the subject seriously enough."[41] While Waquet studied corruption in Florence in the seventeenth and eighteenth centuries, Wim Blockmans focused on the

Burgundian-Habsburg Netherlands.[42] In a study of corruption in sixteenth-century France, Natalie Davis found that "gifts were everywhere," in politics, justice, and in the appointment of political positions even though gift giving was officially illegal.[43]

Hunt Janin, an American historian, described the arbitrariness of judges (sheriffs) in thirteenth-century England in the book *Medieval Justice*, studying cases in France, England, and Germany. Discussing the income of British sheriffs, the author wrote that the sources of regular income from the office of sheriff were not obvious and what seemed clear was that the sheriffs had to resort to different forms of exaction to make ends meet. The author noted that as late as 1260, the men of Nottingham had to pay their sheriffs 100 shillings not to invade their liberty or, in other words, to gain immunity against criminal prosecution. As the author wrote, the sheriffs demanded high "ferms," or fixed annual payments, owed by the bailiffs to the sheriffs in return for holding their offices. The bailiffs received whatever income they could earn or were entitled to from the public, but they were always required to pay ferms to the sheriffs if they wanted to keep their jobs.

As the author mentioned, the sheriffs held other aces as well. Some seized the property of criminals or used the threat of imprisonment to extort money from innocent people. Unscrupulous sheriffs could make a man pay twice for a single offense. They could also demand payment from several persons with the same name, when a fine had been imposed on only one of them. Sheriffs, as the author noted, could compel people to pay higher taxes than were legally required. Sheriffs and bailiffs could summon excessive numbers of jurors, including those who could not possibly serve for reasons of age or poor health, or because they lived in another jurisdiction, forcing these unfortunate men to pay bribes if they wanted to be excused from the onerous task of jury duty. Finally, the sheriffs could pocket money offered by their prisoners in hope of better treatment, while suspected criminals (that is, accused or indicted persons) paid bribes in order to avoid being arrested.[44]

Because of bribes, the number of criminals sentenced for their deeds was quite low. Frederick Pollock and Frederic Maitland found in their study of English law that in Gloucestershire in 1221, 330 homicide cases were heard in court, but only 24 of the defendants were put to death, while most were acquitted. In 1414, King Henry V held special sessions of the central criminal court, during which it was found that in some midland counties the court received more than 2,000 murder indictments, but only three resulted in executions.[45]

Of particular importance was the judicial immunity of officials and rich people in the Middle Ages as well as in post-Soviet society. In both cases, members of the ruling class received immunity from punishment. Writing about the Middle Ages, Trevor Dean suggested that many studies from various places and periods confirm that, in Romagna, Italy, nobles were not punished for their crimes in the fifteenth century. In Brescia, the middle and privileged classes were absent from lists of convictions, and the courts dealt mainly with the violence and unruliness of the poor and rootless. The same situation was found in Venice, where the court records showed only one conviction of a nobleman for theft. In general, as suggested by Dean, the noblemen were more likely to request and obtain pardon for their misdeeds, which explains the disproportionate number of noblemen who petitioned for pardons in Guyenne in southwest France.[46]

Everyday Corruption in Post-Soviet Russia

By the end of the 1990s, corruption was an omnipresent problem in Russia. There were two types of corruption: one in which officials of low level and ordinary people were engaged, and another that included highly ranked bureaucrats and people from big businesses. This section deals with the first type of corruption.

The scope of corruption continued to rise even with Putin at the helm. By the beginning of 2000, half the population was involved in corruption: 55 percent reported that they had bribed officials (50 percent in 2001). As General Prosecutor Yurii Chaika declared in late 2006, "[C]orruption permeates all levels of power and strikes the whole social system."[47] According to Transparency International (a well-respected and widely quoted source), Russia belonged to a group of 22 countries, which included Ghana, Lithuania, Niger, and India, where the number of respondents who reported paying bribes was 11 to 30 percent.[48]

According to a study conducted in 2005, bribes were particularly important to Russian citizens when interacting with the police and courts (40–60 percent of the Russians used bribes). People also used bribes to acquire free medical services from the state (38 percent), to enter desirable high schools or colleges (41–52 percent), or to solve various problems related to land or residential property (34–40 percent). Bribes played a special role in people's relations with military draft offices (58 percent of the respondents were confident that bribes could be used to avoid military service).[49] Transparency International offered similar data. On a scale from 1 (no corruption at all) to 5 (extremely corrupt), the Russians rated the police and judiciary at 4.2, the education system at 3.9, and customs agents at 3.7.[50]

While most people bribe officials in order to urge them to observe the law and satisfy their legal needs, many people resort to bribes in order to receive illegal services. The case of Russian education is a good example. Hundreds of thousands of people bribe officials in educational institutions in order to gain entrance to colleges without the necessary qualifications, to pass exams without preparation, or even to simply receive a bachelor's or PhD degree without attending courses. As one participant of the underground education business said, "Its profitability has reached the level of the oil industry."[51] The activities of Evgenii Volkov, who created a special corporation in Petersburg, serve as a good example. The corporation included several illegal colleges with low-quality instructors and very low academic requirements. The corporation sold bachelor degree diplomas for $5,000 and PhDs for $50,000. Even the driver of one of the corporation's "managers" had his PhD. The corporation was protected by local courts and the Office of the Prosecutor General; those who tried to uncover the business were murdered.[52]

The Normalization of Corruption

Emerging from the near anarchy of early 1990s, the rules of corruption in Russia became more explicit and better orchestrated by the early years of the twenty-first century. According to a survey conducted by INDEM, most people (61 percent) now knew how much, or how little, to pay in bribes to officials (the average individual bribe, according to INDEM, was $90 in 2005, equivalent to half the average official salary); roughly 70 percent of respondents reported that they knew the proper size of the "gift" before making the bribe.[53] Businesses understood the cost of protection (or *krysha,* to use the Russian term). Only a minority of Russians (less than 10 percent) who admitted to making a bribe were disappointed with the outcome.[54] This balance between expectation and results soothed the anxiety associated with corruption. In less than one-third of bribery cases (according to the INDEM data, only 25 percent) the bribe was solicited by officials.

The Russians have acquiesced to the current situation to such a degree that they do not bother complaining about it. Only 23 percent of the Russians regarded corruption as a "major concern" in 2001–2002, down from 40 percent in 1997. In 2006, despite its rise according to various data, corruption had already receded from the list of top concerns. It garnered only 12 percent of the respondents in 2006. The fight against corruption was also absent among the country's ten most important problems.[55] Having been forced to make a bribe for a general service, only 10 percent of the Russians said they had made a formal complaint about a "bad bureaucrat."

Ordinary people were not the only ones who felt at home with corruption. According to a poll by Komkon-2, the wealthiest 10 percent of the population (labeled the "middle-class" in Russia) did not select "corruption" as one of their "top-ten worries."[56] Oligarchs also acquiesced to corruption. Though less politically conspicuous inside the Kremlin than during the previous regime, they retained their dubious fortunes and continued to wield tremendous power within their corporate empires. By the early years of the twenty-first century, they enjoyed relatively stable relationships with the central and local administrations and law enforcement agencies.

There were only a few anticorruption enthusiasts in the country. The famous journalist Yurii Shchekochikhin and the social scientist Lev Timofeev raised their fists against corruption in the 1990s, but neither made any progress in preventing it. In the early years of the twenty-first century, they were joined by a former aid to Yeltsin, Georgii Satarov, who, despite his conspicuous hatred of corruption, never talked about Yeltsin's role in expanding corruption in his numerous publications in the 1990s.[57]

As if struck by collective amnesia, ordinary people no longer associated corruption with some officials who were once seen as Russia's greatest crooks. Investigative journalists have collected and published thousands of facts about the corrupt activities of many officials, including the former prime minister Viktor Chernomyrdin, the current prime minister Mikhail Kasianov, Moscow's mayor Yurii Luzhkov, former deputy prime ministers Anatolii Chubais and Alfred Koch, and several other highly ranked Kremlin officials, not to mention Yeltsin and his family. None of these people have even refuted the allegations set against them.

More harmful to Russia, however, is the fact that Putin is no different from his countrymen. Despite all his declarations about strengthening the state, he has not only avoided taking serious actions against corrupt officials and oligarchs, but also conspicuously ignored the subject in his interviews, informal meetings, and public statements, including his presidential addresses to the Russian parliament in April 2001 and April 2002.[58] Federal agencies have conducted very few investigations into corruption, and no officials have been indicted and brought to trial in a Russian court. The investigations against

Pavel Borodin were closed because "there were no criminal activities found" (I will return to this case later). Putin appointed the former governor of the Far East province Evgenii Nazdratenko, who was known for his corrupt activities, as a member of his government. Putin also appointed Nazir Khapsirokov, another corrupt official, to the Prosecutor General's Office as a deputy to the head of the presidential administration.[59]

EXTORTION

Extortion is treated by some authors as a form of corruption, because it relates to the interaction between the powerful and the weak. However, acts of extortion are different from classic corruption, even if the distinction, in some cases, is not easy to make. Classic corruption supposes that the bribe giver initiates a deal with the bribe taker. In contrast, extortion is initiated by a bribe taker and is imposed on bribe givers (victims) against their will. Bribing a doctor in a Russian hospital to get a surgery done, bribing an army official to avoid being recruited, or bribing a traffic officer to avoid paying fines for a real violation of the law are all acts of corruption.

However, when the individual has no legal option to avoid an illegally imposed payment and faces pure losses, as opposed to an exchange of utilities, it is extortion. When a traffic officer or a sanitary inspector invents a violation, or when an army officer threatens to beat one of his soldiers unless a payment is made, it is also extortion. The relative weights of corruption and extortion clearly reflect the level of lawlessness in society. Extortion, unlike corruption, supposes the use of direct threats to the life or property of the individual. Of course, extortion exists mostly in the criminal realm, but political officials, the members of law enforcement agencies, and other individuals also resort to the violent tactics of extortion.

Extortion was a typical phenomenon in the Middle Ages. Royal soldiers, roving knights, judges, and even priests all participated in extortions and requisitions of various sorts, in some cases using a specious legal pretext, but more often without one. Take, for instance, the conduct of mercenaries. In the fourteenth and fifteenth centuries, kings, princes, popes, and city officials resorted to purchasing the services of mercenary soldiers. The worst evil the mercenaries brought was not their lack of loyalty, but their constant plundering of the countryside. The mercenary bands were permanent bodies organized to bring profits for their members, and when unemployed, they lived off the countryside, taking whatever they could find. A besieged noble or a monastery could usually buy them off by paying a tribute and send them on to the next county, but the peasants had no defense.[60]

Post-Soviet Russia was a society replete with cases of extortion of various sorts. Extortion was a widespread problem among traffic police and an even greater problem in the army.[61] The usual objects of extortion in the army were new draftees. Hazing in the army consisted not only of beatings and humiliating acts, but also the permanent demand for cash from new draftees or the parcels they received from their families. In many cases, rookies, particularly from poor families (youngsters from rich families were usually able to avoid army service altogether), could not meet such demands. The suicides of soldiers who were unable to provide the required payments to senior soldiers, officers, and generals became a sort of epidemic.

Examples of extortion could even be found in the regiment that served the General Staff of the Russian Army in Moscow. In the summer of 2006, the public learned of a case of extortion that ended with the suicide of a soldier who had served as a computer programmer.[62]

Russian generals and officers were among the most active extortionists in the country. In 2006, it was found, for instance, that General Sergei Shpanagel, the head of the Ekaterinburg Artillery Institute, and Colonel Oleg Ledentsov regularly forced their subordinates to give them cash payments.[63]

In the same year, Russian media reported numerous cases of extortion involving businesses. Among the extortionists was a member of the State Duma's accounting office, who demanded money from the head of the air company Transero.[64] Extortion prospered in Russian schools as well. The parents of children in all types of schools were required to bring "gifts" to teachers and make various contributions to the school budget. In higher education, corruption was widespread in the admissions process, and extortion was seen in the area of testing and exams; professors demanded money from their students for good grades. There were numerous such cases in colleges in Tomsk, Novosibirsk, Samara, and other Russian cities.[65] Another example of extortion was the demands of city officials for money from people or businesses who wanted to construct residential houses.[66]

WEAKNESS OF LAW ENFORCEMENT AGENCIES

Trevor Dean, a British historian, offered a clear description of the medieval justice system. He contended that medieval justice suffered from two interlocking defects: the ability of noblemen to commit crimes with impunity, and the extortion/bribery of judges. At the same time, Dean suggested that the social power of the nobility and its connection to judges were but two of the complaints that historians have directed against the late medieval justice system. As Dean explained, there was also a problem with bringing suspects to court. Those who absconded were rarely caught and brought to trial. In fact, the court system could be seen as a machine for producing outlaws and bandits rather than for repressing crime.

In a world of fragmented and competing jurisdictions, there were, as this historian asserts, many means of avoiding prosecution: flight into an adjacent jurisdiction or sanctuary in a nearby church were the two most obvious, but claiming clerical status, and thus immunity from prosecution in the secular courts, was another. Dean noted that even when suspects were detained, the arrangements for holding them securely were often inadequate and prison breakouts were frequent. As Dean observed, it was especially important that at each stage social pressures could be applied to prevent or mitigate the rigor of the law: friends and kinsmen would influence those with duties to denounce crimes, or they and their noble protectors would press or persuade judges for lenience. After being proved guilty, concluded the author, there was a fair chance that the convict would succeed in obtaining a pardon for the crime; the ease with which pardons were granted was often criticized.[67]

The system of justice in post-Soviet Russia was similar in many respects to the medieval system. Law enforcement agencies were extremely inefficient. As suggested by the Russian crime expert Vladimir Pleshakov, the police registered only part of the total number of crimes, which increased the official indicator of crimes solved.[68] According to experts, the number of nonregistered crimes grew significantly after 1991. In addition to the 3.5 million crimes registered by the Prosecutor General's Office in 2005, there were no less than 1.5 million nonregistered crimes committed. The police in many cases simply could not find the culprits. In some regions, the number of such cases reached 25 to 35 percent of all crimes.[69]

According to a survey in 1997, people associated their concerns about crime with their low level of trust in law enforcement agencies; 60 percent of respondents reported a lack of confidence in officers' ability to offer competent assistance. Moreover, 38 percent of respondents wanted to own firearms to protect themselves from criminals. Eight years later, attitudes toward law enforcement agencies had not improved. Eighty-five percent of the Russians regarded "lawlessness and arbitrariness" as typical features of law enforcement agencies. Only 15 percent felt "protected against the arbitrariness of law enforcement agencies." In 2007, up to 70 percent of the Russians felt that "they are not protected by law."[70]

According to data from the Fund of Public Opinion and the Levada Center, between 40 and 70 percent of respondents were afraid of the violence of the police. Only 10 percent of Russians (and 8 percent of Muscovites) fully trusted the police.[71] The Russian courts were regarded with high disdain by most people. Only 15 percent trusted this institution in 2005.

A considerable number of Russians did not make any distinction between the police and criminals. Twenty percent of respondents characterized Russian police officers as people who take bribes, steal, and participate in criminal acts; 8 percent labeled the police as "criminals in uniform."[72] For this reason, many Russians assumed that it was meaningless, or even dangerous, to look for help from the police.[73]

Many people in law enforcement agencies did indeed use their positions to commit crimes. In the process of fighting fires, for instance, police and fire officers often plundered property from the buildings they were supposed to be protecting. For instance, during a blaze in a Moscow building known as Media in February 2006, the officers pilfered several pieces of equipment from the newspaper organizations that were housed in the building.[74]

THE CONSEQUENCES OF CORRUPTION: AN INEFFICIENT STATE

When money from corruption stays in the country, the problem has less of an effect on the country. For instance, in Italy, South Korea, and Japan, corruption has functioned as an impetus (though an illegal one) for the redistribution of national income. As a rule, the damage to a country is far greater when the money from corruption goes overseas. This was what happened in Russia. Between 2000 and 2006, roughly $20 billion, which included "the income" from corrupt activities, left the country each year.

Russian corruption posed serious long-term problems. For one thing, it undermined labor ethics, particularly among young people. The Russian youth firmly believed that bribes and connections were the best and perhaps the only way to become successful. Even more indicative were the data from a survey of Moscow students (the elite of Russian youth) conducted by the Moscow High School of Economics in 2002. When asked about the conditions for success in life, 64 percent of the students said "connections" and 49 percent said "resourcefulness." Significantly fewer students thought that "the quality of education" (35 percent) and "hard work" (27 percent) would bring success.[75]

Probably the most harmful consequence of corruption was its impact on the Russian state machine. Corruption weakened the state apparatus and turned state employees into cynics, who were indifferent toward the national interests of the country. They knew that their current positions and prospects for promotion depended not on their honesty or professionalism, but on their corrupt informal relationships with superiors and oligarchs.

As demonstrated by Russia, widespread corruption created a parallel, semifeudal chain of command that competed with the official hierarchy. While supposedly pursuing national goals, the real motivation of corrupt officials and corporations was at odds with the Kremlin's directives. For example, in an issue of *Izvestiia,* journalists gave a detailed description of Putin's specific directives for organizing the Far East fishing industry and explained how these directives were skirted by government officials who maintained close ties with the so-called fish oligarchs and the "fish mafia." The officials enforced their own commands and openly damaged national interests.[76]

When life in a country is relatively stable, corruption, like some cancers, destroys the society from the inside without producing symptoms or even pain. This was the case for Putin's Russia, where the political arena was calm in comparison to Yeltsin's turbulent years in office. However, the weakness of law enforcement agencies and the army, which was almost totally demoralized, was to a great extent the product of corruption. Igor' Rodionov, the former minister of defense, and Leonid Levashov, the former head of the international department of the general staff, agreed with the current head of the general staff Anatolii Kvashnin when he said that the Russian army was in a catastrophic state and was unable to perform any serious military operation.[77]

The state machine also proved weak in the face of "nonstandard situations," such as the tragic loss of the Kursk submarine and the mass flooding in different regions of the country in 2002. In July and August 2002, floods claimed 200 lives in the Krasnodar and Stavropol regions alone.[78] Equally powerful floods had wreaked havoc in many European countries, particularly in the Czech Republic and Germany in August, but the number of deaths was incomparably lower. German Gref, the Russian minister of economic development and trade, cited data that ranked Russia quite low (107 out of 158 countries) on an index describing state efficiency.[79] As an illustration, an audit of the

Petersburg police in August 2002 found that this agency was totally unprepared "for any cataclysm in the city, such as mass disorder, or a necessity to impose a citywide curfew."[80]

CONCLUSION

The weakness of the central administration represents a core element of the feudal model. The key features of societies in Middle Ages Europe were the autonomy of regional barons; the high levels of criminality, corruption, and extortion; the precarious status of private property rights; and the difficulties in interregional commerce. All these features were also typical for post-Soviet Russia, which justifies the application of the feudal model to the analysis of contemporary Russian society.

As in the Middle Ages, the cause of the country's major problems was the weakness of the state. It was unable to maintain order in society. Corrupted from the top down, the state machine was unable to fight corruption and extortion in its own ranks or in other spheres of social life. It was also unable to fight criminality in society. As in the Middle Ages, the ineptitude of the state and the corruption of its agencies were accepted by the population as normal phenomena. The people also became accustomed to the permanent fear and concern about their lives and property. The weakness of the state and its numerous consequences are deeply rooted in post-Soviet Russia. It would be difficult to overcome these problems in a short period of time. Even if the liberal elements of society improve, the Russians will likely live under conditions that are quite similar to life in the Middle Ages for many years to come.

CHAPTER 4

OLIGARCHS AND CORRUPT
BUREAUCRATS

The Purchase of Political Power

INTRODUCTION

The existence of powerful actors who could confront the central administration or control it through illegal means was a major feature of European societies of the Middle Ages. As discussed earlier, the feudal model is the most appropriate tool (though not the only one) for analyzing this period of history. In the Middle Ages, the most important actors were feudal lords, wealthy bankers, the church, cities, universities, and guilds. Among the major social actors in contemporary society, the president and the corporations are probably the most powerful. Other important actors include the bureaucracy, local governors, political parties, social movements, media, the church, universities, and trade unions. The high role of corporations (in Russian terms, "oligarchs") should be ascribed to the possibility of using big money as a powerful instrument in politics.

Money was an important means for influencing the central administration also in the Middle Ages. While the sale and purchase of territories and offices was a typical phenomenon at this time, the role of money in the interaction between the central political power and the major social players has increased immensely in contemporary society.

In post-Soviet Russia, money played a key role in the political process. The rich spread corruption in society and diminished the efficiency of the central state. The leaders of major corporations, or "oligarchs," became important political actors. The relationship between the Kremlin and the oligarchs was a defining characteristic of post-Soviet Russia. While in the United States the debates over the effect of corporations on society were already well defined by the 1930s and especially in the postwar period, stimulated by the publications of John Galbraith (*The New Industrial State,* published in 1967, among others),[1] in Russia, scholars only recently began studying this phenomenon.[2]

RENT-SEEKING ACTIVITY AS THE BASIS OF CORRUPTION

The idealization of money as a social institution probably explains in part why rent-seeking theory did not emerge until 1967, as described in Gordon Tullock's noted paper.[3] The term "rent seeking" itself, however, was not used until 1974, Anne Krueger says in another influential paper.[4] Rent seeking is usually defined as the political activities of individuals or groups who devote their scarce resources to pursuing the monopoly rights granted by the government. In other words, corporations and other major social actors bribe officials, from the heads of state to local judges and police officers, using cash and gifts such as shares of company stock, apartments, and high-class entertainment. They may also donate funds to the given official's election campaign. In exchange, these social actors receive privileges, including tax exemptions, immunity against criminal prosecution, autonomy in management, licenses for foreign trade, low-interest lines of credit, and the elimination of competitors during the sale of state property. A bank, for instance, may gain a great advantage over its competitors when government officials select it as the agent for the distribution of budget money. A special type of rent-seeking activity is the buying of official positions in political life. Wealthy individuals, or their proxies, have taken control of government positions at almost all levels.[5] Oligarchs and corporations employ a diverse group of people, including corrupt government officials, writers, journalists, scholars, and huge security teams, for this purpose. As in the United States, Russian legislators tended to avoid adopting laws that were aggressive toward businesses (as one Russian author put it, "laws with teeth"), while corporations in their turn did their best to "blunt, co-opt, or altogether destroy" any law that could really fight corruption.[6] The State Duma started to discuss a bill related to the fight against corruption, but by February 2007 it was not yet endorsed, because, as Russians joke, "[T]here are no businesspeople who want to pay deputies for it."[7]

RENT SEEKING IN THE MIDDLE AGES

Rent seeking was practiced on full scale in the Middle Ages as various social actors extricated privileges from the central administration in exchange for money. Military power was the major resource used by feudal lords in their conflicts with kings and other lords. However, the role of money was still quite high. In fact, money played a key role as early as the classic Middle Age, between the eighth and twelfth centuries. It was a powerful means for corrupting and acquiring power.[8] The subsistence economy, which many scholars treated as a leading characteristic of the Middle Ages, was mostly related to the peasants and was only partially relevant to the upper class, considering their consumption of luxurious foreign goods. In general, as suggested by Michael Postan, a famous economic historian, "[E]conomies wholly natural never existed and money always played an important role in Middle Age life."[9]

The royal administration and feudal lords of the Middle Ages badly needed money for various purposes. First, money was required for the expansion of the royal domain (the personal property of the head of state). Second, the central administration needed money for strengthening its military forces. Third, money was necessary for maintaining the high style of life of the king and his retinue. Many luxurious goods were imported from foreign countries, including remote countries such as India.

The central administration received money from many different sources. The king and other major actors (feudal lords and the church) received a significant amount of money from taxes or from extorting cities, guilds, and foreign merchants. The king, with his monopoly on minting money, could "spoil" or inflate money to benefit his interests.[10] Along with taxes, the state frequently could force the bourgeois and cities to "borrow" money. The central administration could also get money from big actors, such as cities and guilds, through negotiations and promises of autonomy and various privileges. Another source of money was the sale of various positions in the royal administration, a common practice.[11] The feudal king's strategies for procuring funds were quite similar to the notorious auctions of state property and the selling of high positions in government conducted by the Kremlin in the 1990s.

MONEY AND POLITICAL POWER IN A TOTALITARIAN SOCIETY: THE SOVIET CASE

The role of money in post-Soviet Russia was similar in many respects to that in the Middle Ages. In both cases, the state was weak and could not (and often did not want to) prevent the coalescence of big money and political power. Money served as an instrument for the coalescence between the central political power and other actors, particularly rich people and corporations. It was responsible, to a great extent, for the lawlessness in society. However, unlike in feudal and post-Soviet societies, the role of money in Soviet society was relatively weak. This does not mean that money was not an important ingredient in Soviet social life. Even in Stalin's times, money played some role in the economy and particularly in the everyday life of the Soviet people. Indeed, the people, as employees of the state, received money in the form of salaries, and everyone wanted to increase their incomes, even if one's social status was more important for receiving goods and services.

The existence of private plots and houses in the countryside and in small cities and the functioning of various "color markets"—illegal (black), semilegal (gray), and legal (pink)—where people could sell and buy goods also made money an important ingredient of life in the Soviet Union.[12] The importance of money increased with each decade of the Soviet evolution. The role of money increased in post-Stalin times when the authorities removed the legal constraints on the private purchase of cars and apartments in cities. The development of the underground economy further enhanced the importance of money in Soviet society.[13]

However, even in the last years of the USSR, money was less important than many other means for achieving high status in society or for enhancing consumption. For this reason, the level of corruption was low. In the 1960s to 1970s, it was mostly concentrated at the lower levels of the state hierarchy. Ordinary people bribed low-level state officials and other people in the retail trade and service sectors. Bribe receivers were typically found among the local officials responsible for the distribution of real estate, the directors of stores and hospitals, low-ranking police officers, theater ticket distributors, and sometimes the heads of educational or research institutions. A special area of corruption was the informal economy, where the managers responsible for fulfilling state plans used bribes to get machine parts and raw materials.[14] Overall, however, bribe giving was not highly prevalent in the Soviet Union. It was more common in non-Russian republics. The number of crimes committed by officials in Azerbaijan surpassed the average level in the USSR by 6 times. In Georgia there were 5 times more crimes of this type than in the USSR, in Armenia 3.5 times, and in Moldova 1.5 times. In the Russian Federation it was about 90 percent of the national level, and in Ukraine, 60 percent.[15]

Most importantly, the role of money in high Soviet politics was close to zero. I do not know of any evidence to support the idea that bribes had the slightest impact on political appointments in Moscow or even in the capitals and regional centers of the European Soviet republics. Corruption at the highest echelons of power in Moscow was extremely rare, and the known facts about such corruption make this phenomenon look like a childish game compared to the corruption in the Kremlin after 1991. The case of Ekaterina Furtseva was unique for the Moscow *nomenklatura* (from Latin *nomenclatura,* meaning "a list of names"). As the minister of culture, Furtseva took bribes of a few hundred dollars from actors traveling abroad.[16] It was discovered in 1973 that she used government funds to build a dacha worth roughly 60,000 rubles (about $6,000, a cost equivalent to her one year's salary). Contemplating the impending scandal and disgrace, she committed suicide in the following year.

In 1983, during Andropov's short rule, Mkhitara Ambartsumian, the director of a local trade office that dealt with the distribution of fruits and vegetables in the central districts of Moscow, was arrested. He was sentenced to many years in prison. It turned out that he had bribed several midlevel officials, the size of the bribes ranging from 720 rubles to 24,300 rubles (about $72 to $2,430, according to the black market exchange rate at the time).[17] These were indeed peanuts compared to the bribes in the post-Soviet society.

None of the Soviet leaders, from Lenin and Stalin to Chernenko, left valuable materials or money for their children. Brezhnev, who had the reputation as a person with an interest in collecting foreign cars (he had half a dozen of them, all gifts from foreign leaders), was essentially not an exception. He was rather irritated by his daughter's infatuation with diamonds.

The situation was different in the Caucasian and Muslim republics, where corruption flourished in the post-Stalin period and where positions in the party and state apparatus could be bought as in the Middle Ages. However, this practice had nothing to do with the highest positions in the national republics, as they were controlled by Moscow.

After 1991, there was a tendency inside Russia, fueled by anti-Communist ideology and the willingness to justify lawlessness in post-Soviet Russia, to magnify the real scope of corruption in the Soviet Union. Some even contended, against conventional wisdom and glaring facts, that corruption was a bigger problem before than after the collapse of the Soviet Union.[18] In the West, authors such as Leon Aron asserted that "corruption reached its apogee under the Communists."[19] Several other authors pointed to the privileges of the party nomenklatura, which, in fact, had nothing to do with corruption.

CORRUPTION IN POST-SOVIET RUSSIA: THE BUREAUCRATS

Rent-seeking activity expanded greatly in post-Soviet Russia. Illegal incomes from bribes soon surpassed the legal salaries of bureaucrats by many times. The illegal or semilegal incomes made people in the state apparatus and deputies in legislative bodies much less dependent on their current jobs. If they were fired or not reappointed, their accumulated wealth from bribes allowed them to continue their high lifestyles or find inroads into lucrative businesses.

In 2005, approximately 41 percent of Russian businesspeople described the level of corruption as "high," 45 percent as "average"; in 2001, the respective numbers were 28 percent and 47 percent. Small and midsized businesses suffered the most from corruption.[20]

All levels of the Russian bureaucracy, including the civil and military bureaucracies, took part in rent-seeking activity in the capital and in the provinces. As data from the research firm Fund INDEM showed, the biggest rent seekers could be found in the executive branch, which collected 87 percent of all bribes from businesses, leaving legislators with only 7 percent and the judiciary with 6 percent.[21] According to a survey by Transparency International, in 2002 Russia ranked among the most corrupt countries in the world, sharing a six-country ranking bracket (places 71–76) with Cote d'Ivoire, Honduras, India, Tanzania, and Zimbabwe.[22]

A Russian author tried to estimate the value of each office from the rent-seeking perspective. As an indicator he used the amount of revenue produced by companies that were under the given office's control. The highest score was given to the head of the presidential administration, who supervised the activities of companies with revenues amounting to more than $10 billion a year. The second place belonged to a federal minister who controlled roughly $1 billion. The next place went to directors of some departments in the federal ministry ($100 million). Other high officials in the ministry handled companies with revenue streams between $1 million and $10 million.[23] This list of offices was similar to the king's ranking of the most and least wealthy areas in the country in the Middle Ages. The king would charge a vassal or a claimant for the position of tax collector in a given area in accordance with this ranking.

The corrupt activities of Russian bureaucrats began in the last years of perestroika, when the Soviet state began to crumble. It increased dramatically after 1991. In fact, it was encouraged by Yeltsin, who, in a frenzy of money grabbing, gave the green light for personal enrichment to the people around him and to other officials. (I discuss Yeltsin's activities in greater detail in Chapter 6, "The Royal Domain.")

The case of Anatolii Chubais, a close aid to Yeltsin, is a good example. In the first half of 1996, a foundation called *In the Defense of Private Property*, headed by Chubais, was given a large noninterest loan that was used for financial speculation and as a source of income for Chubais himself. In order to make this possible, Chubais gave up his position as deputy prime minister temporarily (from December 1995 to July 1996) but was later reinstated in the government.[24]

Chubais and a few other high officials were linked to Oneksimbank, which, by using a variety of tricks (no-interest loans, excessively high honorariums, and other methods), provided them with various perks. The facts surrounding this case were uncovered by media organizations working in the interest of Oneksimbank's rivals, leading to a huge political scandal in Moscow in the second half of 1997.[25]

Another major rent giver, Andrei Vavilov, who served as the deputy finance minister, aided various Russian banks and even helped some (Unikombank, among others) participate in fraudulent operations with budget money.[26] Aleksandr Starovoitov, head of the Federal Agency of Governmental Communication and Information, was also accused of corruption, along with his colleagues (one of them was arrested in 1997), by the media.[27] By the end of the 1990s, it was admitted in Moscow that Gazprom was under the special protection of Prime Minister Chernomyrdin, who was a former boss of this corporation, and who, by all accounts, had a great deal of stock in the company.[28] In Putin's time, another form of rent-seeking activity prevailed in the elections of members of the state apparatus and the Parliament, as well as in the appointment of board members in major corporations. Almost all members of Putin's presidential administration were appointed to the board of directors of the major oil and gas companies, including Gazprom, Rosneft, and Transneft.[29] (I will discuss this subject in detail later.)

The Parliament, following the executive branch's model, ignored any conflict of interest and allowed its members to get involved in private businesses. Even if the officials did not receive formal salaries from the companies, there were, as noted by the Russian politician and journalist Boris Vishnevsky, "dozens of ways to 'reward' these people for their 'work' in a company—from multi-million dollar honorariums for so called creative activity, which were permitted by law, to the transfer of money to relatives."[30]

Encouraged by top officials, corruption embraced all levels of the bureaucracy. Another example of corruption was the case of General Viktor Kazantsev, Putin's emissary in the South District in 2000–2004. While holding his position as a general, he accumulated so much cash and jewels that when his house in Rostov was robbed he could not tell the police what were missing, because "they did not know how much they had." Evidently, using bribes from businesses, the general created several companies in his wife's name. Among these were supermarkets, a meat factory, and a medical center. As a sort of bribe, he received not one but two PhD degrees, one in 2000 from Rostov State Construction University, the other in 1999 from Adygei State University.[31]

THE ABSENCE OF A STRUGGLE AGAINST CORRUPTION

The corruption of officials by big business increased as the state weakened during 1989–1991. The problem did not find serious resistance from state agencies or other social actors. Over 15 years of post-Soviet experience, there were no arrests or trials involving high officials. Only a few second-rank bureaucrats were sent to prison, most of them without public trials. The Prosecutor General's Office, presumably the main agency for fighting corruption, muzzled all serious cases against corrupt officials, acting on the Kremlin's command.

One of the best known cases of corruption involved the actions of high officials who helped the furniture company Three Whales by reducing the tariff on the import of its furniture. The case surfaced in 2002, when it was discussed in detail at a meeting of the Committee on National Security in the State Duma.[32] The minister of internal affairs wanted to sue the businesspeople who colluded with corrupt customs officials, top members of the Federal Security Service (FSB), and the presidential administration. The investigation uncovered sufficient evidence for convicting all of the officials and businesspeople involved, but the prosecutor general, without any public explanation, closed the case and arrested its most successful investigator using a ridiculous pretext. Several people who witnessed or gained information about corrupt activities were killed, including a famous Russian journalist.[33] Four years later, the Kremlin decided to reopen the investigation and a few businessmen (but no officials) were arrested; by September 2006, however, there were no public trials in store.[34]

From time to time, some corrupt officials and oligarchs have even enjoyed a refurbishment of their reputations. For instance, Boris Berezovskii, the epitome of corruption, was praised in 2002 by some prominent journalists, including Andrei Uglanov and Yuliia Latynina, who invented various arguments to clear his name.[35] In 2002, the leading Russian newspaper *Izvestiia* launched a big campaign to refurbish the name of Kirsan Iliumzhinov, governor of Kalmykiia, who was not only well known as one of the most corrupt local barons, but was also involved, in the opinion of many Russian journalists, in the death of their colleague who had collected materials about Iliumzhinov's clan in this republic a few years earlier.[36]

How the Oligarchs Built Their Fortunes

In the early Middle Ages, the feudal lords emerged from various channels. Some belonged to the old families of the Roman Empire. They were able to survive the difficult times after the empire's collapse, just as the nomenklatura survived the fall of the Soviet Union. Others had a humble origin and were elevated to power by the new kings as knights. The continuity of the nobility of the old and new empires and the relative role of each element of the new ruling class were contested in medieval literature as well as in post-Soviet sociological literature.[37]

The origins of the Russian magnates were as diverse as those of the feudal lords in the post-Roman period. The oligarchs included former party and Komsomol apparatchiks, their children, former underground businesspeople, and even scholars.[38] The Kremlin played a crucial role in the process of their rise to prominence. It created their fortunes on the condition that they would share their revenues in one form or another.

As Yeltsin pushed for liberal economic reforms and privatization, he began to see an opportunity for personal enrichment and the perpetuation of his power. Of course, he was not alone in using power to create personal wealth. Members of the ruling elite and the nomenklatura, including the directors of enterprises, had seen the opportunity even earlier, in 1989–1990, when they began to take control of state property. Leaders of the Kremlin and people in the highest echelons of power almost immediately realized that the Kremlin should take privatization under its personal control. They saw the privatization of big firms, particularly those in the extraction industry, as an opportunity to bestow great privileges upon individuals who would reciprocate in the form of cash and other gifts. This process was similar to the creation of the feudal structure in the early Middle Ages, when the king distributed land and peasants among those whom he trusted and thereby installed as his vassals. The auctioning of state-owned oil companies was a good example of how the fortunes of oligarchs were built and exploited by the Kremlin. These auctions were a formality because particular buyers were assured the stocks prior to the auction.[39]

KHODORKOVSKY'S FORTUNE

The origin of Mikhail Khodorkovsky's fortune serves as an excellent illustration of how the Kremlin created its vassals. Khodorkovsky gained his wealth through the famous Menatep Bank and his close ties to the government. He served as a member of the government in his capacity as an adviser to the prime minister of the Russian Federation Ivan Silaiev in 1990–1991, as a deputy in the Ministry of Fuel and Energy in 1992, and as a member of the same ministry in 1998–1999. Because of his influence, Menatep was chosen by officials as the holder of accounts from various ministries as well as from the Moscow City government. The bank was responsible for the import of Cuban sugar and participated in many suspicious transactions with the government.[40] Khodorkovsky's bank was also the first to sell stock to ordinary people, who never received what they were promised.[41] Khodorkovsky was able to manipulate funds from various sources in times of high inflation for big gains. By 1995, Khodorkovsky, without making even the slightest real contribution to Russian economy, became one of the richest people in the country.[42]

In the following years, Khodorkovsky's next move, which added greatly to his wealth, was guided directly by the Kremlin. He transformed himself from a banker into an oil magnate by purchasing state oil companies while still in the government. This was another dark story related to the so-called loans-for-shares auctions, which allowed chosen banks to take control over leading state companies at a low cost in return for lending money to the Kremlin.[43] Khodorkovsky took over the oil company Yukos in 1995 for $350 million, even though its market price was $6.2 billion only eight months later, and $8.1 billion by 2002. His participation, along with other oligarchs and officials, in the financial operation known as Short Term State Obligations in 1996–1998, which brought up to 200–250 percent interest per year, was beyond doubt.[44] Khodorkovsky almost never discussed the origin of his wealth, dropping a remark only once that none of "us" are saints. He also said that "since 1999, we began to accept the international standards of reporting the activities of the company."[45] Khodorkovsky and other oligarchs often argued that they had not violated any law in the process of their enrichment, because such laws did not exist. It was difficult to disagree with Putin when he strongly rejected this argument.[46] Indeed, these people broke many of the laws that existed then, including the law against bribing officials.

VARIOUS FORMS OF RENT-SEEKING ACTIVITY

The origins of their wealth was not the only thing that tied oligarchs to politicians. A certain proximity to political power was essential for the general functioning of any big business in post-Soviet Russia. The fate of big corporations depended not on economic efficiency, but on the privileges they received in the form of budget money, the illegal or semilegal acquisition of state property, and the redistribution of property.[47] With the help of the Kremlin, a few dozen oligarchic structures acquired control over a considerable chunk of the Russian gross national product (GNP). The most wealthy oligarchs were involved in the extraction of raw materials (oil and gas in the first place) or in the area of finance and trade. Almost none of them ran enterprises in the science and technology sector.[48] Rent-seeking activities and close connections with the central and local administrations often allowed oligarchs to hold a monopolistic position at the local or national levels. These monopolistic tendencies were a typical phenomenon in the Middle Ages as well.[49]

OLIGARCHS AS POLITICAL ACTORS: POWER OUTSIDE

At the first stage of their development, oligarchs, like the new feudal lords after the collapse of the Carolingian Empire, were absorbed only with the consolidation of their power using the help of the central and local administrations. However, at the second stage, these actors made an effort to play a role in national and local politics. Oligarchs had several motives for getting into politics. There was a desire for immunity from criminal activity, the hope for developing a full-fledged political career, and the assurance of favorable conditions for their businesses in the given region.

Oligarchs entered the political scene with great fanfare on the eve of the presidential election in 1996. A group of 13 oligarchs (among them, Boris Berezovskii, Vladimir Gusinskii, and Mikhail Khodorkovsky) financed Yeltsin and his family and installed a sort of oligarchic regime known as *semiboyarshchina* (the rule of seven boyars, an allusion to one of the darkest periods in Russian history at the start of the early seventeenth century), which controlled not only the economy but also the law enforcement agencies. The oligarchs appointed, with Yeltsin's help, several ministers and high officials. They also tried to cancel the presidential election of 1996 and were active in financing Yeltsin's election campaign.

Buying Offices

One of the most important features of an oligarchy, as noted by Aristotle,[50] is the exchange of wealth for political positions, which, in turn, perpetuates the oligarchs' economic and political power. This practice not only allows for additional pecuniary revenue but also enhances the social prestige of the buyer. Exchanges range from purchasing nobility titles, as was common in the Middle Ages, to buying ambassadorial offices in the United States. The buying and selling of political offices escalated in post-Communist Russia.[51]

The career of Boris Berezovskii in 1996–1997 can be cited as a classic example of how money can buy political power. Berezovskii was appointed as a deputy secretary of Russia's Security Council, despite a myriad of obstacles that stood in his way. These included his double citizenship (Russian and Israeli), which the law prohibited for state employees of such a high rank, and the evident anti-Semitic sentiments in the State Duma and the security forces. The debunking of his reputation and, more important, his sources of wealth, along with his activities in the United States,[52] did not hurt Berezovskii's standing in the Russian political establishment. Berezovskii continued to combine his commercial and political activities until his showdown with Chubais at the end of 1997, a struggle he lost, and was subsequently fired by Yeltsin.[53] Vladimir Potanin's career stands as another good example of the cash-power nexus. As the head of a big financial empire he was invited to the government as deputy prime minister and served in this capacity for one year (1996–1997).

Oligarchs as Governors and Senators

A confluence of two major feudal actors—oligarchs and local barons—emerged when the Kremlin permitted oligarchs to become governors. The population was not averse to the idea because they saw oligarchs as good managers.[54] The most famous cases included Roman Abramovich, who became the governor of the remote region of Chukotka in 2000. Aleksandr Khloponin was governor in Taymyr in 2000 and then in Krasnoiarsk in 2002, and Sergei Pugachev asserted himself as a senator in the Tuva Republic in 2002. All of these cases occurred after 2000, when Putin was already president.

OLIGARCHS INSIDE THEIR EMPIRES

As feudal actors, oligarchs enjoyed a high level of autonomy inside their empires. When Putin curtailed their influence on national politics, he left their freedoms and autonomy from federal laws inside their fiefs intact. The employees of Russian corporations, particularly if the company was located in a small city or was the single major employer in the area, were not able to defend their rights. As a rule, the existing trade unions served the interests of the corporation, not of the workers. The case of the small Siberian city of Megion illustrated this thesis. The major employer was an oil company called Slavnest-Megionneftegaz. The workers lived in wooden barracks that had been built 30 years ago as temporary houses and still did not have running water. Most of them were close to collapsing. However, the company ignored the workers' complaints and persecuted activists in the independent trade union in various ways (for instance, by depriving them of bonuses).[55] The company also disregarded the rules governing safety in production processes, and in the case of an industrial accident forced the victims to ascribe the accident to factors unrelated to production.[56]

Among other things, the central authorities turned a blind eye to the collusion among business interests, criminal structures, and local political power. For instance, before he became the new governor of the Far East region, Sergei Darkin was widely regarded as a corrupt oligarch and a criminal by the Russian media.[57] Anatolii Bykov combined his control over the aluminum industry with his evident involvement in crime and corruption and his active role as a deputy in the local Duma in Krasnoiarsk. The late governor of Krasnoiarsk Aleksandr Lebed had Bykov arrested on homicide charges. Before his death in an air accident, Lebed wrote a special letter to Putin, begging the president to prevent the intimidation and bribing of the judges who would preside over the trial in Moscow. His plea was forwarded, but to no avail.[58] Bykov was given a five-year suspended sentence. He left the courtroom that day, boarded a black Mercedes, and headed for the airport where his jet awaited.[59] Also notable was Bykov's interview with NTV, a Russian TV station known for its liberal views. A leading anchorman spoke to Bykov with full respect, as if he was talking to a noble public figure.[60]

"THE WAR OF ALL AGAINST ALL"

Hobbes' famous characterization of the Middle Ages supposed, among other things, a war between feudal actors and the royal power. Post-Soviet Russia fits this formula well.

Feudal Wars: The Kremlin and Oligarchs

The relationship between the central administration and autonomous agents in post-Soviet Russia, as in the Middle Ages, was both mutually beneficial and at times deeply conflictual. The conflicts between the government and some oligarchs began in March 1997 with the arrival of Boris Nemtsov to the Kremlin. Together with Chubais, he persuaded Yeltsin to curb the rent-giving activity of the bureaucracy and the arbitrariness of oligarchs, particularly Gusinskii and Berezovskii. The battle that roared between Chubais and Berezovskii in 1997 was at the center of political life in the country. This conflict had two dimensions. On one hand, it was connected with the competition between Berezovskii and Potanin, whom Chubais supported. On the other, there was a struggle between the state and the oligarchs who wanted to control the president, whom they had helped in his reelection campaign in 1996. Chubais, of course, focused on the second aspect of this struggle, presenting himself as a politician who wanted to save the state from the control of oligarchs.[61] Both conflicts initially ended with some success on the part of the government (Berezovskii lost his position in the Security Council, while Gazprom and a few other big companies were forced to pay their taxes, at least partially), but it was evident that with their great wealth still intact and their control over the media, the oligarchs would regain practically all of their might by the beginning of 1998. Another conflict arose between Nemtsov and Gazprom, which was partially owned by the government and whose stock also belonged to the Chernomyrdin family.[62]

Putin versus Khodorkovsky

If under Yeltsin the oligarchs felt quite confident in their positions, the situation changed drastically with Putin's rise to power and his move to curtail their independence. The Kremlin offensive against Khodorkovsky was symbolic in this respect. Until 2000, Khodorkovsky had remained preoccupied with his business and the accumulation of wealth. After 2000, however, he declared his interest in entering politics. As he suggested in July 2003, "I never said that big business should be outside politics."[63] He even dared to publicly argue with the president and accused his administration of improprieties during face-to-face confrontations with Putin.[64] What is more, the oligarch promised a stupefied Russian public that in the next years he would leave business and go into politics.[65]

As a matter of fact, he picked up the torch from Boris Berezovskii as the most powerful oligarch in the mid-1990s. Khodorkovsky argued that the people who run the country's economy should control the country politically as well.[66] He suggested that if the oligarchs were able "to unite political power and financial opportunities . . . Russia would be a happy country in comparison with the current society," which Khodorkovsky equated with societies based on slave ownership.[67] The Russian public was also surprised by his declaration that he would rather be jailed than flee Russia.[68] The direct conflict between Putin and Khodorkovsky was triggered by the upcoming 2008 presidential election.

In his duel with the oligarch, Putin had numerous advantages. The main asset that helped him to prevent Khodorkovsky from intruding into politics was, of course, the might of the state. The developments in the summer and fall of 2003 showed how the president was able to use the Prosecutor General's Office and police to bring Khodorkovsky to his knees. The Kremlin terrorized several of Khodorkovsky's people by arresting them and by summoning the oligarch himself to be interrogated at the Prosecutor General's Office. The prosecutor showed him a warrant for his arrest on the spot. There were also numerous searches of Khodorkovsky's offices (they even searched the home of his friend). They surrounded his house with tanks, broke down the gate of his yard with firefighting equipment, and sent an FSB agent to the school where the oligarch's 12-year-old daughter studied. His arrest only crowned the chain of harassment started in July 2003.[69]

However, even Stalin needed ideological support for his actions against those whom he considered active or potential enemies. This was true as well for Putin, who needed the backing of the public and the elites and also some understanding from the West. He wielded several different ideological weapons for this purpose. Designing the game against the oligarch, Putin's team recognized first of all that Khodorkovsky's trump cards could be neutralized by his shady past. What is more, Khodorkovsky and several of his collaborators, including Leonid Nevzlin, his first deputy, were Jewish. The Jewish dimension was mildly, though rather successfully, used in the campaign against Yukos. For instance, the company was often compared to its major rival, the state oil company Sibneft, which was headed by an ethnic Russian.[70] As an article in *Izvestiia* suggested, the assault against Yukos had a clearly anti-Semitic overtone; some people claimed that because of Yukos the "Russian people cannot fully use their oil resources."[71]

The purchase of a British soccer club by Roman Abramovich only increased the popular anger toward Jewish tycoons. The decision of Nevzlin to apply for Israeli citizenship also provoked negative public sentiments.[72] While the Jewish factor should not be dismissed in the analysis of Russian politics, big money could neutralize it, as demonstrated by the experiences of Berezovskii and Abramovich. For this reason, Khodorkovsky's ethnicity was not a total guarantee for Putin.

Putin also had a file full of information about the semicriminal origin of Khodorkovsky's wealth. Khodorkovsky did not have the reputation as a great advocate of democracy, like Sakharov or even Sergei Kovalev, a known human rights activist in Russia. Putin was also unconcerned about Khodorkovsky's political moves abroad. With his sober assessment of the international situation, including the policy of the United States, Putin was confident that his support for the American efforts in the fight against international terrorism and the proliferation of nuclear weapons, along with Russsia's tremendous oil and gas resources, would ensure a hands-off approach in the West when it came to the internal processes in Russia. This assessment was reasonable, even as the *Washington Post* muttered that "[t]he preservation of democracy in Russia is more than an ideal; it is a crucial U.S. interest."[73] Putin did not get irritated by the statements in favor of the jailed businessman, even those by the highest American officials, including Secretary of State Colin Powell.[74] Putin was probably glad that the Davos Forum (a prestigious gathering of politicians and businesspeople) almost ignored Khodorkovsky's plight. He nonchalantly dismissed all rebukes against his domestic policies and defiantly equated Russia and the United States on all issues (for instance, he compared Stalin's terror to McCarthyism and the investigation of

Yukos to the cases of Enron and WorldCom). He simply lied about several developments in Russia, such as the situation in Chechnya and the case of Levada.[75] What is more, with his love-hate relations with the West, Putin began to flirt with the Eurasian ideology, which characterized Russia as different in various ways from the West.[76]

Putin felt quite confident in his conflict with Khodorkovsky also because he had the Russian public on his side. While Khodorkovsky's numerous defenders in the West and in Russia tended to ignore the origin of his wealth, this issue was not forgotten by many ordinary Russians. Having crushed the oligarchs' role in national politics, Putin in no way tried to eliminate oligarchs as a stratum of the population. He supported those who demonstrated their loyalty, such as Roman Abramovich, Mikhail Friedman, Vladimir Potanin, Aleksandr Mamut, and Oleg Deripaska, and aided a new generation of oligarchs who were not interested in becoming independent political actors. In 2006, there were 33 Russian billionaires on the *Forbes* list, compared to only seven in 2002.[77]

The Wars between Oligarchs

As in feudal times, the shifting of the Kremlin's "favorites" resulted in major political events during 1991–1997. Yeltsin's "pet politicians" (Gennadii Burbulis, Aleksandr Korzhakov, Anatolii Chubais, Boris Berezovskii, Boris Nemtsov, and several others) were in a continual struggle for "the ear of the tsar." Conflicts between corporations in any country are always bitter. Corporations compete for the leading position in the market and for a favorable influence over the central administration. This form of competition involves only "the few" and there are high barriers for new actors. In Russia, the ethnic factor played a role in some oligarchic conflicts. Supposedly, there was fierce competition between "Jewish" (Gusinskii, Berezovskii, Nikolai Smolenskii, Khodorkovsky) and "Russian" (Vladimir Vinogradov, Potanin, Lebedev, and others) oligarchs.[78] However, much more, often the oligarchs clashed over economic or political matters.

The feudal wars between oligarchs began in the early 1990s, when the battles between Berezovskii and Gusinskii, Smolenskii and Potanin, as well as between Potanin and Berezovskii raged.[79] The hottest areas of the conflict revolved around the auctions organized by the government, which sold huge chunks of state property in 1995–1997.[80] One of the fiercest battles among oligarchs was waged in 1997 for control over the gigantic state communication company Sviazinvest. In the opinion of Dmitrii Travin, a well-respected Russian journalist, this battle, which included Boris Berezovskii and Vladimir Gusinskii on one side and Anatolii Chubais and Vladimir Potanin on the other, defied all legal and moral norms as the two sides fought like criminals.[81]

Another important battle was that waged between the Moscow financial and political groups and the regional oligarchs.[82] A major conflict was also seen during Putin's regime when the old oligarchs from Yeltsin's era clashed with Putin's new circle.[83]

OLIGARCHIC SOLIDARITY

The fierce conflicts did not, however, stop the oligarchs from developing temporary alliances against a common enemy from time to time. Such was the case during the presidential election of 1996 when the oligarchs united in order to prevent the imminent victory of the Communists. They issued "The Letter of 13," which called on the Kremlin to cancel the election. Oligarchs as a group, in their attempts to seize power, supported the existing state of lawlessness and obstructed the attempts of people such as General Aleksandr Lebed, who promised to fight against corruption.[84]

With Khodorkovsky's arrest and the strengthening of the central administration under Putin, oligarchic solidarity was destroyed. Khodorkovsky's talk about "the maturity of big business" and its determination to defend him simply did not hold water.[85] The leaders of big businesses dropped to their knees and asked for mercy for Khodorkovsky in a letter to Putin in July 2003, but they did not even mention the name of their disgraced confrere.[86] In their next letter to the president, this time after the magnate's arrest, they sounded a little less obedient, but still refused to call a spade a spade.[87] In fact, none of the famous oligarchs, including Oleg Deripaska (who accompanied the president on a trip to Italy in November 2003 to promote Western investment in Russia), Roman Abramovich, and Vladimir Potanin (who, incidentally, declared his support for the president), uttered a single word in public to support Khodorkovsky.[88] As a Russian journalist noted, big businesses capitulated without taking a single shot at Putin.[89] The famous historian Roy Medvedev quite reasonably contended that the pusillanimous behavior of the oligarchs should be ascribed to their inferiority complex, which is generated by the dark origins of their wealth.[90]

Later, as the Kremlin continued to redistribute property in favor of Putin's people, the oligarchs remained passive with respect to the misfortune of their colleague. Only in rare cases would an oligarch beg the Kremlin to change its mind about Khodorkovsky or other businesspeople. Anatolii Chubais, the ideologue and implementer of privatization, despite his reputation as someone who spoke his mind, mostly kept silence on the Khodorkovsky case. After Khodorkovsky's arrest he uttered only a few words of condemnation and warned that big business could unite against the president, but he did not propose any specific collective action.[91] Chubais' friend Yegor Gaidar, the other "young reformer," was no less acquiescent, even though he regarded Khodorkovsky and other oligarchs as allies during the time of the country's major transformation.

CONCLUSION

The Russian oligarchs may be seen as the contemporary version of feudal actors. As in the Middle Ages, they continually challenged the laws and fueled the corruption of the central administration. The oligarchs could not function without help from high state officials, whose support they purchased with cash, gifts, and company stock. The relationship between oligarchs and the central administration changed over time. In some periods, the oligarchs could almost impose their will on the Kremlin, while at other times they retreated to the obedient role of faithful vassals. Unable to perpetuate sturdy alliances, they tended to fight each other, though, on occasion, they came together in opposition to the Kremlin.

CHAPTER 5

THE OLIGARCHIC IDEOLOGY AND ITS OPPOSITION TO THE LIBERAL AND TOTALITARIAN IDEOLOGIES

INTRODUCTION

Since ancient times, there has been a view that only rich people can effectively run society. The oligarchic ideology supposes that the rich tend to be hardworking, virtuous, and talented, while most poor people are lazy and prone to drinking and committing crimes. The oligarchic ideology has rarely been defended publicly in modern history. It was first formulated in ancient Greece. Critias, the cruelest of the "Thirty Tyrants," who governed the defeated Athens after the Peloponnesian War (404-403 B.C.), drew heavily on the oligarchic ideology. Several decades later, "Old Oligarch," written in the time of Socrates and attributed to his friend Xenophon, criticized the Athenian democracy.[1] Finally, it was Plato who discussed the oligarchic ideology in *The Republic*. In post-Soviet Russia, with cynicism dominating the public mood more than in other countries, the advocates of the oligarchic ideology had the opportunity to delineate the elements of this ideology publicly.

The contemporary oligarchic ideology, or "corporate ideology," recognizes several elements of the liberal ideology, including the role of the market, private property, and political freedoms. At the same time, supporters of the oligarchic ideology often justify, directly or indirectly, the corruption and violation of laws by oligarchs and major corporations. They tend to share the negative values of capitalist society, such as consumerism, greed, and narcissism, as suggested by the authors of *White Collar Crime*[2] and *The Bourgeois Virtues*.[3] They generally accept the reckless behavior of people inside corporations as a normal part of their tense and competitive life, even if such behavior brings harm and even death to others.[4]

Russian oligarchs and their advocates are more open than their Western counterparts in promoting these values in their public speeches. However, Russian novels, such as Yulii Dubov's *Big Ration*, Yuliia Latynina's *Steel King*, or her *Hunting Manchurian Deer*, are probably best at penetrating the mentality of the oligarchs.[5] Noted American novels, such as Theodore Dreiser's trilogy *The Financier*, *The Titan*, and *The Stoic*; F. Scott Fitzgerald's *The Great Gatsby*; and Tom Wolfe's *The Bonfire of the Vanities* and *A Man in Full*, also describe the mentality of wealthy people.[6]

ANTISTATE ATTITUDES

The oligarchic ideology, which in some ways overlaps with the libertarian ideology, is hostile toward the state, the totalitarian state in particular, even if it promotes the use of the state machine for achieving corporate interests and for the rent-seeking activity. The ideology is generally antibureaucratic, as clearly demonstrated by the case of Russia, where rich people, entrepreneurs, and their ideologues were deeply antistatist in the first years after the collapse of Communism. These ideologues talked about the state only as an inimical force on the economy.

The state was never discussed as an important agency for establishing and enforcing the rules of the new economic system (particularly in fighting monopolies and enforcing laws); it was never seen as a promoter of science, education, technological progress, and the arts. The advocates of oligarchic ideology ignored the importance of state support in some sectors of the economy, such as transportation, that were needed for satisfying public interests.[7] Larisa Piiasheva, an eloquent theorist of privatization during perestroika and in the first years after the collapse of the Soviet Union, was one of the most consistent foes of the state. She condemned the social function of the state and called for the privatization of all public services. Piiasheva explained that with economic progress, "social expenditures should dwindle" and people should pay for education as well as medicine and health care directly.[8] She claimed that "private farmers will assert themselves, new houses will be built, as well as new roads. During this time normal supplies of all goods . . . will be set up." In 1991, Piiasheva said that these changes would take only one year to implement.[9]

Oligarchs evidently held bureaucracy in contempt. They saw its leaders as incompetent and easily corrupted. Vladimir Perekrest, a Russian journalist with close ties to the Kremlin, offered the following description of the oligarchic ideology in an article that strongly criticized Khodorkovsky in particular: "The oligarchs set up patterns of nihilistic attitudes toward the state and they stimulate illegal activity in the economy. They consistently fight the rules in business and widely use their influence in the government for their interests, to violate judicial norms and as a major source of corruption."[10]

Justification for Corruption

The disregard for corruption is an essential element of the oligarchic ideology. The authoritarian and democratic ideologies, unlike the oligarchic ideology, strongly oppose corruption and the unrestrained use of money for political purposes. The Russian liberals of the 1990s, who often advocated the oligarchic ideology, tended to ignore the problem of corruption or downgrade its importance. Yegor Gaidar, the symbol of liberalism, avoided the subject entirely in his many works.[11] Other liberal authorities talked about the problem of corruption as a hopeless fight. Anatolii Chubais was one of the advocates of the "cultural origin" of corruption, which exonerates bureaucrats and oligarchs.[12]

Another way to justify corruption was to praise it as an important institution, as the "grease" for the proper functioning of the state machine, or as an antidote to the inefficient organization of society and bad state policy, as formulated by the defenders of corruption. Gavriil Popov, the former Moscow mayor and a prominent liberal, was a pioneer in proclaiming this theory in the early 1990s.[13] Oleg Deripaska, a great admirer of Popov, argued that public officials could not survive on the "miserable official salary," and therefore the money they received from corporations should not be seen as corrupted but as a normal part of their income. Deripaska applied the term "corruption" only to cases where bureaucrats took money from businesses against the will of the businesspeople.[14] The usefulness of corruption under some conditions was theoretically elaborated by the Moscow economists Viktor Polterovich and Aleksei Makarov—both members of the Russian Academy of Science.[15]

Another major argument is that corruption in Russia does not necessarily jeopardize its economic growth. Those who look at corruption in Russia with gloomy eyes should be reminded of how South Korea created a vibrant economy, notwithstanding its serious problems with corruption. Likewise, Italy made gigantic economic leaps in the post–World War II period long before the operation "puli mani" began its crackdown on corrupt officials at all levels in the Italian government.

JUSTIFICATION FOR VIOLATING DEMOCRATIC PRINCIPLES

The oligarchic ideology, which praises the rule of the "few" as opposed to the rule of "one" or "many," is inimical not only toward a strong state, but also toward a democratic society. The ideology justifies the large donations made to candidates and negatively influences democratic processes and political equality in society. It also justifies rude violations of law and is generally tolerant of corruption and the manipulation of elections and the media. It regards this form of manipulation as the only way to get realists (as opposed to idealists, demagogues, or populists) into the legislature who can work with big businesses.[16] As Robert Dahl wrote in his recent book *On Political Equality* (2006), in countries like the United States and Britain, the high role of "minority money" in political life makes no sense of the idea of fair democratic competition and at the same time makes elected politicians answer more to money and less to voters.[17]

In the Russian context, the ideology does not hide its contempt for democratic procedures. Compared to American or West European oligarchs, Russian oligarchs more openly promulgate their negative views of the general public and democracy.

THE ELITIST VISION OF THE RUSSIAN PUBLIC

The elitist image of the masses as "lumpen and uncivilized people" was elaborated in detail by sociologists from Yurii Levada's polling firm. This model describes the Russians as uncivilized people who are unable to live under democracy and whose opinions have no value for those who are trying to build a normal society. Lev Gudkov's article "Negative Identification," published in one of the best sociological journals in Russia, clearly defined this model.[18] Gudkov described the Russians, particularly those without higher educations, as an archaic and primitive people. He suggested that the workers were lazy drunkards and thieves, who refused to work hard and honestly but constantly complained about their salaries. They lacked motivation and were unable to work creatively. They needed a strong "organizational standard and technological control."[19] At the same time, they tended always to exaggerate the success of their work. Gudkov characterized the Russians as passive and resistant to change. They idolized "weak, poor, and suffering people—failures of all sorts. They like to quarrel with family members, colleagues at work and neighbors."[20] They used the halls and elevators of their residential homes as toilets. As human beings, Gudkov said, they were unaccustomed to "lofty motives" and prone only to "deviant and deeply individualistic actions." They maintained inferiority complexes and were permanent pessimists (he suggested that only 4–5 percent were optimists). They disliked themselves and lacked self-respect. The Russians, particularly those above the age of 40, were resentful, grudging, and discontent (in 2000, according to the VTSIOM data cited by Gudkov, only 17 percent reported being satisfied with their lives).

In some cases, Gudkov contended, the Russians' visions of themselves bordered on fantasy. They believed, for instance, that "collectivism" (*sobornost*) played a central role in their lives. The Russians supposed, without grounds, that they were highly spiritual and hospitable people, who were ready to make sacrifices for others. Another sociologist from Levada's polling firm, Boris Dubin, added to Gudkov's tirade, suggesting that the Russians were at a very low cultural level; only 50 percent of the Russians were interested in foreign culture and history.[21]

HOSTILITY TOWARD SOCIAL EQUALITY

One of the pillars of the oligarchic ideology is the hatred of social equality and the cultivation of greed. In this respect, it is clearly different from authoritarian ideology, which often gravitates toward socialism and social equality. On this issue, the oligarchic ideology also differs from liberal ideology, which has its focus on social and political equality.

However, this was not the case in post-Soviet Russia, where enmity toward social equality was openly discussed by the advocates of the elitist approach. The liberal establishment of the 1990s virtually discarded such words as "equality" or "social fairness" from its lexicon. These words were almost completely absent from the speeches made by Yeltsin and his ministers in 1992–1998, who were strongly influenced by the oligarchs. These issues were also neglected in the articles and essays that praised the regime in the 1990s.

The disdain for social equality after 1991 marked a historical break from Russia's cultural traditions. The elite's acceptance of inequality, for example, was deeply at odds with classic Russian literature. Since Aleksandr Radishchev, one would be hard pressed to find a single Russian writer imparting sentiments with even an inkling of admiration for wealth and the privileged lifestyle. It suffices to mention the giants of the Russian literary tradition such as Gogol, Turgenev, Dostoevsky, Tolstoy, and Gorky.[22]

Between 1992 and 1998, Yegor Gaidar, the architect of Russian liberalism, was consistent in his justification of the existing social polarization. He declared that anyone who really wanted to make money could do so.[23] Yet, after 1998, Gaidar entirely avoided the subject in his long articles about the developments in Russia.[24] Many social scientists and cultural figures followed Gaidar's lead, by ignoring the issue, shifting the blame for it onto the people, or focusing on the so-called positive aspects of corruption.[25]

Another leading liberal, Anatolii Chubais, who served as a top member of Yeltsin's government in 1997, was even more outspoken. Trying to put an end to questions about the huge poverty-stricken segment of the populace, Chubais said, "You cannot expect everyone to live a comfortable, pleasant life. It is simply impossible."[26] In the writings of Aleksandr N. Yakovlev, a leading ideologue of the new regime and former head of the Department of Propaganda at the Central Committee of the Communist Party, one can find condemnation of Soviet egalitarianism, but nothing against social polarization in post-Communist Russia.[27]

The economic problems of 1998, even the financial catastrophe in August 1998, did not enhance social sensitivity and the empathy of the liberals. In that year, Aleksei Uliukaev, a known liberal economist, called on poor people to blame only themselves for their mishaps.[28] However, even stronger words were used by Alfred Koch, the former vice prime minister, who declared on American radio that "the Russians deserved their miserable fate."[29]

Over the entire course of privatization, not a single leading liberal politician or ideologue stepped forward in the name of fairness and equality or criticized the conspicuous consumption by the elites. The blatant injustice that pervaded privatization was left unacknowledged by political elites such as Yegor Gaidar, Aleksandr Yakovlev, and Yeltsin.[30]

Presumably, the lack of concern on the part of the "old liberals" for the problems of inequality can be attributed to the formative years (1991–1993) of the new regime and the strong antipathy toward the still "fresh" Soviet system with its shameless demagoguery surrounding the subject of social equality. However, this same attitude continued throughout the years 1995–2006. The old liberals balanced their analysis of social reality, ridding it of the "Bolshevik-style" promarket fanaticism of the early years. They amended their image of the world and included—besides their beloved "universal" economic variables—an assortment of contextual variables that were thought to influence the developments in Russia, including the importance of the past, the complexity of social relations, and the emergence of the global economy.[31]

The "new liberals" who came to power in the mid-1990s were uncritical of the first wave of liberalism, which had disregarded social equality. For example, Boris Nemtsov, a typical new liberal, confronted the Russian oligarchs, accusing them of trying to control and manipulate society. Nemtzov did not, however, portray the oligarchs as the perpetrators of social inequality, nor did he mention their social insensitivity, their impropriety, or their undying will to flaunt their wealth and power at every opportunity.[32]

With Putin's coming to power and the increase of the leftist elements in the official ideology, the Russian oligarchs became less active in praising inequality. Most of them avoided the subject, assigning their ideologues to find a new, less arrogant way to justify the polarization of society. Nikolai Uskov, the editor of the magazine *GQ*, at the Russian Economic Forum in London in 2006, proposed a new formula to explain social stratification: "There is no right or left. There are only winners and losers."[33]

The insensitivity of the liberal establishment was predicated—or so the liberals contended—upon the irrefutable theoretical pillars of liberal capitalism. The "anti-egalitarian" mind-set of the liberals was rooted in their conviction—which was not without merit under special circumstances—that inequality propelled economic progress and represented an integral part of a free society. Inversely, complete equality, when forced upon the people, was feasible only within the framework of an authoritarian or totalitarian society. It precluded democracy and hindered efficient performance by the economic mechanism.

In defending social inequality, the "trailblazers" of privatization in Russia cited Friedrich Hayek, who argued that even if inequality cannot be justified on the grounds of variations in "innate abilities," inequality was still beneficial if only because it was conducive to the growth of the "total pie."[34]

Aleksandr M. Yakovlev, a prominent lawyer and at one time the president's envoy in the Duma, stated that "any society based on the rule of law engenders inequality of wealth and equality before the law."[35]

Unfortunately, Yakovlev seems to imply that inequality always benefits civil society.

THE CULT OF GREED AND HIGH STYLE OF LIFE

The idolization of money and the cult of greed are very important features of the oligarchic ideology. While these features can be found in any society, the veneration of wealth was particularly strong among Russian oligarchs. No group of people in the world were as interested in their places on the *Forbes* list of the richest people in the world as the Russian oligarchs were.[36]

The cult of money was linked to another tenet of the oligarchic ideology—the claim that rich people have the right to conspicuous consumption and should not be concerned about the impressions of the rest of the society. Two circumstances influenced the passion with which the rich people indulged in luxury after the collapse of Communism. First was their inferiority complex in regard to their Western counterparts.[37] Second, the life of the Soviet political and cultural elites was regulated by the many restrictions imposed by the Soviet regime. After 1991, rich people were suddenly free to enjoy a life of luxury commensurate with their Western counterparts. By the end of the 1990s, the oligarchic ideology had incorporated a new "theoretical element"—the praising of all things "glamorous," including "glamour cars," "glamour telephones," "glamour dresses," "glamour journals," "glamour romances," and even "glamour foods."[38]

The members of this establishment demonstrated their conspicuous consumption and wealth with their many galas, anniversary receptions, weddings of their children, consumption of expensive foods and liquors, use of newest luxury automobiles and private jets, and trips to the most expensive casinos and foreign resorts.[39] These demonstrations were covered extensively by Russian TV news and other programs in 1992–1996 and only somewhat less frequently in the following years. At the Russian Economic Forum in London in May 2006, there was a discussion on "luxury as a Russian national idea." The editor of *GQ*, a magazine addressing the richest segment of the population, talked about "the emergence of a class of 'golden collars' for which the consumption of luxury goods became a priority." As an argument, he mentioned that "Putin's love of luxury goods is well known."[40] In 2005, the sale of luxury goods in Russia was three times higher than in 2000, reaching $300 billion.[41]

Not surprisingly, the new liberal ideology, with its contempt for equality and insensitivity toward the suffering of ordinary people, often helped to justify this luxurious lifestyle in the eyes of the elites and the public. Russian media, including "serious" newspapers, described the lifestyle of rich people in Russia without even a modicum of moral condemnation. For instance, *Izvestiia* published a rapturous, two-page description of the lifestyles of oligarchs' mistresses. The oligarchs' expenditure on their "main lovers" included an apartment (a charge of $450,000 once every three years), a car ($70,000 every three years), casual expenses ($120,000 per year), gifts and entertainment ($130,000 per year), and vacations ($260,000 twice a year). The total yearly expenditure was estimated at $660,000. The expenditures on "reserve mistresses" were significantly lower, $150,000 per year.[42]

Russian oligarchs particularly showed their love for the glamorous life at Western resorts, especially in Austria and southern France. They vacationed at these resorts, celebrated birthdays, and threw New Year's Eve parties, sometimes inviting hundreds of guests from Russia. A French resort called Courcheville became particularly popular among Russia's nouveaux riches. Here they would pay up to 10,000 euros for a one-night stay and spend up to 700 euros for a bottle of champagne, "which flowed like a river" at this resort.[43] At Courcheville, Mikhail Prokhorov, one of the richest people in the world, was arrested in January 2007 for allegedly hiring and entertaining a ring of prostitutes at a party with several guests. Prokhorov was released after a few days of detention, but the incident showed the whole world how some of Russia's wealthiest people "s'amuse" (entertain themselves).[44] Another oligarch, the metals and media tycoon Vladimir Potanin, gained the attention of the international media when he invited the British pop singer George Michael to give an hour-long concert at his New Year's Eve party, paying him $3 million.[45]

Another typical example of conspicuous consumption was the public wedding of the oligarch Yan Abramov and the pop singer Alsou. The event took place at the famous Moscow hotel Rossia. During the wedding, the hotel was circled by six rings of police. Moscow mayor Luzhkov presided over the ceremony of signing the contract and the wedding itself. Several other dignitaries, including the speaker of the Federal Council, Mironov, honored the wedding with their presence, along with dozens of VIPs. The gigantic hall in which the wedding was celebrated was adorned with innumerable flowers costing several hundred thousand dollars. Champagne and caviar were offered to the several hundred guests. Among the highly valuable gifts (they were guarded by six men) the couple received a Bentley automobile from close friends.[46]

Almost no one among the leading Russian liberals raised even the faintest voice against the oligarchs' "feast in the time of pest."[47] Complacency toward the problem of inequality and its social ramifications could perhaps be tolerated if the country enjoyed a high standard of living—or at least a standard of living that provided a "respectable" subsistence for those "left behind" by liberal capitalism. In present-day Russia, however, a major segment of the population remains severely impoverished.

CONCLUSION

The oligarchic ideology was deeply hostile toward the authoritarian and liberal ideologies. As a rule, the oligarchic ideology was not publicized by those who followed its prescriptions. The characteristics of this ideology could be seen in the behavior of wealthy people, as well as in works of art and fiction. The role of the oligarchic ideology was generally underestimated by the Russians, and its critics could be found only among Marxists and in the radical literature. The ideology supposed that only successful businesspeople could run the country efficiently. It disregarded the conflict between the egotistical interests of the ruling elite and the interests of the nation. It also justified rent-seeking activity and the corruption of the bureaucracy, as well as encouraged contempt for ordinary people and democratic processes.

CHAPTER 6

THE ROYAL DOMAIN

The Thin Line between the Nation's Assets
and the President's Private Wealth

INTRODUCTION

A key characteristic of societies of the early Middle Ages was the vague division between the private property of the leader (the "royal domain") and the property of other lords and the nation's assets. The situation was similar in post-Soviet Russia, where the personal wealth of the president and his control over the nation's assets had a tremendous impact on the country's social and political landscapes. The concept of the royal domain is far less relevant to democratic or totalitarian societies.

In societies with strong feudal elements, the domain serves three main purposes: (1) it guarantees the wealth of "the family" and of the leader after leaving office; (2) it provides the leader with the necessary resources for maintaining power and getting reelected; and (3) it allows the leader to suborn officials and legislators with various privileges, such as apartments, hospitals, and trips to vacation resorts. In feudal-like societies such as Russia, the leader's domain systematically weakens democratic institutions, even if they continue to play some role in society. In such a society, state-owned companies and particularly mixed companies (state and private ownership) are important sources of enrichment for the heads of state.

Given the murky border between the leader's private property and state assets, the leaders tend to exploit their office for gaining control over a big chunk of the country's wealth. The leader's domain, which can be detected in most post-Soviet states, as well as in many developing countries, is created through various illegal means and can easily be used as the basis for future indictments. The concept of domain links the concept of feudalism to Russia—an observation mentioned many times in the last years by Russian media.[1]

THE LEADER'S AMBITIONS IN SOCIETIES WITH WEAK STATES

There is no chance for a leader in a democratic society to stay in power after the term limit runs out. In a totalitarian society (though not always in an authoritarian one), as soon as a leader reaches the top, he is almost guaranteed to hold the position for life without requiring to take any special step. Most totalitarian leaders in history were relatively unconcerned about the stability of their positions. The cases of removal of a leader in an independent totalitarian society, such as the Soviet Union, China, Cuba, or North Korea, are quite rare in history. The change in rulers in Soviet satellites was more common as Moscow could replace any leader at any time. In all of Soviet history, however, only Khrushchev was forced to resign when a political struggle emerged at the top of power. The Russian movie *Brezhnev* (2005) showed very eloquently how the frail general secretary, who would indulge publicly in a childish game with pigeons, was nevertheless protected from his rivals by the iron wall of legitimacy. The general secretaries in the USSR would solidify their positions by gradually diminishing the power of the politburo. This task was accomplished quite easily by Stalin, Khrushchev, Brezhnev, and Gorbachev without help from social actors outside the Kremlin. With his policy of repression, Stalin eliminated the possibility of outside individuals and organizations participating in political life. This policy was maintained by his heirs. As a result, political life in Soviet society was reduced to the relations between the politburo and the general secretary. Power shifts were only seen in the relative roles of individual politburo members with respect to each other and with respect to the leader.

THE ROYAL DOMAIN IN THE MIDDLE AGES

In the Middle Ages, the royal domain—that is, the private or semiprivate property of the leader—played a major role in the struggle for power. There was a tendency for the leaders to prioritize their personal wealth over the nation's interests. This focus was inherited from the first barbarian states in which a distinction between "private" and "public" did not exist.[2] A king in the early Middle Ages had his own property, which was managed by his retinue. The notion of "res publica" (public assets), inherited from the Roman Empire, was mostly ignored in this period, until the beginning of the ninth century, and the border between the king's property and that of the feudal lords and free peasants was recognized by the king himself.

In France, until the fourteenth century, there was no such thing as "public finance," and the king was not held accountable to public needs; he was only allowed to collect taxes when "the nation" was at war.[3] The royal domain played an important role in the expansion of power of Hugh Capet, the first king from the Capetian Dynasty.[4] At the end of the tenth century, his power was limited to his own domain. The same was true for his successors over the next century. Their principalities served as their only source of real authority.[5] The kings used every opportunity to increase the property under their direct control. Louis VI marked the end of the Capetian weakness when he rose to power in the beginning of the twelfth century, strengthening his control over his own domain and making his word the law within it. After the French king Philip II crushed the heretics at Languedoc in 1229, this part of France was incorporated by him and his son Louis VIII into the royal domain. In France, according to Martin Wolfe, "the royal domain lands just before the Hundred Years' war had spread to include virtually two thirds of France."[6]

According to the noted Russian historian Vasilii Kliuchevskii, Prince Ivan Kalita of Moscow, in the first half of the fourteenth century, behaved exactly like a French king. Yearning for the leading role in Russia, he increased his role as a Moscow prince and expanded his principality, which he treated as his own property. He was able to fill his coffers with more money than his rivals could and use it as a weapon to dominate Moscow. He bought the land of impoverished landlords in order to expand his domain. Kalita also made transactions with the church and other princes, buying whole cities and expanding his power. This use of the prince's personal money for maintaining and expanding power continued throughout the fourteenth century, but later it was with the help of military force and the

Tatar masters of Russia, for whom Kalita served as a sort of "capo" against other Russian princes, that Kalita's heir could expand the nascent Moscow state.[7] The role of Russian princes' personal money in expanding their kingdom was also noted by Sergei Platonov, another prominent Russian historian.[8]

The situation changed in the seventeenth century when Russia became a full-fledged absolutist monarchy. Then the Russian tsars were seen as the ultimate owners of all material and human assets. The special political role of the tsar's domain no longer existed, as the whole country was, theoretically, the tsar's property. Fernand Braudel, writing about this period in Russian history, suggested that in Russia the state was very powerful and compared it with "a rock in the middle of the sea." He wrote, "Everything would come down to its power, strong police and its self-imposing rule on the towns and on the conservative Orthodox Church and mass peasants (that were primarily the Tsar's 'property' and only then the property of their particular owner)."[9] In this respect, Russia was behind the Western European absolutist monarchies, which recognized a separation between the property of the king and the property of "others."

However, the Russian tsars possessed their own property until the fall of the monarchy in 1917. Livadia's famous castle in Crimea (where the Yalta Conference was held in 1945) was the property of the tsar's family. However, the tsarist property did not play any role in the political life of the monarchy.

THE LEADER'S DOMAIN AND THE TOTALITARIAN STATE

Unlike Russian emperors and post-Soviet presidents, the Soviet leaders did not own any major property. None of their children inherited significant assets, even if they enjoyed various material comforts while their fathers were in power.[10] This was true even for Brezhnev, who had a reputation for being interested in material goods. Property simply did not play any political role in the Soviet society. None of the Russian leaders (neither the tsars nor the general secretaries) used their personal wealth and money to keep or expand their political power.

THE DOMAIN OF POST-SOVIET RUSSIAN PRESIDENTS

Both Yeltsin and Putin, as leaders of a weak and lawless state, from their first moments in power engaged in relentless activities, most of them illegal, to secure their positions against their rivals, to extend their power and accumulate personal wealth, as well as to plan for a secure departure from the Kremlin. The expansion of their personal domain helped them achieve these goals.

The presidential domain in contemporary Russia included property that formally belonged to the presidential administration and that was completely or partially controlled by the administration. It also included state or private property that was grabbed by members of "the family" or given as "donations" by private businesses.

Yeltsin's Domain

When Yeltsin came to power, he immediately found ways to fill his pockets. His policy reflected the famous slogan "enrichessez-vous" (enrich yourself) proclaimed by Guizot, a minister under the French king Louis Philippe in 1830. The major motor of Yeltsin's personal enrichment was his family, particularly his daughter Tatiana. One of his main techniques was to sell state property at a negligible price to oligarchs who would pay the family back in company stock, real estate abroad, and cash. The most prominent cases included the auctions of major oil companies in 1995–1997, including Yukos, which was taken over by Khodorkovsky.

The real size of Yeltsin and his family's material assets is unknown because Putin, agreeing to become Yeltsin's heir, promised not to divulge anything about them. In his first interview as acting president, Putin acknowledged that Yeltsin gave him "an election gift." He even mused about his intentions to treat Yeltsin the way a grateful child treats his parents.[11] It was not accidental, of course, that Putin devoted his first edict to Yeltsin's immunity and to the well-being of his family.[12] There are only small bits of information about the wealth of Yeltsin's family, such as the existence of a castle in Germany that belongs to Tatiana and the luxurious lifestyles of the family, which are often discussed by various media.

Yeltsin created his own commercial enterprise—"the household of the presidential administration"—which was involved in various commercial transactions. The manager of the Kremlin household received a special presidential decree that allowed him to run the firm without paying taxes or customs duties. *Moskovskii Komsomolets,* a Moscow newspaper known for its impertinence, in an article titled "Under the 'Roof' of Boris Nikolaevich: Warm and Clean," suggested that Yeltsin had created "the most prestigious and corrupt commercial firm in the country."[13]

As in the early Middle Ages, when power was established more on the basis of personal relations than on a formal, legal basis, in Russia, people close to the president did not represent the nation. Figures such as Aleksandr Korzhakov, Mikhail Barsukov, or Pavel Borodin (the Kremlin "butler") were not accountable to the Parliament or government. The situation was similar in France in the early Middle Ages when the housekeeper of the king, the *majeurdome,* was a leading figure in the royal administration.

Yeltsin served as a "roof" (protection) for hundreds of people in his administration. If he lost his grip on power, these people would likely be prosecuted when their rivals took revenge. While some of them might have been able to find another roof if the president fell (just as some feudal vassals did in times of crisis in the Middle Ages), most of Yeltsin's inner circle saw a threat to the president's power as a personal threat to their livelihoods. For this reason, they would do almost anything to perpetuate Yeltsin's tenure and remained generally unconcerned about the nation's interests.

Yeltsin's Domain as a Source of Physical Security

In Yeltsin's time, the state machinery was so inefficient and unreliable, particularly after the events of October 1993 when Yeltsin used tanks against the Parliament, that the president created his own security structure. This structure represented part of his royal domain. In the past, the special guard of the head of state was part of the KGB. Yeltsin broke this tradition and created a network of security bodies that reported only to him. He established the Kremlin Guard, which was headed by his personal friend Aleksandr Korzhakov.[14] Yeltsin also controlled the Main Administration for the Protection of the Russian Federation. This body was autonomous from all formal (legal) government structures. Moreover, in August 1995, Yeltsin issued decrees that withdrew the three power ministries—defense, internal affairs, and the federal security service—from the government and included them instead under the presidential administration. Moscow newspapers assessed this act unanimously as a sort of anticonstitutional coup.

The Domain and Yeltsin's Struggle for Power

As soon as Yeltsin reached the apex of power, his personal interests became his top priority. Yeltsin's personal motivations and his willingness to retain power by all means necessary were often overlooked by Moscow observers during several key moments of his rule, including his violent confrontation with the Parliament in 1993, the falsification of the presidential election in 1996, and the scheme to privatize oil companies. Only a few authors insisted on the crucial role of personal interests behind Yeltsin's most important decisions.[15] As Vitalii Tretiakov noted, "Yeltsin manifested serious concern about life in the country only if it pertained to the preservation of his power."[16] Yeltsin used the money from his personal domain to bribe members of Parliament, a maneuver that may have saved him from impeachment. He also used his money to win reelection in 1996.

Putin's Domain

Putin's domain turned out to be quite different from Yeltsin's. Certainly, the property of the Kremlin administration still played a pivotal role in politics. As in the past, the Kremlin was deeply involved in commercial activities, including the use of numerous estates for business transactions and the sales of state land. The revenues from these activities were not controlled by the Duma or any other regulatory body.

However, unlike in Yeltsin's times, there was not an open appropriation of state assets; Putin's "family property" played a much smaller role than in the case of Yeltsin. Still, since 2003–2004, Putin's critics have increasingly accused him of expanding his personal property. As in the classical case, he accumulated property in part by diminishing the border between his personal property and that of the Kremlin. The case of the mega yacht *Olympia,* which was valued at $50 million and formally belonged to the Kremlin administration, stands as a good example. The real owner of the yacht was the subject of much speculation, though most of Putin's critics gravitated toward the theory that the ship was a gift from the oligarch Abramovich to his "friend." The critics were confident that Putin was the only one who had access to the yacht. Of course, it was unclear as to what would happen to the ship once Putin left office.[17]

The most important source of Putin's domain was his personal control over the major oil and gas companies. The gigantic gas company Gazprom and the oil company Sibneft, along with several other related firms, with all their financial resources, were under the complete control of Putin and his close circle. Yuliia Latynina, a prominent economic analyst, discussing the mysterious circumstances surrounding the auction of the oil company Yuganskneftegaz (a big part of Yukos) in December 2005, could not help but allude to the president's participation in this semicriminal business deal and his use of KGB techniques.[18] Garry Kasparov, the former world chess champion and a liberal activist, ascribed the government's attack on the mobile telephone firm Vympelkom to the intrigues of the rival company Megaphon, which was "closely connected with Mr. Putin."[19] Many Russians were sure that Putin kept money in foreign accounts.[20] Stanislav Belkovskii, a Moscow political analyst, was among those who insisted that the accumulation of personal wealth was the primary goal of Putin's presidency.[21]

Property through Proxies

As mentioned, unlike Yeltsin, Putin expanded his domain not through his family, but through his proxies—people from Petersburg, mostly Chekists, who became members of the boards of directors of leading monopolies in oil, gas, electricity, and railway transportation. While Yeltsin's two daughters and their husbands played a major role in his domain, Putin's daughters were still teenagers and remained far from politics.

Andrei Illarionov, a former economic adviser to Putin, who knows the inside workings of the Kremlin firsthand, discussed the developments in the Kremlin after his resignation. Instead of "domain," he used the term "corporation" to describe the enrichment of the Kremlin people. This corporation, according to Illarionov, saw the whole country and particularly the economy as its private property.[22]

Indeed, as the economics department of a respected Russian newspaper suggested, eight persons (seven Kremlin officials and the president) controlled "the assets of these companies, which were equal to three Russian national budgets, while the owners of the companies were so loyal that they were ready to give almost everything to the Kremlin."[23] Deputy Prime Minister Dmitrii Medvedev was the chairman of the board of directors at Gazprom (valued at $30.1 billion). Igor' Sechin, a deputy of the head of presidential administration, was the head of Rosneft (worth $57 billion), and Vladislav Surkov, another deputy, served as the chairman of the board at Transneftproduct (worth $400 million). Three aides to the president—Igor' Shuvalov, Viktor Ivanov, and Sergei Prikhodko—took control of companies worth $2.29 billion, $2.19 billion, and $1.2 billion, respectively. Evgenii Shkolov, an aide to Medvedev, was in charge of a company valued at $4.1 billion.[24]

One of the ways to acquire direct control over a profitable company and use its revenues for private purposes was a new type of nationalization that transformed the company's state-ownership status to mixed ownership (partly private, partly state-owned). This allowed the Kremlin people to access the company's assets. This happened to Rosneft in 2005.[25] The Kremlin's domain (or "the corporation," to use Illarionov's term) not only controlled the energy industry but could also influence most major corporations in the country. Using the state apparatus, tax leverages, the police, and courts, "the corporation" punished some companies and helped others. They imposed illegal taxes on businesses whenever the Kremlin needed money. For instance, the Kremlin charged private businesses in Petersburg $300 million for repairing the Konstantin Castle, which was to be used for a G-8 meeting in July 2006.

CONCLUSION

A leader's private property (domain) plays an important role in societies with strong feudal elements. As described in this chapter, the leader's domain was particularly important in contemporary Russia and several other post-Soviet republics. The leaders of some post-Soviet states, including Nazarbayev, Akayev, Shevardnadze, Niazov, and Aliev, were well known for their personal fortunes and the extent to which their domains influenced their actions and the general political climate in their countries.[26] But the key role of the leader's domain could be seen outside the post-Soviet space as well, particularly in some African and Asian countries.

The domain in Russia was commonly used for political purposes and was therefore incompatible with democratic institutions and clearly made a real fight against corruption impossible. As suggested by Yuliia Latynina, Putin did not confront the country's problem with corruption, because he himself was deeply enmeshed in it.[27] Drawn to protect their large domains, the post-Soviet leaders were intolerant toward free and fair elections and always limited the independence of Parliament with investigative committees. The dark origins of the domain pushed the leaders to stay in power for as long as possible, or appoint an heir who would guarantee their immunity and protect their personal wealth.

CHAPTER 7

THE LOCAL BARONS AFTER THE SOVIET COLLAPSE

Ideology and Practice (1989–1996)

INTRODUCTION

The characteristics of the period that followed the collapse of the Soviet Union, particularly the relationship between the weak central administration and the local barons, can be explained well with the
feudal model. In the Soviet period, the powerful state had controlled
each region and each non-Russian republic. After 1991, the situation
changed drastically, and most governors and republican presidents
tried to free themselves from the Moscow rule. The developments in
Russia in the first half of the 1990s were remarkably similar to those
in Western Europe after the fall of the Carolingian Empire. The feudal model explains almost perfectly the struggle between the center
and the provinces for property, taxes, and customs duties, as well as
many other developments in this period, such as the increase of bartering, the emergence of local currency, and the alienation of provincial Russians from the capital, a tendency that increased their hostility
and contempt toward Moscow.

The Center and Provinces in Soviet Times: No Sign of Feudalism

Before the revolution, in the second half of the nineteenth century, a few attempts were made, particularly in Siberia, to develop a sort of regional ideology (*oblastnichestvo*). This inspired a powerful social and cultural movement focused on the specific characteristics of the individual Russian regions and promoted local customs and culture. The most active figures in this ideological campaign were labeled "separatists" and were punished severely by the tsarist government, but the regional ideology continued to play a part in cultural life in some Russian regions until the October Revolution.

During the civil war, the central administration weakened and the separatist movement and regional ideology gained new life. A few regions proclaimed themselves independent "republics," such as Siberia and Kaluga. Moscow itself initiated the creation of "independent republics," if it could not control the given territory, as in the case of the Far East Republic. For a time, the Kremlin was forced to tolerate the "arbitrariness" of the local authorities, who were irritated by any direct intervention from the center in their region's way of life.

As soon as the Bolsheviks consolidated their power, however, any attempt to create regional autonomy or profess the regional ideology was harshly persecuted. The mass terror of the mid-1930s completely destroyed the regional ideology and quelled any action associated with separatism in all its forms. "Localism," or *mestnichestvo*, became a serious political crime. It meant that those who were focused on local issues in this way demonstrated their disregard of national interests, an accusation that could easily land the culprit in the Gulag. Stalin claimed that local separatism was among the many threats to the Soviet system.

Various provocative measures were taken against the local officials found guilty of attempting to separate from the center, and these usually ended in violent reprisals. In the late 1940s, the Leningrad leadership fell victim to a provocation concocted by the Kremlin. Stalin accused the party leadership at the city and district levels of organizing the all-Russia wholesale fair without the permission of the union government. The Kremlin charged some of the Leningrad leaders at the all-union level with conducting separatist activities. It was stated in the politburo's decision that Leningrad was guilty of "attempts to build a partition between the Central Committee and the Leningrad organization and in this way to separate the organization from the rest of the party."[1]

All of the major Leningrad leaders and 200 others were fired and excluded from the party. Many were executed by firing squad and hundreds were imprisoned. The city party organization was subjected to a purge, in the course of which thousands of Communists suffered.

After Stalin's death, oblastnichestvo began to slowly revive itself, mostly in the realm of culture, literature, and the so-called *kraevedenie* (the study of local lore), and later in the emergence of publications on the history of the regions. However, the Soviet ideologists were often hostile even toward these innocent publications, requiring their authors to write, for instance, not about "Siberian literature" but about "the place of Siberia in Soviet Russian literature."

In Soviet times, the role of provincial leaders (the first secretaries of the regional or republican committees of political parties) fit the totalitarian model. They were full-fledged bosses of their regions, but had to follow strict directives from Moscow, with a narrow freedom of action. Although the party secretary had a powerful image before his subordinates and the population of the region, he could not act alone on any domestic or foreign policy issue. He even lacked leeway in the interpretation of political directives. In case of any doubt, he had to consult the central committee. During the major political campaigns in Stalin's time and after, all party secretaries strictly followed Moscow's orders regarding the number of peasants who should be enrolled in collective farms during collectivization, as well as the approximate number of "enemies of the people" who were arrested in their regions. Of course, exceeding these political targets was usually, but not always, greeted positively by the Kremlin.

The power of the party secretary was also limited when it came to the selection of cadres. The second secretary, other leading officials of the party regional committee, the chairman of the Soviet Executive Committee, the chiefs of the regional branches of the KGB and the Ministry of Internal Affairs, the procurator, the representative of the Ministry of Procurement, and the directors of large industrial enterprises of union importance were all appointed by Moscow as the nomenklatura of the central committee. However, along with the rest of the huge army of officials, the first secretary of the regional party committee did whatever he wanted; he appointed them, dismissed them, and transferred them to other jobs. It was not infrequent that the service list of one person in a district (regional) nomenklatura included the posts of the heads of industrial, cultural, and trade organizations. The everyday life of top regional leaders was organized along the same lines as in the capital.

THE CENTER AND LOCAL BOSSES DURING PERESTROIKA: THE START OF FEUDALIZATION

As perestroika began in 1985 and the central administration gradually weakened, the country entered a long period of decentralization, which can be best described with the feudal model. In these times, as the central authorities gradually lost their absolute control over the country, the local party leaders became more and more like the barons of the Middle Ages. They oscillated between demanding total autonomy or even independence and supporting the idea of a strong center for defending and maintaining order in society. At the same time, the supreme leader, similar to a feudal king, in his struggle with rivals in the capital or in the provinces, was also torn between allowing a weakening of his power and recruiting allies among the local barons.

In 1988, as demonstrated by the Nineteenth Party Conference, the local bosses evidently wanted to use the process of democratization and the weakening of the Kremlin for the enhancement of their autonomy. They ignored the potentially negative impact of decentralization on the future of the state. Their critiques of the central authorities were as acerbic as their attacks on the mass media. Local party officials clearly regarded the ministries and the Moscow press as enemies who could potentially reduce their power and limit their ability to make arbitrary decisions.

When Gorbachev confronted his opponents in Moscow he tried to rely on local bureaucrats to support him in his fight against the Stalinists, who saw decentralization as the road to anarchy and the disintegration of the empire. However, with the dismantling of the Soviet system, the local apparatchiks began to worry not so much about their autonomy, but about the fate of the totalitarian state. In 1990, almost all of them strongly opposed the Kremlin at the last party congress in July 1990. At this point, the conflict between them and the general secretary had grown intense. It was only natural that during the August 1991 putsch against Gorbachev and the subsequent reform, the local party apparatchiks almost unanimously supported the conservatives. However, only a few regional party secretaries, without any tradition of independent political activities, were bold enough to support the putsch openly. Almost all of them waited to see who would come out on top before proclaiming their positions.

THE TRIUMPH OF THE REGIONAL IDEOLOGY UNDER YELTSIN

The anti-Communist revolution of 1991 and the victory of the liberals accelerated the process of decentralization. Two factors were accountable for this process: the objective changes in the country and the attempts of local elites, using ideological arguments, to expand their power at the expense of the center.

Aside from the Soviet collapse itself, certain developments in 1991–1995 accelerated decentralization. The abrupt fall in the standard of living and the evident inability of the central administration to prevent it served as the basis for the popularity of regionalism among Russians living in the provinces. It was reminiscent of the period of the Roman Empire's collapse when local bosses suddenly became socially responsible for the survival of the population. Millions of Russians in these years stopped receiving their salaries, and their savings were decimated due to the astronomical inflation. Under these circumstances, regional leaders claimed to be the country's saviors. Local leaders resorted to barter exchanges in order to provide food for their people. In some regions, the government started to issue its own money and carried out trade agreements with other regions and even with foreign countries.

The ideological struggle in the aftermath of the collapse of the Soviet Union also contributed a lot to the growth of feudal tendencies. Indeed, calls for the expansion of regional rights corresponded with the democratic ideology that dominated the Kremlin in 1992–1993 and was dear to the regional leaders who emerged after 1991.

As with any other ideology, the regional ideology was advanced and promoted by elites—mostly local elites and some liberal politicians who saw regionalism as an ally against the totalitarian state. The regional ideology was closely intertwined with the non-Russian nationalist ideologies that were also growing in strength during this period in all non-Russian republics, particularly the relatively big Tatarstan, Bashkortostan, and Chechnya.

Indeed, the thrust of the liberal ideology was directed against the totalitarian state, which, by definition, was a strongly centralized one. For this reason, the attacks against totalitarianism in the Russian context encouraged the regional ideology. During this period, the ideology focused on the negative role of the centralized state and even on the state in general. The democrats saw the Soviet Union as a totalitarian state that ignored the interests of the regions.

One of the most powerful arguments for regionalization in this period was the accusation that the center was plagued by bureaucratism, ineptitude, and incompetence, all of which stifled development in the provinces. The decadence and corruption of Moscow politicians and the general moral decay of Muscovites were included in almost all major texts or speeches that defended regionalism.

The regional ideology of that time further supposed that not only was the center unable to run the country through centralism, but also only the regional leaders, through joint efforts, could preserve the unity of the country.[2] The primacy of the Russian nation-state was being replaced with the idea of Russian Confederation. In 1991–1995, several regional leaders served as the mouthpiece not only for their own regions but also for the country as a whole. The advocates of the regional ideology differed in their desire for autonomy. Some would have been satisfied with a modest level of freedom in minor domestic affairs. These elites were generally from economically weaker regions that received subsidies from the center. The other group, which came from regions with stronger economies, especially large, non-Russian republics, advocated full separation from Moscow.

The advocates of regional ideology were united in their critique of the center, but split on the way to rule the regions. Regionalists with liberal backgrounds insisted on self-government in the regions and the honest election of governors and local parliaments. The slogan "democratism and centralism are incompatible" was a principal battle cry for many regionalists. References to the Western experience, particularly the autonomy of the American states and the German lands, were a necessary appendage to any ideological justification of regionalization. The liberal regionalists supported the liberal reforms that Yeltsin's regime tried to bring about in 1992–1995. They also supported political freedoms, including the freedom of media. Nizhniy Novgorod and Ekaterinburg were the bastions of liberal regionalism in the early 1990s.[3] The regionalists with authoritative views wanted to see their territories governed in the same way as in the Soviet Union. They were mostly enemies of the liberal reforms and wanted to preserve a Soviet-style order in their respective regions.

The regional ideology of the 1990s was criticized by the centralists (mostly Communists and nationalists), as well as by some democrats who saw the local elites as the enemies of liberal reforms. The foes of regionalization rejected the idea that the growth in local bureaucracy was beneficial. They pointed out that it was becoming even more arbitrary and greedy than the central government. For them, regionalization meant the expansion of the bureaucracy and a significant deterioration in the protection of individual rights. The critics of regionalization also argued that without a powerful central bureaucracy with an army and law enforcement agencies at its disposal, a nation cannot pursue its national goals, maintain order and unity, and protect the country against foreign enemies.

THE POWER STRUGGLE IN MOSCOW AS A CAUSE OF FEUDALIZATION

Another powerful factor that pushed the country toward feudalization was the conflict inside the ruling political elite. Indeed, the apogee of regionalism came in the early 1990s when Yeltsin, trying to consolidate his power in the Kremlin, encouraged the regional ideology by all means, which ultimately led many regions to proclaim their independence as republics, a move that jeopardized the existence of the Russian Federation.[4]

In his fight against the central administration in the last years of perestroika, when the Soviet centralized state was still relatively strong, Yeltsin, as a typical feudal king, looked for additional allies in the regions. He encouraged each ethnic region, particularly Tatarstan and Bashkortostan, and then pure Russian regions within the Russian republic "to take as much sovereignty as possible," an offer he came to regret one year later. Feeling insecure as the master of the Kremlin after the collapse of the Soviet Union in 1991, Yeltsin continued to look for support from local elites.

The tone for these steps toward feudalization was set by the ethnic republics, which extricated various privileges from the Kremlin, particularly in state tax revenues and subsidies. These special privileges enjoyed by the ethnic republics became the local Russian elites' main argument for justifying the need to elevate their regions' status. This tactic was used to place pressure on the center, as well as to persuade the local populations to support the elites in their struggle with Moscow.

ACTIONS AGAINST THE CENTER, 1991–1993

In early 1992, one region after another began to demand an extension of its conditional sovereignty. It soon became evident that the regions' efforts to obtain greater autonomy bordered on separatism, which was considered the greatest threat to Russian unity.

Following the example of the non-Russian republics, the ethnic Russian regions began to abolish or ignore the laws adopted by the Parliament, the president's edicts, Constitutional Court decisions, and the government's directives. The regional elites, particularly non-Russians, ostensibly adopted laws that were at odds with the constitution, exerted their control over law enforcement agencies, maintained relationships with the military units located in their territory, introduced customs duty for goods arriving from other regions of the country, introduced their own regional money, used bartering as a major form of interregional economic relations, and entertained their own relationships with foreign countries. In some ways, the regional elites now had more power than in the Soviet times, because ordinary people could no longer address their complaints about various aspects of their lives to Moscow, as was the case in the Soviet Union. The regional elites were free to manipulate elections, control the media, and maintain connections with criminal structures.

A FEUDAL STRUGGLE FOR TAXES AND PROPERTY

As in the Middle Ages, the fight between the center and the regions over taxes held special importance. After 1991, demands for the redistribution of tax incomes became one of the most important elements in the regionalists' programs. The regions, especially the so-called donor regions (economically powerful regions), demanded a radical reduction in the taxes paid to the center. Economically weak regions that depended on the center's subsidies were much less aggressive in this respect. The powerful regions were prepared to reject the center's subsidies, which were usually less than the funds sent from the regions to the center. In the struggle for financial independence, a few regions achieved some significant success in 1993–1995.

Ultimately, a number of regions (Volgograd, Yaroslavl', Samara, Krasnoiarsk, Altai, and several others) either stopped paying taxes to the federal treasury or sharply reduced the amount contributed.[5] By mid-1993, 30 regions had not remitted their taxes to the federal treasury on time.[6] The non-Russian republics were the most aggressive in the tax war. Chechnya, Tatarstan, and Tuva virtually ceased paying their taxes in 1993.[7] In this year, the Krasnoiarsk authorities decided to sue Moscow for various laws that had been passed to encumber the region's budget with additional expenditures, which the regional authorities saw as the center's responsibility to pay.

Another confrontational issue between the center and regions was property. As soon as regionalization took its first steps, the local elites put the question of regional property rights before Moscow. Non-Russian republican elites made the strongest demands for the extension of their control over the means of production in their units. In

1991–1992, the national republics tremendously increased the amount of production facilities and utilities under their jurisdiction. Whereas in Soviet times up to 80 to 90 percent of all enterprises in the republics were run by the ministries, in 1993–1995, 60 to 70 percent were directly controlled by the local, republican authorities.[8] The Russian and particularly non-Russian regions also fought with the center for various individual "exemptions." For example, they demanded (and in many cases received) export privileges, the profits from which would go to the regions. Irkutsk, for instance, demanded special quotas for the export of timber, and Tiumen received oil and gas concessions. Many other regions, such as Kaliningrad, Arkhangelsk, Kemerovo, Ekaterinburg, Murmansk, Cheliabinsk, and Chita, also demanded quotas for the export of their products.[9] (This issue will be discussed in detail later.)

THE ALLIANCES OF LOCAL BARONS: ANOTHER FEUDAL ELEMENT

Yeltsin's leadership was forced to acquiesce, as in the Middle Ages, when the regional barons came together against the central administration. The leadership even formally supported the Association of Governors and the Siberian Agreement even though these alliances were hostile toward Moscow. Many other alliances of regional politicians emerged in different corners of Russia. Some were relatively solid and coherent groups, while others were loosely formed bodies. Among them were the following: Alliance of Russian Cities; Alliance of Northern Cities; Association of Regions and Republics of Ural; Far East Regional Association, centered in Moscow; Northwest, in St. Petersburg; Central Russia; Association of the Regions of Central Russia, centered in Belgorod; Siberian Agreement, located in Novosibirsk; Association of Territories and Districts of the North Caucasus, concentrated in Rostov on Don; Great Volga, active in Samara; Ural Regional Association, with its center in Ekaterinburg; and Association of Eastern Territories, located in Khabarovsk. By the end of 1995, eight interregional associations appeared to be quite active.[10]

With the restoration of presidential power in the aftermath of the election of December 12, 1993, the activities of the interregional associations declined almost immediately. They forgot about their ultimatum to Moscow, which they had been bold enough to send only a few months earlier.[11]

CALLS FOR SEPARATISM

The local elites were always looking for more and more independence from Moscow. In 1991–1993, the local administrations continued to complain, as in the past, that they were "deprived of a real leverage on power," as mentioned in 1993 by Ivan Shabunin, the head of the Volgograd administration. Many regions in this period composed various statutes and constitutions that did not even mention the Russian Federation.

During this period, several regional leaders declared, as did the chairmen of the Altai and Cheliabinsk Soviets in early 1993, that "they have the right to cancel any edict of the president on their territories." Also, in early 1993, the political parties of the Kuzbass, for instance, vehemently discussed a draft of a regional statute that, among other things, declared political strikes against the Moscow authorities to be legal actions. Further developments prevented some local politicians from realizing their plans, yet the relationship between the center and the regions had already been fundamentally altered. It became normal to hear and read throughout the year about the regions' appeals for separation from Russia and even for the creation of independent republics. Siberia and the Russian Far East proved to be the leaders of the pack in this move. Conferences that met to discuss regional separatism, directly or indirectly, meshed with the contemporary political landscape of the new Russia. One of them, the Congress of the Deputies of Siberian Regions, convened in Krasnoiarsk in March 1992. The federal government seemed to be undisturbed by the conferences.

The dominant feeling in the periphery in 1991–1992 was that Moscow lacked a coherent political power and that the only way to save the regions was for the local elites to take total control. As suggested by Valentin Fedorov, the then governor of Sakhalin, "The state has been destroyed and if there is some power it is only in the hands of local administrators. Foreigners have realized it and want to deal not so much with the government but with the regional authorities."[12] Another prominent regional ideologist, Eduard Rossel, a politician from Ekaterinburg, created a movement called the Transformation of Russia, which was based on the idea that progress in Russia would be possible only if the regions became a leading political force in the country.

The Movement toward Disintegration in 1993

Without meeting significant resistance from Moscow, the regions increased their efforts, particularly after March 1993, to probe the limits of their autonomy. In the summer of 1993, in an article titled "The Brown Movement in Russia," one columnist from a Moscow newspaper stated, "In July the Russian regions ultimately abandoned their submission to central bodies."[13]

As key participants in the drafting of the new constitution, regional leaders sent one ultimatum after another to Yeltsin and threatened to boycott and disrupt the constitutional process if their demands for equal status with the ethnic republics were not met. The emergence of eight interregional alliances in 1989–1992, all of which were evidently aggressive toward Moscow, also indicated the growth of regionalization in Russia.

Throughout the winter and spring of 1992–1993, several regions tested just how far they could go. Siberia (one of the regions where oblastnichestvo had emerged) was a leading force of regionalism. For instance, during this period, a few regionalists in Tomsk formulated a draft of the constitution of the Tomsk Region, which was inspired by the "advocates of *oblastnichestvo* with its idea of the sovereignty of Siberia."[14] An article in a Siberian periodical denounced "Russian imperialism" and called for the creation of the "Siberian Federative Republic" as "the best flower among the flowers of one hundred independent states" to emerge from the territory of Russia.[15] In Tomsk, which was regarded as the spiritual capital of Siberian regionalism, the emergence of the Party of Siberian Independence headed by Boris Perov did not surprise many Russians.

In 1993, several regions, both non-Russian and Russian, declared that they would not participate in the national referendum on the public's confidence in the president and the Parliament and in other discussions that were being hotly debated since the end of 1992. As a result of these and other developments, a few regions did indeed prevent their subjects from taking part in the April 1993 referendum.

The idea of creating republics based on the unification of several districts had already emerged in 1992 but did not climax until early 1993. A number of Russian regions, represented by politicians of various ranks, in one way or other declared their intention to elevate their region's status to that of a republic. A new wave of events began on May 14, 1993, when Vologda, an agricultural region close to the White Sea, declared "*urbis* and *orbis*" that it wanted to be a sovereign

Russian republic. However, this bold declaration of the Vologda rulers was ignored by Moscow and the "republic" gradually evaporated from public consciousness. However, further developments showed that this idea did not completely disappear.

An epidemic of sorts swept across several regions, a regionalist domino effect that seemingly progressed without consultation with the president or other central bodies, and without an announcement by the regions either on their new political status or on their intention to make such a proclamation in the near future. The new republics mushroomed everywhere. European Russia saw the formation of the Pomor Republic, centered in Arkhangelsk; the Central Russian Republic, presumably formed of 11 regions, centered in Orel; the Leningrad Republic, centered in St. Petersburg; and the city republic in St. Petersburg known as the Neva Republic. In the Urals, the Ural Republic was formed around Ekaterinburg and the Southern Ural Republic grew up around Cheliabinsk. In Siberia there were the Siberian Republic, centered in Novosibirsk, and the East Siberian (or "Enisei") Republic, centered in Irkutsk. In the Far East, the Maritime Republic was formed with its center located in Vladivostok. Of all these republics, only the Ural Republic and, to some degree, the Vologda Republic developed politically.

No local leader, Moscow theorist, or law expert, including those who were close to the Kremlin, seriously considered this trend until the summer of 1993. One of them, Sergei Alekseev, wrote an article, "The Province Wants Freedom: Do Not Dramatize the Creation of Regional Republics," in defense of the creation of the Ural Republic. Alekseev argued that with a growing number of republics, such as "the Middle Russian, Moscow, Ural, Siberian, Maritime Republics and the 'free' city of St. Petersburg," "the recitation and the blossoming of the Russian people" will become possible.[16]

MOSCOW AS A FEUDAL FIEF

In the aftermath of the anti-Communist revolution, Moscow had an ambivalent position within the Russian state. The city clearly lost its dominant position as the capital of a highly centralized totalitarian state. The provinces no longer respected Moscow, which became an object of hatred and contempt. At the same time, Moscow was still the location of the central administration, which held tremendous political and financial power. These circumstances made the political struggle in the capital, as in Paris or London in the Middle Ages, for control over resources intense. In the 1990s, as a result of the weakening of the central administration, Moscow was transformed into a sort of feudal fief that could challenge the Kremlin.

After 1991, Moscow was not only the capital of Russia but also the leading semifeudal fief, ruled by Yurii Luzhkov. In the 1990s, he ran the city with his network of vassals (i.e., heads of Moscow districts and the highest Moscow officials), making the Moscow parliament an instrument of his personal power.[17] The obedient courts always protected Luzhkov, whatever his role in a trial, defendant or plaintiff. Luzhkov and his retinue combined their political power with their direct control over the extensive municipal property, including banks and car manufacturers. Luzhkov entertained close relations with several oligarchs (Vladimir Gusinskii, the owner of Most Bank, among others) and had political allies among the members of the elite who dominated the State Duma. He also controlled the media through newspapers such as the popular *Moskovskii Komsomolets,* which always described Luzhkov's deeds in a positive light.[18] With their massive administrative and financial resources, Luzhkov as well as the governors in many other regions were able to secure his reelection by a much greater margin than incumbents in Western democratic countries.[19]

AN ATTEMPT TO CURB FEUDALIZATION

The policy of the central administration toward the regions proved to be quite ambivalent and indecisive, as was the case in Middle Ages France. While watching the centrifugal processes, as well as the local authorities' animosity toward Yeltsin during the abortive coup of August 1991, the Kremlin quickly undertook actions to check regionalism in the provinces, hoping to stop its growth. One of the first actions was a presidential edict, endorsed by the Russian parliament on November 1, 1991, that gave the Kremlin the right to appoint the heads of the administration, a decision that was received with hostility by the local Soviets.

During the next few years, Yeltsin tried to preserve his right to appoint the heads of the administration and the governors for as long as possible by postponing the elections on several occasions. However, he did not object to the presidential elections in the non-Russian republics, a fact that angered the local elites in many Russian regions. It was not until the summer of 1995 that he permitted gubernatorial elections, first in the Sverdlovsk Region and later in other regions.

Another measure used to counteract the growing autonomy of the local authorities was the creation of the position of "presidential representative" in the regions in 1992. This official was responsible for ensuring the proper execution of the laws and commands of Moscow in the regions.

Despite these measures to restore the center's authority, the Kremlin did very little to curb the impertinence of regional leaders, especially the heads of the local councils (Soviets), who were popularly elected and thus felt particularly independent from the Kremlin. They challenged, usually successfully, the actions of the governors and of the president and his government. The press was full of articles describing the conflicts between the various branches of government in the regions.

FEUDALIZATION AND THE POLITICAL STRUGGLE AMONG ELITES IN MOSCOW

While early on (1990–1991) the feudalization in Russia was fueled by the conflict between Gorbachev and Yeltsin for power, in the next years (1992–1993) it was stimulated by a new conflict among elites, this time between the liberals led by Yeltsin and the Parliament headed by the Communists. The confrontation between the executive and legislative branches in 1992–1993 became the axis of the country's political life. Indeed, the peak of feudalization in Russia was reached during this confrontation. The closest parallel in the Middle Ages was the struggle between the German emperor and the Catholic Church. Like the Russian parliament, the church could damage the legitimacy of the head of state.

During this period of intense struggle with the Parliament, the Kremlin did much to ingratiate itself with local leaders and to elevate their status, even against their own desires. The president and other high officials began to convene various meetings of "consultation" with local bosses, who, like Viktor Stepanov, chairman of the Karelian Supreme Soviet, were behaving more and more impertinently toward Moscow.

Ruslan Khasbulatov, the chairman of the Parliament, and Vice President Rutskoi, who had headed the opposition against Yeltsin in 1993, actively looked for the regions' support in their political struggle with the center. During his visit to East Siberia in late 1992, Rutskoi demanded that the Russian regions have the same rights as the ethnic republics. Khasbulatov also traveled across the country attending various meetings and doing his best to enroll the support of the local elites. At one such meeting (the Conference of Deputies from All Levels, from the district Soviets to the All-Federation Supreme Soviet) in June 1993, he encouraged the local Soviets to resist the executive power in their regions as well as in Moscow.

The regions' crucial role became evident in March 1993, when the confrontation between Yeltsin and the Parliament reached its first climax. Both camps did their best to gain the support of the regional elites as well as the masses. The president and the Parliament attempted to outmaneuver each other, reduce the other's power, and generally present the other as the enemy of the people. In the meantime, the regional leaders felt that their time had come and that they should establish themselves as the real power holders.

By March 1993, the differences in attitudes among and within the regions toward the conflict intensified. The local councils in many of the regions favored the Parliament, whereas the heads of the administration demonstrated their loyalty to the president. Interestingly enough, most of these heads were appointed by Yeltsin, including the mayor of St. Petersburg, Anatolii Sobchak, and the governor of Nizhniy Novgorod, Boris Nemtsov. Such a split also occurred in Samara, where the head of the local administration, Konstantin Titov, supported Yeltsin's edict against the Parliament while the so-called small council of the local Soviet refused to comply. Similar developments occurred in Tomsk, Voronezh, Tula, Krasnoiarsk, Khabarovsk, and other places. These developments also revealed with great clarity how fragile the regional political structure really was. Until the showdown in October 1993, the Parliament certainly enjoyed greater support from the regions.

Even though internal conflicts were raging almost everywhere, the political sympathies in some regions and cities were focused primarily on one of the rivals. For instance, Krasnoiarsk, one of the largest Siberian cities where the Communist and Russian nationalist movements were quite strong, was one such locus of support. Russian nationalists were also active in 1992–1993 in Vologda, Irkutsk, Perm, and a few other cities. Only in a few regions and cities, including Moscow and St. Petersburg, did the president's faction prevail.

IN FEAR OF THE COUNTRY'S COLLAPSE

The movement toward autonomy and separatism in Russia was so unusual and alarming that the fear of an imminent collapse spread throughout the country in 1992–1993. Most politicians and journalists saw the major threat to the Russian Federation not so much in the separatist rhetoric of the ethnic republics as in the aspirations of the Russian regions, whose views were also supported by some Western observers. Nikolai Travkin, a prominent politician, said at the end of 1992 that the disintegration of Russia was "an evident fact."[20] A typical article of this period was titled "Will Russia Collapse?"[21] Leonid She-barshin, the former KGB chief and head of the Soviet foreign intelli-gence services, was also very pessimistic in mid-1993. He wrote: "Unfortunately, the process of the splitting of Russia is continuing and the fears of some sincerely concerned people that Russia will break up into several independent principalities do not seem fantastic to me."[22]

Andranik Migranian, a member of the presidential council and a prominent political scientist, in late 1992 also lamented the impend-ing collapse of the country. Protesting against the possible dissolution of the Russian parliament by the president, Migranian said, "The dis-integration is going on its own, but without the body [Parliament] which is the symbol of the unity of the Russian state; it is difficult to imagine how Moscow will be able to keep control over the regions and republics."[23] The same feelings were expressed by dozens of other politicians.[24]

Pessimists were especially concerned about the effect of regional-ization in the regions that bordered foreign countries, such as those in the Far East. Pointing to the tremendous economic and social dif-ferences between regions, they envisioned interregional conflicts, ini-tially based on economic disagreements, which would escalate into military confrontations as part of an overall civil war. Russian pes-simists also imagined regional alliances directed against Moscow, an idea once found only in science fiction that had now become a poten-tial reality. In addition, they raised questions about the ability of re-gional leaders to guarantee the safety of nuclear power stations, chemical plants, and oil pipelines. In the view of these critics, region-alization would hardly serve the population, because its beneficiaries would be the regional elites and the mafia.

In a survey of 200 experts conducted by the Moscow Center of Public Opinion Studies in April-May 1993, 53 percent envisaged "a growing number of regions that would proclaim their sovereignty," and 5 percent even predicted the full disintegration of Russia. Whereas 52 percent predicted that separatism would grow or at least remain at the same level, only 18 percent believed in the integrative process. In another survey of "the leaders of public opinion," con-ducted by Boris Grushin's polling firm Vox Populi in November 1993, 38 percent of those polled, who answered the question "What is the probability of the division of Russia into several independent states?" responded "very high" or "high."[25]

THE WEAKENING OF FEUDALISM
IN THE MID-1990S

The confrontation between the Kremlin and the Parliament ended when Yeltsin ordered the shelling of the Parliament building and the arrest of the leaders of the insurrection on October 3–4, 1993. With the defeat of his rivals, Yeltsin strengthened his position with respect to the local barons. Soon after his victory, he radically changed his attitude toward the regional leaders, forgetting his declarations about their special role. The president declared war on the regional elites and their administrative bodies. Most of the elites were terrified as they watched the shelling of the White House. Yeltsin's administration purged many regional leaders and regional Soviets. The president then declared that all governors would be appointed by him.

Yeltsin also signed a decree on the use of economic sanctions against the territorial formations within Russia that failed to pay taxes to the state treasury. This decree gave the government the right to stop financing the enterprises located in those districts, territories, and national republics that underpaid their taxes to the federal budget.

However, the Kremlin could only afford to keep its contemptuous stance toward the regional leaders for a short period after the October 1993 debacle. A few months after his October victory, Yeltsin, as a typical feudal monarch, realized that he could in no way assume that the country was now stable and under his control. In fact, the extremely poor economic situation, the key factor in the political processes in Russia, persisted in 1994–1995. As it soon turned out, Yeltsin's October victory only temporarily strengthened his regime. His base of support among the Russian population gradually waned in 1994–1995 and his regime weakened. Thus, it did not come as a surprise that the December 1995 parliamentary elections brought about the opposition's victory. This victory forced the current regime to make a number of concessions to the Communists and nationalists, who, during the election campaign, tried to present themselves as the provinces' defenders against a Westernized and corrupt Moscow.

With the regime's internal weakening in 1994–1995, regionalization entered a new phase. The public was already accustomed to the regions' growing role in the country's political and economic affairs, leading to the media's disinterest in this issue, in comparison to the events of 1992–1993. However, the non-Russian republics continued in 1994–1995 to gradually gain greater autonomy.

THE NEGOTIATION OF PACTS BETWEEN MOSCOW AND THE REGIONS

One of the most important events in this period was the signing in February 1994 of a treaty stipulating 12 special agreements between Moscow and Kazan. This treaty was purportedly to recognize both the "statehood of Tatarstan" and the republic's subordination to international law. The treaty was also seen as a method to demarcate the powers of federal and local authorities.

However, the treaty did not satisfy the extremist groups in Moscow or Kazan. Russian centralists, preaching the Russian nationalist ideology, denounced the treaty as too large a concession to the Tatar separatists. Tatar nationalists saw the treaty as indicating the Tatar elite's retreat from its previous position, because the term "sovereignty" was not even mentioned. In addition, they considered the treaty, which regarded Tatarstan as an ordinary subject of the Russian Federation, as contradicting with the Tatar constitution.

Despite this debate, the treaty between Moscow and Kazan became a desirable model for all the other republics. In 1994–1995, Moscow signed similar agreements with Bashkortostan, Buriatiia, Kabardino-Balkaria, Sakha-Yakutiia, Udmurtiia, and North Osetiia. As a rule, the separation of power between the republics and Moscow in these treaties was quite ambivalent, leaving both parties the opportunity to interpret the treaties as they wished.

Many Russian regions also required similar relations with Moscow. Following the events of October 1993, the Kremlin initially rejected the pressure exerted by most of the larger regions, such as Nizhniy Novgorod and Ekaterinburg, to sign a special pact with them. However, two years later, Moscow retreated from its position and started to make similar agreements with the pure ethnic Russian regions. Remarkably, Sverdlovsk was the first such region. Then, in late 1995 and early 1996, special agreements "on the separation of powers" with the Kremlin were signed by Nizhniy Novgorod, Orenburg, and Kaliningrad.

At the same time, several regions, mostly those with weak economic potential, declared in 1993–1994 that they were not seeking special agreements with the center and preferred standard rules in their relations with the center. They assumed that such a procedure would not put them in a disadvantageous position in comparison with the stronger regions.

A REVERSED COURSE: THE WAR AGAINST CHECHNYA

While in the first half of the 1990s the Kremlin was still weak and avoided confrontation with the regions—as seen, for instance, in the conflict between Moscow and the boss of the Maritime Territory, Evgenii Nazdratenko—in the middle of the decade it moved toward a more assertive policy. The turning point was 1994, when Moscow decided to declare a war against General Dzhokhar Dudaev, the president of separatist Chechnya, and pacify this republic, which had openly proclaimed its independence. However, it turned out to be a disaster, and before the presidential election in 1996 Moscow signed a peace treaty with the Chechen leader and recognized Chechnya's de facto independence.

However, despite the defeat of the Russian troops in Chechnya, the blood bath in this republic sent a signal to the regional bosses, and particularly to the elites in non-Russian republics, that the cost of their separatism would be very high. In any case, after 1996, the movement toward disintegration of Russia was halted. What is more, with Putin's rise to power in 1999–2000 and with the start of the second war against Chechnya, the center's offensive against the regional barons resumed with new force across the country.

PUBLIC ATTITUDES TOWARD REGIONALIZATION IN THE 1990S

The attitudes of ordinary Russians toward the ideology and practice of regionalization in the 1990s were quite contradictory. Two circumstances shaped these attitudes: the deep indifferences of the Russians toward public life, and their contempt for the central authorities.

The mood in Russia after the collapse of the Soviet Union was similar to the mood in Europe after the collapse of the Roman Empire. In both cases, people struggled to survive and lost interest in public issues. The privatization of state offices and the absorption of state officials with their private interests—a feudal process that has almost nothing in common with the capitalist transformation—only enhanced the people's indifference toward national issues. Indeed, according to data collected by VTSIOM in 1994, no more than 3 to 7 percent supported any particular "ideological slogan," including "social justice" (no more than 3 percent) and a "strong state" (7 percent).[26] The Russians in this period demonstrated their lack of concern for the fate of the country. They were openly hostile to

Moscow and refused to see it as the capital of a united state. Patriotism, a leading Soviet value shared sincerely by the majority of Soviet people, probably reached its nadir in 1994. Although the Russians were nostalgic for the "old country" (the Soviet Union), in 1992–1995, they did not want to accept even the slightest sacrifice for the restoration of the empire. For this reason, ordinary Russians were lukewarm about the possible reunification with Byelorussia and Ukraine, seeing both of these Slavic republics as poor relatives whose alliance with Russia would only fuel inflation.

Given the mood of "jungle individualism" and with private concerns trumping interest in public affairs, the Russians refused to trust any national political institution or Moscow politician. In the eyes of the people, almost all politicians, especially those in Moscow, were corrupt and concerned only with their own private interests and enrichment. Less than 10 percent of the Russians trusted Yeltsin as a leader in the 1990s.[27]

Most Russians did not identify with any single national political party in the country, a circumstance that contributed to their alienation from the center and aided the spread of the regional ideology. According to various surveys, in 1992–1995, no more than 5 to 10 percent of the Russians considered themselves members of a political association or even sympathized with any particular politician in the current government or in the opposition.

The people were not only disinterested in restoring the Soviet Union, but they were also rather indifferent toward the integrity of the Russian Federation. Most Russians did not support the official justification of the Chechen War as an action necessary to save Russia as a nation. They refused to sacrifice their sons and money for this purpose. In fact, most favored the expulsion of Chechnya from Russia. Only a minority of the Russians (no more than 20 to 25 percent) accepted Yeltsin's justification of the war as a necessary condition for the preservation of the territorial integrity of the country.[28] The people were evidently unafraid of the idea of an almost independent Chechnya and would not make the sacrifices needed to stop national separatism. The media castigated the Kremlin, denouncing Yeltsin's policy in the North Caucasus not only in the non-Russian republics but also in the pure ethnic Russian regions.[29]

Considering the public's hostility toward national institutions in general, the people in the provinces were somewhat less hostile toward the local authorities, in spite of being aware of their corrupt activities. Indeed, according to a June 2000 survey, 60 percent of Muscovites saw their Moscow bosses "as more responsive to their needs and interests" than "the Russian state authorities"; 10 percent held the opposite view. For St. Petersburg, the respective ratio was 2:1. The resounding victory of Rossel in August 1995 in the governor's race in Ekaterinburg was quite remarkable, as this politician was the founder of the Ural Republic. However, in other regions included in the survey, the "arbitrariness" and "aloofness" of the regional power holders were considered higher than that of the central administration (in Novosibirsk, for instance, the ratio was 0.7:1; in Dagestan, 1:9).[30]

With the Russians absorbed with their private lives and considering their distrust of political institutions and ambivalence toward the regional leaders, both the centrists and regionalists had a chance to persuade the public to join them in their struggles. As further developments showed, with the reassertion of presidential power in Moscow and the Russians' yearning for order as a supreme value, the Kremlin gained public support in its move toward centralism.

CONCLUSION

Russia started its move toward a polycentric, decentralized society under the impact of the liberalization of the monocentric Soviet society during perestroika. The withering of the totalitarian state immediately triggered the process of decentralization. The local elites started to expand their power. Clashes in the capital between different factions and the emergence of several centers of power only increased the level of decentralization. At the same time, the weak center expanded the power of regional elites, because it could not satisfy the basic needs of the local populations nor maintain order in the regions. These social and political processes were quite similar to those in Europe in the early Middle Ages.

CHAPTER 8

THE LOCAL BARONS UNDER PUTIN'S MODERATE FEUDALISM (2000–2006)

INTRODUCTION

With Putin's rise to power, Russia entered a new phase in its history. Putin strengthened his position at the expense of the local barons, whose national power declined though their authority remained strong in their own regions. The same trend could be seen in the Middle Ages as the royal power strengthened and the level of arbitrariness and chaos in the country diminished. This happened, for instance, during "the Caroling renewal" following the rule of the last Merovingian king in the eighth century. It was Charlemagne (768–814) who restored the power of the central administration by demanding, among other things, an oath of fidelity from the local lords. Louis the Pious, Charlemagne's son, introduced in the early ninth century the official term "res publica" as a sign of the preponderance of the interests of the state over private ones.[1]

PUTIN RESTRAINS LOCAL BARONS

Putin's first steps as president were devoted to restraining the power of the local barons and oligarchs. The population was mostly ambivalent toward the relations between the Kremlin and local autocrats. In 2006, according to a survey by the Fund of Public Opinion, one-third of the population endorsed their local leaders, one-third was indifferent toward them, and 17 percent disliked them. At the same time, 52 percent of the Russians were dissatisfied with the state of affairs in their regions, and almost the same number believed that local leaders systematically violated the law.[2] With such mixed attitudes toward governors and presidents, Putin could hardly expect to meet resistance to his decisions to curtail their political role.

Putin proved that he was capable of undermining the power of any of his potential rivals and not only of politicians in Moscow, such as the liberal Grigorii Yavlinsky, the Communist Gennadii Ziuganov, and oligarchs such as Berezovskii, Gusinskii, and Khodorkovsky. He also ousted local barons including the Kursk governor Aleksandr Rutskoi and the Petersburg governor Vladimir Yakovlev. Although Putin did not follow suit with the presidents of non-Russian republics, he did weaken their role in national politics. Putin also curbed Yurii Luzhkov's arrogance, and by the first years of the new millennium the Moscow boss had been reduced to an obedient feudal baron.

Evgenii Nazdratenko, governor of the Maritime Territory (Far East), was also quite insolent toward the Kremlin during the 1990s. All of Moscow's attempts to dislodge him, particularly Chubais' endeavors in 1996, had failed. But Putin solved the problem by ousting Nazdratenko from his position as governor and bringing him to serve in a position in Moscow.

Until 2004, several governors and presidents of non-Russian republics, such as Nikolai Fedorov from Chuvashiia, could express their views even if these contrasted with Putin's. Soon, however, challenges to Putin's authority by local governors or republican presidents totally disappeared. After the terrorist attacks in 2004 on a high school in Beslan (in North Ossetiia), the president cancelled the election of governors and began to appoint them instead. Putin's move eliminated the last relatively independent institution in the country. The governors could no longer assert themselves as "elected leaders."[3]

THE DECLINE OF THE FEDERATION COUNCIL

In 1993, in order to ingratiate with local leaders, Yeltsin had created the Federation Council, a body consisting of regional leaders. Whereas the regional bosses saw this body as a new institution that could effectively run the country, unlike the inept Parliament and the government, the president saw it as an antidote to the increasingly rebellious Parliament.

The first meeting of this council, whose existence was not stipulated in the acting constitution, took place in September 1993, on the eve of a direct confrontation between the president and the Parliament. It was evident that Yeltsin, attempting to exploit the local barons in his fight against his Moscow opponents, wanted to replace the Parliament, the instrument of his foes, with this new body, to which he had personally appointed a significant number of members. At the same time, feeling their powers growing, local leaders, Russian and non-Russian alike, went so far as to demand that future presidents be elected from among their ranks. It looked as if Russian governors wanted to follow the example of the Holy Roman Empire in the Middle Ages when German princes elected the emperor. One of Putin's first actions as president was to radically change the role of the Federation Council and exclude the governors from any serious role in national politics.

Making the Federation Council a ceremonial organ, Putin appointed his myrmidon Sergei Mironov as its head. Mironov was ready to take on any task for his boss, including the rather bizarre role as Putin's fictitious challenger in the presidential election of 2004. During the election campaign, Mironov actually supported Putin. He was also among the courtiers who proposed changing the constitution in order to provide Putin the possibility of a third term.

PRESIDENTIAL EMISSARIES

Before discussing Putin's presidential emissaries, let us return to the Middle Ages. In order to offset the power of the local administrations, Charlemagne extended the use of *missi dominici*—that is, envoys who served as liaisons between the central government and local agents and who were responsible for keeping the latter in line. To strengthen his control over the population, Charlemagne attempted to develop intermediary bodies and use both vassalage and immunity as means of government—in the first instance by creating royal vassals and giving them control of public offices, and in the second by controlling protected institutions such as monasteries and the Jewish community.

Using similar maneuvers, Putin created an institution of interregional envoys to supervise the seven interregional districts in order to curb the power of the local barons. He signaled his determination to place each governor and president of non-Russian republics under the control of his emissaries. The major task of this new institution was to make the local laws compatible with federal laws and first of all with the constitution. There was no doubt that the presidential emissaries made some progress in unifying the law on the territory of the Russian Federation. However, in the opinion of most experts, they did not seriously curtail the power of local governors or the presidents of non-Russian republics.[4]

The case of Dmitrii Kozak is particularly interesting. With a reputation as one of the best of Putin's administrators, he was appointed as an emissary in the South District, which included the North Caucasian region. However, he clearly was unable to even superficially curb the arbitrariness and corruption of the local barons. He had almost no influence on the conduct of the Chechen leader Ramzan Kadyrov, or the Dagestan rulers, or the president of Adygei, Khazret Sovmen.[5]

Contrary to Putin's pledge to enforce social order and federal laws across the country, the Kremlin allowed the regional leaders to act like feudal lords as long as they demonstrated loyalty to the Kremlin and remained ready to support Putin against his rivals. Putin almost never removed a governor for improper or illegal actions committed in the governor's own territory. As described by various sources, the governors who were forced out by Putin had shown disloyalty or were deemed untrustworthy.

Why the Moscow "Tsar" Gave So Much Power to Local Barons

Having pushed the local governors and presidents out of national politics, Putin did not, however, attempt to control their actions inside their own regions. An expert on Russian domestic politics contended, perhaps with some exaggeration, that none of Putin's edicts were taken seriously by the governors.[6] There were several explanations for why Putin did not interfere in the internal life of the regions and republics and in many cases tolerated the arbitrariness of the local barons.

The Lack of a Loyal and Effective Apparatus

Putin did not have a state apparatus or political instrument like the Communist Party of the past that could supervise the implementation of Moscow's policies in the provinces.[7] The replacement of one local leader by another did not lead to a serious change in the state of corruption or criminality in a region. The substitution of Nazdratenko with Sergei Darkin in the Maritime Territory, for instance, did not improve the political climate in the region. Both were deeply corrupted officials with direct links to the organized crime in the region.

The Special Support of Presidents of Non-Russian Republics

In its attempts to create order in society, the Kremlin supported any leader in non-Russian republics who could maintain order, turning a blind eye to their egregious violations of law. This policy reflected the conviction that Moscow was unable, as it was in the Soviet times, to maintain order in the non-Russian republics, given the high level of local nationalism. While many non-Russian republics learned the lesson from the bloody repressions in Chechnya, the Kremlin also realized that even if Chechnya could be pacified with immense effort and financial resources, the same could not be done with all the other republics if these republics decided to challenge Moscow. For this reason, Putin's Kremlin did not abandon Yeltsin's feudal policy of securing special agreements between Moscow and the republics, which stipulated various issues, including taxes and the state languages.[8]

At the same time, the Kremlin allowed the leaders of non-Russian republics to act quite freely within their territories. For instance, Mintimer Shaimiev was allowed to do almost everything he wanted inside the Tatar Republic on the condition that he did not challenge the Kremlin or the major corporations it protected. Understanding Shaimiev's problems with local nationalists and even Muslim extremists,[9] the Kremlin permitted Shaimiev to treat Tatarstan in its constitution as a "state" and "subject of international law." The Kremlin also allowed its residents to keep a special page in their passports that contained Tatarstan's official insignias and recognized Tatar (along with Russian) as a state language.[10] The Tatarstan authorities often ignored the federal constitution. Kazan created its own Tatar postal system to serve inside the republic. Telephone communication was also under the control of the local authorities. Reviewing these developments, a Moscow journalist noted, "The republic has its own communication company, its own oil and its own energy system and now its own postal service. It is evident that Tatarstan is slowly but consistently turning into a new state."[11]

The Kremlin, despite its support of the Russian nationalist ideology, turned a blind eye to the discrimination of the ethnic Russians (and other ethnic groups) living in non-Russian republics.[12] This was in stark contrast with the Soviet policy from the early 1930s until 1985, which promoted Russification in all the national republics and made sure that the leading positions in the party and state apparatus, as well as in culture and education, were held by ethnic Russians. Moscow cruelly punished anyone who even remotely undermined the leading role of the Russians, the so-called senior brothers, in the regions.

Discrimination was seen in the hiring and firing practices and in the various benefits given to people who knew the local language. Ethnic discrimination was quite strong in almost all non-Russian republics. In Chechnya, due in part to the war, the proportion of ethnic Russians decreased by eight times between 1989 and 2002; in Daghestan, by two times; in North Osetiia, by 29 percent; and in Kabardin-Balkar Republic, by 27 percent.[13]

The Kremlin did not object to the fact that some leaders of non-Russian republics ruled their territories like fiefs over many years and suppressed any challenge to their position, using various means including violence.[14] In many cases, Putin did not use his power, which he acquired in 2004, to replace old presidents with new ones. He even persuaded them to stay in power—for instance, in the case of Shaimiev, the Tatar president, whose third term expired in 2006.[15] Indeed, Putin allowed Shaimiev to hold his position as the Tatar president for four terms in a row. During practically the same period, President Murtaza Rakhimov reigned in Bashkortostan and President Kirsan Iliumzhinov in Kalmykiia.

Kadyrov's Case

A good example of the Kremlin's need to rely on feudal lords in non-Russian republics was the case of Chechnya, which represents a clear parallel to the Middle Ages. Unable to pacify the rebellious republic after years of war, Putin assigned Akhmet Kadyrov in 2000 as a boss with almost unrestricted power. After Kadyrov was murdered in 2004, his position was taken over by his son Ramzan. Relying only on his clan, while ignoring federal laws and resorting to unrestrained violence against anyone who resisted, Ramzan Kadyrov was indeed able to install some level of order in the republic. Russian journalists talked about Chechnya as "leased by Moscow to Kadyrov," a pure feudal case.[16] Expecting political loyalty from the local bosses, Putin was tolerant toward most aspects of their conduct inside Chechnya, particularly when it came to corruption and nepotism. What is more, Yuliia Latynina, a prominent journalist who followed the developments in Chechnya for several years, suggested in her article "One Day with the Master of Chechnya" that the relations between Putin and Ramzan Kadyrov were in some ways reversed. It was Putin who paid a "levy" to Kadyrov for maintaining order in Chechnya. Putin permitted Kadyrov to control the revenues from locally produced oil and the federal budget. He made him almost independent from the federal authorities, including the federal troops stationed in Chechnya.[17]

WHAT THE MOSCOW SUZERAIN EXPECTED FROM HIS BARONS

Social Order in the Regions

The local bosses were called on to release the president from various obligations. This was the policy of Putin's government in 2003–2006 when, trying to reform its programs for welfare, health services, and real estate management, it tried to hold the regions responsible for satisfying the population's basic needs. Many experts saw the notorious benefits reform of early 2005 as an indication of the Kremlin's plan to shift social responsibility (medical and transportation in the first place) onto the shoulders of the local administrators, knowing fully well that regions' budgets were insufficient for performing these functions.[18]

The Kremlin tended to appoint wealthy individuals as new governors, hoping that they would use their personal resources to improve life in the regions, as demonstrated by the case of Roman Abramovich, the governor of Chukotka. One Russian journalist wrote in 2005 that "[t]he center has shifted the responsibility for solving the complicated problems in the regions on the newly appointed leaders, relying on their personal financial resources and connections in political circles and the state apparatus."[19] It was obvious that such an approach deeply contradicted Putin's attempts to centralize management in the country.[20]

The Importance of Loyalty in Presidential and Parliamentary Elections

The Russian governors were expected to deliver a majority of the votes in the presidential and parliamentary elections in favor of the ruling leader. The governors and presidents of non-Russian republics were obliged to support the president in all his domestic and foreign actions. The collection of votes had already been established as the major obligation of the local barons under Yeltsin. Indeed, in 1996, the Kremlin expected governors and presidents to do everything they could to get Yeltsin reelected in 1996. The Kremlin demanded that the local barons be ready to rig the elections. The bosses in Tatarstan and Bashkortostan and several other regions did, in fact, rig the elections in order to guarantee Yeltsin's victory in the second round, because, as demonstrated by the first round of the election, Gennadii Ziuganov, the Communist candidate, had a significant lead and should have been elected as president.[21]

It was remarkable that the president of the Chuvash Republic, Nikolai Fedorov, submitted his resignation to Yeltsin (though it was not accepted), because he had not been able to fulfill his duty of ensuring Yeltsin's victory in his territory.[22]

As suggested by Sergei Dorenko, a prominent Russian journalist, "[W]e live under feudalism"; the governors can do whatever they want, so long as they support the presidential party and guarantee successful results in the parliamentary and presidential elections.[23]

THE CENTER'S INDIFFERENCE TOWARD LOCAL CORRUPTION

If the governors and presidents showed their loyalty to the Kremlin, the center remained indifferent toward their efforts to enrich themselves and their relatives and friends. Governors in Putin's Russia were similar to the German ministerials (lower-ranking knights in the Middle Ages with temporary positions at a prince's court) who tried to accumulate wealth whenever possible. This was not, however, an easy task because land was the most important asset and it was totally controlled by the feudal lords. In post-Soviet Russia, the task was much easier because money played the leading role in political and economic life.

The Russian newspaper *Kommersant-Daily* analyzed 11 cases of criminal acts committed by governors between 1996 and 2006 (nine of the cases occurred after 2000 when Putin became president). None of the 11 governors were incarcerated for even one day. Either the accusations against them were found to be unsubstantiated or the accused governors were saved from prison by amnesty.[24]

In 2006, the Kremlin initiated some judicial actions against a few governors and mayors, including the governor of the Nenets Region Aleksei Barinov and Volgorgrad's mayor Evgenii Ishchenko, but these actions did not change the general climate of tolerance toward the corruption of the local bureaucracy.[25] In some rare cases, governors and mayors were prosecuted for their corrupt activities as a result of the conflicts among local political elites, or because of the discontent of the Kremlin with a particular local politician for reasons not related to corruption.[26]

There were different ways to accumulate fortunes, aside from direct embezzlements of state money. Most importantly, governors and republican presidents had tremendous power over local businesses. As a rule, no company could function if the head of the administration was hostile toward it. As Yuliia Latynina noted, "If a governor was replaced by another, any company, aside from those controlled by oligarchs, could lose its factory on the territory of the region." As an example, she discussed the plight of the company Renova, which lost its electrode factory in Novosibirsk when Governor Vitalii Mukha was replaced by Viktor Tolokonskii, who was friendly toward a rival company called TWG.[27] The local Russian barons were particularly active in regions like the Far East and Siberia that possessed rich natural resources, oil and gas in particular. These resources attracted foreign investment—an important asset for rent-seeking activity. It was easier for governors to generate illegal income from oil and gas companies than from the embezzlement of budget money.[28]

Among other devices that governors used to enrich themselves, or their relatives and friends, was to make some private company, without any form of bidding, responsible for providing various services to city dwellers. For example, in Krasnoiarsk, Governor Aleksandr Khloponin forced the public to pay the real estate company Kraskom, which was under his protection, for providing maintenance services in their apartment complexes. In order to increase the income of this company, the governor increased the maintenance payment in 2006 by 30 percent, while the national rate of increase was only 20 percent. The action infuriated the residents of the city, but no actions were taken, because Moscow supported the governor in this case.[29]

In some situations, the local bureaucracy, under the guidance of the governor, created a sort of mafia that established rules for its activities. It enriched itself collectively with regular bribes and embezzlements. A good example was seen in the Orlov Region, which was ruled by Governor Yegor Stroev for 15 years. Corruption was prevalent during the entire period of Stroev's governorship. In 2006, the level of corruption rose to the surface when Moscow moved to fight it. In April 2006, several dozen leading officials, including former deputy governors and former mayors, were detained and accused of taking bribes. The officials in Orlov had organized a group that collected bribes in a common pool, as criminal organizations do, and then distributed the money according to the position of each group member. All these people, as noted in a Moscow newspaper, "felt totally immune to prosecution for many years."[30] At the same time, Stroev was not harmed by "the pogrom" of bureaucrats in Orel.[31] Stroev also made his daughter a Russian senator, which did not surprise many people in the region.[32]

The situation in Chukotka was similar to that in Orel. The region was mostly ruled by Governor Abramovich's people from Moscow and other cities in the European part of Russia. All of the major positions in the bureaucracy were given to the relatives and friends of high officials. These people usually only worked for one to two years, collected their money, and moved back to their original places to avoid exposing themselves to criminal activity in the region.[33] The officials themselves raised their personal salaries to astronomical levels and paid little attention to their duties. Instead, they entertained themselves with expensive parties, hunting expeditions, and sexual activities.

A typical strategy used by governors and mayors for personal enrichment was to create government funds that were not controlled by the local legislators. For instance, the governor of Belgorod Evgenii Savchenko created the "extra budget fund," which was generated mostly by "donations" from local businesses. It was completely outside the control of the local legislators. He also established fictitious public institutions that were financed by the state budget but controlled by Savchenko himself.[34]

When the mayor of Volgograd Evgenii Ishchenko was incarcerated in July 2006, the public learned that he was the owner of an airplane and a yacht worth 3 million euros, which he kept in Monaco. On the eve of his arrest, he negotiated the purchase of one of the Maldives Islands. His luxurious apartment in Volgograd cost $500,000, yet his official salary was only $18,000 per year. As soon as he became mayor, Ishchenko began to protect his own company, Souzneftegazstroi. This corporation created a new firm called Tamerlan, which ran a building operation, and the mayor provided it with the best municipal land.

THE CASE OF BOOS

Georgii Boos belonged to Putin's cohort of feudal barons. He was appointed as the governor of Kaliningrad Region by Putin after the president canceled the election procedure for governors. Many people in the region expected the new governor to change the deeply corrupt and criminalized climate in the region. Their expectations were indeed wrong. Under Boos, the judicial system remained as corrupt as it was in the past. His spouses and children worked simultaneously as judges, prosecutors, and lawyers. Ordinary people were completely defenseless. Boos invited Moscow businesspeople to work with him in Kaliningrad. Local businesspeople were also invited to cooperate with the new administration if they did what the governor expected from them. If they did not cooperate with the administration and were not eager to send money to it for "social projects," they were harassed by the Prosecutor General's Office, which could easily find a way to send them to jail. In this corrupt climate, the election of local legislators became a complete farce.[35]

LOCAL BARONS AND CRIMINALITY

Putin displayed indifference not only toward the corruption of local barons but also toward their direct connections with criminals. In 2000–2006, the Moscow media published numerous articles about the arbitrariness of local barons, the recruitment of their cadres (based on commercial interests), their connections with criminals, and their successful war against the independent media, which included the murder of journalists.[36]

Sergei Darkin, appointed by Putin as the governor of the Maritime Territory, was a good example. Darkin was denounced many times by the Russian media as a person who maintained, in spite of his new position, criminal connections.[37] One of Darkin's close confidants, Yurii Kopylov, who also had a long criminal record, was with Putin at the prestigious meeting in Moscow on the eve of the presidential election as a leading activist in Putin's party, "United Russia"; he was later elected as the mayor of Vladivostok in July 2004 and finally arrested in 2006 for criminal deeds.[38]

The criminal record of Dmitrii Fotianov was common knowledge in his native city, Dalnegorsk, in the Far East, but his record did not dissuade the ruling party, "United Russia," from helping him get elected as the mayor of this city in 2005 and support him in the mayoral election of 2006. As it turned out, it was not the party but his colleagues in the local mafia who put an end to his political career by killing him on the eve of the election.[39]

The immunity of the local and central elites to criminal prosecution became a fixture of life in the post-Soviet period and a clear reminder of the situation in the Middle Ages. A typical example could be seen in the exemptions these people received when they got involved in car accidents, even when the collision resulted in death. For instance, in August 2006, the mayor of Piatigorsk, a city in North Caucasus, in an obvious case of reckless driving, killed five people. Yet, in the face of decisive evidence, he was practically exonerated from any liability in the case. In 2006, the son of the minister of defense Sergei Ivanov, in a similar case, killed an old woman in Moscow and went free from any civil or criminal case in court.[40]

ARBITRARINESS TOWARD THE POPULATION

As governors and presidents were useful people to Putin, their power over the local population was rarely checked. In many respects, their independence from Moscow was greater than during the Brezhnev period, even if the regional party secretaries had been quite free to do as they pleased during Soviet times as well. However, the Soviet people could complain to Moscow, and in some cases they even won their case against the local authorities. This was not the case under Putin. When the system of supervision over the local administration disappeared, the residents of the regions were totally helpless before the local leaders. Only the media could help local residents, though the freedom of the press was weak in post-Soviet Russia and particularly weak in the provinces. In short, the chances for provincial victims to voice their complaints were very low. By 2006, only a few liberal newspapers in Moscow—*Novaia Gazeta* in the first place, with its modest circulation (less than 100,000)—continued to publish critical articles about life in the provinces.

Kirsan Iliumzhinov, the president of Kalmykiia, one of the poorest regions in the country with 50 percent of its people unemployed, once boasted to an American journalist that he built with his "personal money" 38 Buddhist temples, 22 Orthodox churches, a Polish catholic cathedral (the only one of its kind in the republic), a mosque, and a luxurious chess palace that cost him $40 million.[41]

The opposition in the republic had been severely persecuted. A prominent journalist who was critical of the regime was murdered.[42] Iliumzhinov turned the republic into his own fief. While the population remained extremely poor, he turned Elista, the administrative center of the republic, into the "chess capital" of the world. He paid Bobby Fisher, a former world chess champion and an exotic personality, 100,000 dollars as a sign of his "personal recognition of his contribution to chess." He issued an executive order that placed chess in the curriculum in the first three grades of school. The total arbitrariness of the presidents in Bashkortostan and Tatarstan was also well known in the country.[43]

LOCAL BARONS AND DEMOCRACY

The governors, almost without exception, became enemies of democracy with the Kremlin's full consent. Before 2005, the governors had been "elected," though in most cases a victory at the polls was gained with blatant populism and the cynical use of the local bureaucratic apparatus, as well as with the support of businesses and even some criminal structures.

In those regions where the candidates for the position of governor were incumbents, the elections were comparable to those carried out in Soviet times.[44] The most shameful were the elections to the Moscow Duma. Moscow major Luzhkov, in blatant violation of the law, was directly involved in the election process and managed to block certain candidates from entering the elections. What is more, there were serious doubts about the validity of the Moscow elections in 1997. However, because Luzhkov had a great deal of control over all Moscow political institutions, it was almost impossible to file complaints.[45] The abolishment of gubernatorial elections in 2004 only increased the governors' and republican presidents' contempt for democracy and decreased their concern about the attitudes of the people toward their activities.

It was only natural that in most regions, particularly in the national republics, the leaders of the provinces reduced the role of the local parliament to almost zero. In most places, the provincial leaders held strict control (reminiscent of the Soviet era) over the elections in the local Dumas to ensure complete obedience. This practice started in the second half of the 1990s and continued under Putin when Moscow demonstrated total indifference toward the observation of election laws in the provinces.[46] Sergei Darkin, governor of the Maritime Region, filled nearly the entire list of candidates of the governmental party "United Russia" with people from his close circle. Darkin's actions aroused anger among the leaders of the party in Moscow who were forced to acquiesce to the governor's arrogance.[47] Eduard Rossel, governor of Ekaterinburg, also manipulated the elections in his parliament. He did not allow, for instance, certain parties to participate in the elections.[48]

The Lack of Freedom of the Press

In the 1990s, the freedom of local media was quite high. By the beginning of the twenty-first century, however, media freedom in the provinces was curtailed significantly. The Kremlin remained indifferent toward the issue and never defended the press. According to the Fund for the Defense of Glasnost, in 2006, none of the 89 regions in Russia could claim to have completely free media. In three-quarters of the regions, media were rated as "relatively" or "completely" "not free." The freedom of media was absent in 19 of 21 national republics (the Chuvash and Altai republics were exceptions).[49] The debates on this issue, which the Public Chamber carried out in Kazan in November 2006, were indicative in this respect. Nikolai Svanidze, a member of the RF Public Chamber, named specific regions in which the freedom-of-speech situation was abominable. These regions included Mary-El, Bashkortostan, and Saratov.[50] The arrests and murders of journalists became a fixture in many Russian regions, particularly non-Russian republics. The arrests of the Bashkir journalist Viktor Shmakov in May 2006 and the journalist Vladimir Korolev from Perm in September 2006 became known to the local public only because the media in Moscow covered the story.[51] Pavel Gusev, the editor of *Moskovskii Komsomolets,* talked on the radio station *Ekho Moskvy* about the dozens of local journalists working for his newspaper who were beaten, arrested, or murdered, or simply disappeared from their homes in the middle of the first decade of the twenty-first century.[52]

The Cult of Local Leaders

Feudal elements in the regional governments were also seen in the cult status of the local leaders. They were awarded various titles and prizes. For instance, the president of Tatarstan Mintimer Shaimiev, who served four terms in office, was awarded The Kind Angel of Peace prize, an award in a journalism competition, a medal for achievements in chemistry, and a medal in commemoration of the October Revolution. Shaimiev's seventieth anniversary was celebrated in the republic as an official holiday. Shaimiev was greeted during his jubilee by Putin and dozens of other dignitaries.[53] The president of the Udmurt Republic Aleksandr Volkov received the medal "Statehood" (*Derzhava*) and the titles "Outstanding Builder," "Outstanding Engineer," "Outstanding Worker of Public Transportation," and "Honored Academician." The president of Chuvashia Nikolai Fedorov also received dozens of medals and titles.[54]

Conclusion

By 2004–2005, a new balance of power emerged between the Kremlin and the local barons. The governors and presidents of non-Russian republics abandoned their previous roles as active politicians in the national policy arena, but preserved their control over their respective regions. The leaders of the regions were autocratic rulers appointed by the president, who almost completely ignored democratic principles. They ran their regions like fiefs in the same authoritarian way as

Putin ran the whole country. The feudal model, with its focus on polycentrism, is the best instrument for describing the relations between the central administration and the periphery of the country. Neither the liberal model, which supposes the existence of democratic elections, nor the totalitarian model, which supposes an almost absolute control of the center over the provinces, can be used for this purpose.

CHAPTER 9

THE PRECARIOUSNESS OF PROPERTY
IN CONTEMPORARY RUSSIA
AND THE MIDDLE AGES

INTRODUCTION

In Soviet times, private property did not play a crucial role in social life. The means of production, as well as most city apartments, were owned and controlled by the state. The number of objects considered "private" (or "individual" in the Soviet phraseology) was indeed limited. It was not until the 1960s that Soviet citizens received the right to buy a car or own an apartment in a city. In the countryside, the Soviet system tolerated the private ownership of peasant houses, but even here, individuals were not allowed to own a horse or a truck for use in a household; these assets were considered part of the means of production. There were some important differences between various types of public property—for instance, between the property of state versus that of collective farms, or between the property controlled by the central administration and the property of local bodies.[1] The most socially important difference, however, was between public property in general and the private property of individual citizens.

A form of semiprivate property that was especially important to the Soviet people were the small plots of land where peasants grew vegetables and fruits and raised a limited number of farm animals (one cow, a few pigs, and a few dozen chickens). Formally, however, the Soviet peasants leased their parcels of land from the state, which could, for any reason, withhold the property. The peasants, of course, had no right to sell their land. Indeed, plot holders in the USSR were similar to the vassals of the Middle Ages, whose rights to the land were based on the condition that they would loyally serve their suzerain. If the Soviet peasants left the farm or abandoned their duties as collective farmers, they lost their right to the land.

The Soviet state, until its collapse, could not settle the issue of regulating the size of private plots and household agriculture. In Brezhnev's time, with the growing food shortages, the Kremlin moved from harsh to mild restrictions against private plots, a softening of their policy that contrasted with Khrushchev's measures to curtail the size of plots and the number of cattle available to peasants.

Another link to life in the Middle Ages was the fact that the Soviet authorities reintroduced a sort of subsistence agriculture that was typical for the preindustrial era. Indeed, small plots and gardens provided food for millions of Russians. Making up no more than 3 percent of the arable land in the country, these plots produced no less than one-third of all agricultural production, mostly for consumption by peasants, before 1985. The role of private plots was particularly important in the 1990s, when the Russian economy was in shambles after the collapse of the Soviet state. Two-thirds of the population supported themselves with small plots of land and gardens.[2]

The fate of semiprivate plots and gardens was always on the minds of the Russians, particularly in the countryside. The country anxiously watched the changes in the official policy toward the rights to own or use private plots. However, the real outburst of interest in property relations occurred during perestroika, when the issue of property became a leading political and theoretical topic in the Soviet Union. Private property began to expand, and the regions began to increase their autonomy. After 1989–1991, Russian society entered a period in which property relations became deeply unstable, a situation similar to that in Europe during the early Middle Ages. The instability of property in Russia turned out to be one of the most important factors of social and political life in the country during 1991–2007.

THE WEAKNESS OF PROPERTY RIGHTS IN THE MIDDLE AGES

In the early Middle Ages, property rights were conditional and precarious. In fact, the conditional character of the property bestowed by the king or feudal lord on those who were supposed to serve them was an essential feature of the classic feudalism of the early Middle Ages. The property rights system contrasted sharply with the Roman type. It was heavily qualified rather than absolute. The "customs of the manor" represented a set of expressed or implied contracts for an interrelated series of reciprocal rights and duties. As the British historian William Kingston described, *villeins* or *cottars* held strips of land for themselves on the condition that they will provide an agreed amount of work to the lord of the manor, who in turn provided a specified amount of manpower for military service to a greater lord. The author added that these duties corresponded to rights in a set of complex and carefully balanced property arrangements.[3]

In the early Middle Ages there was not a unified definition of property. As the famous British historian Paul Vinogradoff suggested, in early feudalism there were "two elements in the notion of ownership. Roman property (*dominium*) was characterized during the best period by uncompromising unity. A person having dominium over a thing, including an estate in land, had it alone and excluded everyone else." Vinogradoff further contended that medieval lawyers, in contrast to those in Roman times, came to deal with plots of land that normally had two owners, a superior and an inferior, one having direct ownership (*dominium directum,* or *dominium eminens*), and the other having useful ownership, the right to exploit the land (*dominium utile*). The need to reckon with these two kinds of rights contributed indirectly to a weakening of the notion of absolute land property. Instead of trying to ascertain who ought to have the absolute right of ownership, the English courts came to concern themselves with the practical question of which of the two litigants had a "better" right (*ius merum*) to an estate or tenement. The process of feudalization, as Vinogradoff asserted, was in general very complicated and controversial because of the property that generated conflicts in the early Middle Ages.[4]

The confiscation of property by the king or a strong lord was a "normal" element of life in the Middle Ages. Even the church was not immune to the loss of property. For instance, in the eighth century, following Carl Martel's ascendancy and military reforms, Martel's successors, citing a military necessity, confiscated a great deal of ecclesiastical land. The church tried to present this alienation of its land as a "precarial" grant and hoped that the land would be returned later. These hopes, however, went unfulfilled. The monarchs and magnates who received the land had no intention of returning it. However, under Charlemagne, who protected the church directly, church property became more stable.[5]

As for the case of order in the Middle Ages, particularly in the early stages, there are two schools of thought on the role of violence in solving property disputes. Norman Cantor, speaking about the early Middle Ages, mostly talked about the role of power in solving property conflicts. William Kingston insisted that, even during the Carolingian Empire, the "law of the jungle" was dominant.[6] As suggested by the historian Christopher Dawson, after the death of Charlemagne, "the rule of law and the political authority of the state had disappeared, and the only remaining principle of social cohesion was the direct personal bond of loyalty and mutual aid between the warrior and the chief, and that of service and protection between the serf and the lord."[7] In England, it was possible in the twelfth century to purchase from King Henry Plantagenet a writ for the restoration of disputed land.[8]

Frederic Cheyette and Stephen White offered another vision. They wrote about the efficacy of the legal system and the high role of compromise even in the eleventh and twelfth centuries in France. These authors recognized the absence of "real law" after "the disappearance of Carolingian judicial institutions"—something that also happened in Russia after the collapse of the USSR. At the same time, they tried to suggest that informal arbiters were able to solve land disputes in a peaceful way.[9]

The objective here is not to establish the relative roles of power, coercion, and fair judges in solving property conflicts. There is a consensus that property relations in the Middle Ages were in serious turmoil, which makes it appropriate to draw parallels between post-Soviet Russia and Western Europe in the early Middle Ages. I am persuaded by Markus Fischer, who insisted on the existence of a large gap between "the discourse of unity, heteronomy, community, and justice" imposed by the church and the real practices that relied on "forceful conflict resolution."[10]

INSTABILITY OF PROPERTY RELATIONS BETWEEN THE CENTER AND PROVINCES IN RUSSIA

Midway through the period of perestroika, the destabilization of property relations was seen in three spheres: (1) the demarcation of public property between the center and the provinces, (2) between public and private property, and (3) between the owners of private property. Indeed, the regional bureaucracy's struggle to expand the property under its command was one of the most important dimensions of regionalization. It increased immensely after the collapse of the Soviet Union. As one Moscow author contended, the whole issue of "sovereignty" in the 1990s was nothing more than "a fierce struggle for property that embraced the entire former Soviet society."[11]

If the division of resources between the federal and local authorities was of secondary importance in Western countries (the lion's share of resources belonged to private owners), in Russia, the volume of public property was much greater and the administrative control over the means of production and natural resources was vast. For this reason, the struggle over the distribution of state property between the central and local elites was of the highest importance in the political life of the country since the beginning of perestroika.

Indeed, as soon as the feudalization of society took hold, the local elites immediately put the question of regional property rights before Moscow. As mentioned, in the 1990s, facing the need to revise property relations between the center and the periphery, Moscow was under strong pressure from regional movements to shift responsibilities for economic development onto the provincial authorities. Ultimately, the Kremlin accepted many of the demands made by the republics and regions on property issues.

At the same time, the central administration tried not to lose control over the country's major natural resources. The Russian constitution of 1993 (Article 72.1) acknowledged that "the possession, usage and disposal of land, minerals, water and other natural resources are in common control of the Russian Federation and the subjects of the Federation." The vagueness of this article, exemplified by the term "common control," reflected the fact that property relations among various levels of the administrative hierarchy, in the first years of the post-Communist era, remained unresolved and continued to cause tension and conflict between the regions and the center.

The National Republics

As discussed, the elites in non-Russian republics were the most outspoken in their demands for control over the means of production. On several occasions, the leaders of these republics openly declared that for them the distribution of property rights between the republics and the Russian Federation was the most important issue. In 1991–1992, the national republics greatly increased the amount of production facilities and utilities under their jurisdiction. In the Russian Federation, in 1993, "the subjects of the Federation" possessed, on average, 22 percent of all "privatized property," but some localities had a much greater percentage under their control: Kalmykiia had 96 percent of all assets under its control, North Osetiia possessed

83 percent, Yakutiia and Altai had 81 percent each, Dagestan controlled 65 percent, Tuva gained 52 percent, Mordoviia commanded 41 percent, and Komi had 38 percent.[12]

Of special importance was the control over natural resources. Yakutiia, for instance, demanded and actually received partial control over its diamond and gold resources, with only one-third of these resources going to Moscow. Yakutiia also obtained access to the international diamond market. Bashkiria gained control over much of its natural resources, including its oil and a considerable part of its oil-processing and chemical industries.

On one hand, Moscow formally accepted the republics' claims for almost full control over their resources. The respective treaties signed in early 1995 between the Russian Federation and Tatarstan, Bashkortostan, and three other republics acknowledged that the land and its resources belonged to the concerned republics. On the other hand, these treaties, stating that the federal authorities had common control over at least some portion of the republics' natural resources, left Moscow with the legal opportunity to preserve or even increase its command over the resources in these administrative units.

The Russian Regions

The Russian regions followed the pattern of the republics and also declared in the 1990s their need to control their resources. In these cases, however, Moscow was much more adamant in protecting its monopoly on natural resources than in its confrontation with the republics. The case with the Orenburg Region was typical in this respect. In October 1994, the legislators of this region included in a statute an article concerning the rights to natural resources similar to the article in the national republics' constitutions. However, the Russian Ministry of Justice refused to accept this article, and Orenburg was allowed only limited control over its resources.

Similar issues arose in the relationships between Moscow and Ekaterinburg, the administrative center of Sverdlovsk Region. In the aftermath of the parliamentary defeat in 1993, the local legislators included an article in Sverdlovsk's statute that was similar to the article in the new constitution, which vaguely spoke of "the Federation and region's common control over natural resources." However, later in 1995, particularly after Eduard Rossel's victory in the gubernatorial elections, the legislators went on the offensive and began to fight Moscow, demanding its permission to include in the statue an article similar to the one in the republican constitutions underscoring the territory's full control over its own resources.

In addition to the larger regions' claims on their resources, the smaller ethnic districts began to claim sole ownership over their territories' resources as well. In 1994–1995, for instance, the Khanty-Mansy District fought for these rights with the Tiumen Region (their superior regional authority), which was itself "a subject of the Russian Federation." Under the leadership of Sergei Sobianin, the chairman of the local parliament, the Khanty-Mansy District demanded full control over its natural resources, oil in particular (the district supplied Russia with 30 percent of its hard currency at the time), and direct contact with Moscow regarding the distribution of revenue.

The antagonistic interests of the center and provinces over property were wholly revealed during the process of privatization of state property in 1992–1995. Each side fought for control of this process. As the composition of the Russian parliament, in many cases, more accurately represented the interests of the provinces and not those of the center, several of the laws adopted by it helped the regions gain control over this process. One such law was the "Law on the Privatization of State Enterprises and the General Principles of the Privatization of Municipal Enterprises of the Russian Federation," adopted by the Duma in October 1995.

By the end of the 1990s, as the central administration strengthened, property relations between the center and the provinces stabilized. Only Chechnya, drawing on the center's interest in pacifying the republic, continued to extract concessions from the center (in the area of oil production, for instance), in the early years of the twenty-first century. However, it is obvious that property relations between the center and regions, particularly the national republics, could result in hot conflicts with the first sign of weakness in the central administration.

PRIVATE VERSUS PUBLIC PROPERTY: THE PUBLIC'S CONTRADICTORY ATTITUDES

The turmoil that emerged as a result of the changes in private property relations was even greater than the problems that arose in the separation of federal and regional property. The collapse of the existing property relations in the late 1980s and 1990s was similar to the developments in the post-Roman empire. The privatization of the means of production was not a smooth development. It diversified property relations and became a major source of instability.

This instability was enhanced to a great degree by the population's contradictory attitudes toward various forms of property, which could also be seen in the early Middle Ages when Roman laws ceased to function and property of all forms was put in question. Indeed, one of the most spectacular victories of the Russian Communists was not the abolishment of private property as a means of production, but the successful persuasion of most people about the positive character of this development and about the superiority of public property over private property. On the eve of the collapse of Communism, most Russians believed, as demanded by propaganda, in the superiority of Russian culture, the preeminence of the planning system, and the virtue of public property. Only 10 percent of the Russians wanted in 1989 to "legalize" private businesses.[13] Two years later, on the eve of the collapse of the Soviet state, half the population still voted against the privatization of state property, even if the long-term consequences of privatization were still unknown.[14] In the mid-1990s, the negative attitudes toward privatization became even more pronounced. The majority rejected the private property of big enterprises and about one-half preferred socialism for Russia; one-third of the respondents were staunch advocates of capitalism.[15]

The belief in the fundamental advantage of public property over private property was combined with behavior that belied the genuine attitudes of the Russians toward public and private property. Indeed, the Russians regularly stole from their workplaces, despite the efforts of the Soviet state to protect public property.[16] While pilfering from factories, collective farms, construction sites, and offices was perceived as morally acceptable, stealing the belongings of individuals was strongly condemned. The Soviet people did not care about the maintenance of equipment or vehicles that belonged to the state. The waste of resources in state enterprises was enormous. At the same time, the Soviet people were extremely concerned about the state of their personal material objects, from small plots of land and gardens to cars and television sets.[17] The Soviet people, as shown in surveys in the 1990s, had different attitudes toward the property of large versus small businesses. They supported private property rights for small but not large businesses. These observations supported the idea of Soviet liberals that the Soviet public had a hidden admiration for private property,[18] but they turned out to be only partially right. The people's attitudes toward public and private property did not change radically after the anti-Communist revolution in 1991.

THE NOMENKLATURA AS FUTURE FEUDAL LORDS

The nomenklatura (i.e., party apparatchiks and bureaucrats in various bodies), even more so than the general public, supported the idea of public property, even for small businesses. They saw public property as their raison d'être before 1991. Several authors—among them Yegor Gaidar, the famous reformist—retrospectively suggested that the apparatchiks were greedy thieves who dreamed about living the Western style of life, longed for privatization, and therefore initiated perestroika.[19] However, this was a grossly inaccurate assessment. In fact, until the last years of perestroika, the majority of the nomenklatura were strongly against privatization. Gorbachev avoided the use of this term until the last year of his rule.[20] Later he gradually privatized state property. In 1987–1988, Gorbachev's team issued several decrees that radically diminished the control of the state over economic affairs. The decrees included the influential "law of cooperatives" (March 1988), "the enterprise law," which expanded the autonomy of production units (1987), the decree on the "leasing of enterprises by their workers," which permitted enterprises to set prices on their products (started in 1986).[21] A radical break with the planning system took place in 1989, when the Kremlin publicly accepted the market economy as its objective for the next period.

The apologists of privatization were sure that state property would fall into the hands of "effective owners," efficient managers, and active investors. As it turned out, these "effective owners" were the members of the nomenklatura who had directed the economic transformation. In short, they used their connections and status to turn the state's property into their own personal property.[22]

ATTITUDES TOWARD PRIVATE PROPERTY IN POST-SOVIET RUSSIA

In post-Soviet Russia, privatization and strong social polarization had a tremendous impact on people's attitudes toward property. The response to privatization after 1991 can be compared with the feelings of Roman landowners who watched in the sixth to eighth centuries the barbarians grab their property after the collapse of the Roman Empire. By the end of the 1990s, only 3 percent of the Russians were engaged in private economic activity.[23] In early 2000, three-quarters of the population considered the privatization of big business in Russia as "illegal."[24] Indeed, no less than half the population in this time favored a revision of privatization.[25] Only the privatization of small businesses and apartments was well accepted by the majority of the population.

THE PRECARIOUS CHARACTER OF PROPERTY IN A LAWLESS SOCIETY

At the beginning of the twenty-first century, property rights in Russia were quite unstable, a condition caused by two major factors: the refusal of the population to recognize the legitimacy of privatization, and the lawlessness of society. Indeed, ten years after the peak of privatization, the Russians were still hostile toward big businesses, though they were much more positive toward the property rights of small businesses and the private ownership of apartments. According to a Fund of Public Opinion survey conducted in 2000, 49 percent of the Russians were in favor of private property; 42 percent were opposed to it.[26]

At the same time, the weakness of the state and the lawlessness in society enhanced the feelings of instability in property relations. In the first decade of the twenty-first century, almost all forms of private property could be expropriated by the state, private companies, or individuals. As in the early Middle Ages, property rights had become at least somewhat "conditional."

It was remarkable that many publicly owned corporations did not issue an official document to their shareholders. The shareholders' rights to the stock were supposedly kept by the board of the company.[27] Many owners of property who acquired their land or capital investment during "wild privatization" were not confident in the security of their assets. They assumed, as Yurii Borisov noted, that their property was a sort of a "feudal fief" that could be taken from them at any time because they [did] not have the documents confirming their rights to it.[28] With the lack of law and order in society, many members of the state apparatus, as well as criminal organizations, began to "grab" various forms of state and private property, using an array of legal, semilegal, and illegal techniques.

THE TECHNOLOGY OF RAIDING

A sophisticated technology, referred to here as "raiding," was elaborated for the purpose of taking control over various forms of property. The concept of raiding is close but not equivalent to the term "hostile takeover" used in the West.[29] In the Russian context, the strategies of raiders included the use of tax mechanism to set up artificial bankruptcies, various forms of pressure placed on stockholders to sell their shares, the falsification of documents, the bribing of courts and police, the harassment of companies with various government inspections (fire, sanitation, and others), the confiscation of commodities sold by companies as counterfactual, the physical elimination of owners, and the laundering of illegally acquired property by selling it to proxy companies. The bribes made up roughly 17 percent of the value of the seized property.[30] This technology was quite comparable to the strategies used by kings and feudal lords for the capture of somebody's land.

THE STRUGGLE FOR LAND

In many cases, the coveted target of raids was not so much a production resource or even a building, but the land used by or belonging to a company. The fierce struggle for land, particularly in or near big cities, had the same flavor as the feudal battles for estates and manors in the Middle Ages. The desire to seize land, regardless of what was built on it, was particularly strong in Moscow and in the districts not far from the capital.

The struggle for land was no less fierce in the countryside. After 1991, with the partial dismantling of collective farms, the status of land had become as confused as it was after the collapse of the Roman Empire. In post-Soviet society, millions of peasants found themselves in a situation in which their right to own land became quite vague. In some areas, the peasants did not want the collective farms dismantled, and the situation remained as it was before 1991 (most arable land was regarded as a commonwealth). In other areas, the collective farms were broken up into separate parcels. However, the bureaucracy created many obstacles for peasants to formalize their rights to a parcel of land. By the end of the 1990s, millions of peasants still did not have a formal document certifying their right to the land. According to official data, by 2006, there were 40 million plots, but only 20 percent of them had officially recognized owners.[31] This situation was similar to that in the early Middle Ages, when, for instance, French peasants worked their lands for years without knowing whether they held formal property rights.

This situation was seen in the Moscow Region in 2006, when many peasants discovered that their rights to a parcel of land, as members of collective farms, were transferred, without their knowledge, to the owners of new agricultural companies and real estate firms. The courts and the local offices of the general prosecutor did not defend the peasants who lost their land. The Peasant Front, an organization created by former members of collective farms in the Moscow Region, desperately tried to save their property rights, but encountered, as described by the famous journalist El'vira Goriukhina, complete indifference from the local authorities.[32]

THE PERPETRATORS OF RAIDING

Various companies emerged that specialized in seizing property or protecting it from raiders. According to data from the Ministry of Internal Affairs, there were no less than 100 raider companies in the country in 2005.[33] Even if some authors saw positive elements in this activity,[34] most raider companies were predators, reminding one of the Middle Ages when lawyers were used by a strong lord to seize the property of a weaker lord, as Rabelais vividly described in his *Gargantua and Pantagruel*. Yurii Borisov, an expert on raiding, suggested that the profitability of these companies was often astronomic.[35]

One company in Moscow, known as Vedomosti, accomplished a series of raids, seizing land from their owners or users in the Moscow Region. The head of the company, Il'ia Dyskin, became successful, as suggested by the investigative journalist Aleksandr Travin in his article "Raiders: How It Is Done," by generating close relations not only with members of the Moscow business elite but also with the highest federal officials (one of them, for instance, received a BMW from Dyskin). Dyskin had a strong connection with the Moscow Directorate of Justice, which registered all business transactions. For the implementation of his schemes Dyskin used the Russian courts on full scale, not only in Moscow (several cases against him were dropped), but also in other cities, such as Kazan. At the same time, Dyskin recruited several former judicial workers and police officers who helped him take people's property.[36]

RAIDING FOR PRIVATE COMPANIES

The redistribution of property was an important part of the political and economic landscape of Russia at the beginning of the twenty-first century. One expert, Andrei Illarionov, a former economic adviser to the president, even contended that the redistribution of property in favor of the Kremlin was the "major motor" of Putin's regime.[37] The judicial system in post-Soviet Russia in many respects was similar to that in Western Europe in the Middle Ages, when judges often solved property disputes in favor of those who offered bribes. There is much evidence that Russian oligarchs and governors almost completely controlled the courts and other law enforcement agencies in their regions. In the 2006 Russian movie based on Latynina's novel *The Hunt for Siberian Deer*, the filmmakers vividly described how a giant metallurgical complex located in a Siberian city became the center of a fierce struggle involving the owner of the factory, a Moscow bank, and the local governor. All three participants pressured the judge presiding over the case, who finally yielded to one of them. The permanent redistribution of property, mostly by an alliance of criminal structures that included corrupt police and high officials, was the subject of another movie called *Bandit Petersburg*, directed by Vladimir Dovgal in 2003.

An article about the case of businessman Sergei Odinartsev vividly showed how the raiders operated. Odinartsev arrived at work one morning to find that armed thugs had taken over his tea-and-coffee warehouse in Tula, located 150 miles south of Moscow. He knew that complaining to the police would be useless. The corporate raiders who stole his business possessed several officially stamped papers confirming that they were the new owners. The raiders, according to Odinartsev, were well connected. "They have powerful supporters," Odinartsev said. "I could apply to the court but I already know it is going to be just a waste of time."

In another case, "the victim" was a businessman who attempted to play the role of raider, but failed, because his administrative roof (*krysha*) was not strong enough. Moscow businessman Vladimir Moiseev tried to make a takeover bid for a large Moscow hairdressing salon. He already owned 30 percent of the shares in the company and, most importantly, had good friends in the Interior Ministry's Organized Crime Unit. Unfortunately for Moiseev, there was another bidder with connections to the presidential administration. As in a card game, Moiseev was trumped by his rival's superior connections.[38]

Quite resourceful were the attempts of a company called PATM to take control of cement firms in Siberia. Among other devices, the company lodged false complaints in the courts against the targeted firms.[39]

MOSCOW AGAINST THE PROVINCES

In the struggle for property, Moscow corporations, which generally had closer ties to the central administration and its "administrative resources," including military power, often attempted to seize assets in other regions. A good example was the change in ownership of a meat-producing company known as Samson located in St. Petersburg. The company's most coveted asset was a piece of land. A Moscow company, Salolin, wanted to use this land for building residential houses and office space. The Petersburg company did not recognize the right of the Moscow firm, referring to a previous court decision in its favor. Using its connection to the "power structures" (the *siloviki*), the Moscow firm then recruited a special military unit from Chechnya to physically oust the directors of the Petersburg company.[40]

CONFISCATION OF GOODS

In 2006, even retail networks were raided. Stores that sold mobile phones or microwave ovens were raided under the pretext that these commodities were counterfactual. These events showed that raiding, which had previously been concentrated on big industries, had entered a new sphere of the economy.[41] The goods confiscated during the raids created a tremendous source of illegal income for officials. They would sell the goods illegally on the open market or buy them at very low prices.

Customs officers often confiscated imported goods using the most ridiculous pretexts (for instance, any type of mistake in documentation). The criminal activity of Russian customs officials was acknowledged by the highest officials, including the president. Confiscated goods would be sold at auction to a chosen firm at a minimal price.[42]

THE RAIDING OF PUBLIC INSTITUTIONS

In Moscow and other cities, where the value of land was quite high, raids on public institutions, such as clubs, libraries, and theaters, became commonplace in the new millennium. The heads of cultural institutions who resisted a seizure were often threatened with physical violence and other forms of pressure. Arson was a common method used to coerce public institutions. A few facts about these cases emerged in 2005 and in the first months of 2006. In March 2005, the chairman of the Composers Union in Moscow, Vladislav Kazenin, received a warning from the raiders who wanted to seize his building: The windows of his car were broken and a bomb was placed on the seat of the car. In 2005, another form of pressure was used on the art director of the famous Moscow theater Hermitage. There was an attempt to break into his apartment, after which the director ended his involvement with the theater. In March 2006, arson was used to force the Moscow Center for Folk Crafts to yield its territory to criminal elements. Arson was also used in May 2005 to take control of the building of the famous Stanislavsky-Nemirovich-Danchenko Theater in Moscow.[43]

CONFISCATION OF PRIVATE APARTMENTS

The precariousness of property rights was extended even to privatized apartments. This issue is extremely important for the Russians because a significant number of them own apartments (in Moscow, in 2001, half the population owned an apartment). Two authors who discussed this subject named their article "The New Feudalism: In Putin's Russia, the Nexus of Payoffs and Patronage Is Almost Medieval, Touching Every Aspect of Life."[44]

Private companies and state institutions, as well as individuals, were involved in taking over private apartments. These takeovers were supported by law enforcement agencies, the courts, and criminal structures. The Russian media was full of examples of the seizure of residential property. The authors of the above mentioned article described the following typical case: When armed police showed up last Wednesday night at Zurab Dzhaparidze's Moscow apartment, he knew immediately why they had come. Dzhaparidze's crime, the policemen claimed, was that his apartment's purchase documents had not been completed properly, so they had come to kick him out. But the 34-year-old film-festival organizer knew better. His real sin was to be Georgian. Ever since the Kremlin declared its disapproval of Tbilisi following an espionage row the previous month, Russia's police and bureaucrats had declared open season on Georgians, their businesses, and their property. Dzhaparidze paid a hefty bribe to get the police to go away.[45]

The case of a private apartment complex in Butovo, located on the outskirts of Moscow, aroused the attention of the whole country. The Moscow government decided in 2006 to demolish the houses in this district for unclear purposes, seemingly because the land in this area was extremely valuable. The owners resisted the takeover. The conflict involved the court system, police, the State Duma, and other organizations. Media treated the "Butovo conflict" as another evidence of the precariousness of property in the country.[46]

RENATIONALIZATION OR FEUDALIZATION OF PRIVATE PROPERTY

One of the most powerful agents in changing ownership was the state itself. Beginning in the new millennium it started renationalizing private property. As described by Sergei Gureev, a professor at the New

Economic School in Moscow, World Bank studies indicated that the government's share of the industrial output and employment had grown to 40 percent in 2005, from about 30 percent in 2003. "The feeling is actually much worse," he said, "as even private owners know that their property rights are contingent on their relationships with the Kremlin."[47]

Unlike all renationalization cases in history, the seizure of companies by the Russian state was dictated by the personal interests of the ruling political elites. The renationalization was essentially a sort of reprivatization, this time in favor of a new group of "feudal owners," who comprised Putin's ruling elite. In fact, it was a sort of feudal privatization, an antipode to capitalist privatization, because, while in the second case the property became a basis for the market economy, in the first case the property was turned into a part of a feudal estate that was controlled by members of the elite. The feudalization of private property, under the guise of renationalization, unlike the true nationalization of the 1920s, had nothing to do with the centralization of management of the economy, as it occurred after the October Revolution when the new planning system emerged. Indeed, a typical argument used to justify real nationalization was that it would make the economy more efficient. However, after 2000, official ideologues almost never talked about the importance of renationalization of big companies for the enhancement of their efficiency.[48]

Quite often, the Russian state used the same raiding technology as private and criminal businesses. The case of Yukos was a typical example. Sending its head to prison, the Kremlin put the company out of business and then organized the absorption of Yukos by the state company Rosneft.

In 2005–2006, the Kremlin orchestrated the consolidation of several struggling state and private aircraft manufacturers into the newly created Unified Aircraft Corporation, which was under the supervision of Putin's appointed prime minister. This corporation swallowed a number of independent private air companies, including Pulkovo and GTK Rossia. The Kremlin also appointed its own directors from the country's military export arm to oversee the largest automaker, Avtovaz, which became a semiprivate enterprise.[49] As discussed previously, the Kremlin, at the beginning of the twenty-first century, stationed its people on the board of directors of several large corporations.

REDISTRIBUTION OF PROPERTY AND CHANGES IN POWER

The precariousness of property in post-Soviet Russia became especially obvious when new officials come to power. The appearance of a new figure in the central or local government was always followed by a significant change in the property structure of the country. As Grigorii Yavlinsky, a prominent Russian politician, mused in his interview with *Izvestiia,* any move from one position to another meant "a change of control over financial streams." He added that under such conditions "no owner in the country can look to the future with certainty."[50]

Indeed, under Putin's regime, property relations changed radically. In early 2007, when this book was being written, the ruling elites in Russia nervously waited for 2008, the year Putin, according to the constitution, should step down and yield control of the country to a new president. None of those who made their fortunes between 2000 and 2008, or even earlier, could be confident in their property rights under the new leader. For this reason, most elites belonged, in 2007, to "the party of the third term" and wanted Putin to stay in power indefinitely.[51]

CONCLUSION

The instability of private property relations and the use of physical coercion in property disputes represent key aspects of life in the Middle Ages and of the feudal model that best describes this era. At the beginning of the twenty-first century, a series of new battles for the redistribution of property erupted in Russia. Almost everyone supposed that illegal methods and direct violence were being used. The Western term "hostile takeover" does not adequately explain the technologies used in Russia. The powerful raiders could rely on the courts, governors, police officers, special forces of the Ministry of Internal Affairs, the FSB, tax agencies, all bodies that had the right to inspect buildings and offices, the media, and, of course, criminal structures. In post-Soviet Russia, as in the Middle Ages, almost all property owners, from the holders of company stocks to the owners of private apartments and residential houses, were vulnerable to the semilegal manipulations of their property rights and the illegal takeover tactics of criminal structures.

CHAPTER 10

PERSONAL RELATIONS AS A CORE
FEATURE OF FEUDALISM

INTRODUCTION

One of the most important elements of feudalism in contemporary society is the role of personal relations in politics, the economy, and other spheres of public life. Personal relations can be separated into two types. One is based on the interaction between independent subjects who try to achieve their goals through mutual help, and the other is based on clientele principles (or suzerain-vassal relations), which suppose a hierarchy in the relations between people. The second type of relations is more socially important and will be the main subject of this chapter.[1]

The high role of personal relations and kinship in social life is one of the main characteristics that separate Middle Ages societies (or societies close to the feudal model) from the totalitarian and liberal societies. This circumstance should not be considered a plus or a minus of Middle Ages societies or other primitive societies where these relations were so important. In some cases, personal relations help organize social life and create order. For many people, even in the United States, the high impact of the personal factor on decisions in the economy or politics is considered a normal aspect of life and not a form of corruption, with which personal relations are often linked. Adam Bellow, in his book *In Praise of Nepotism: A Natural History*, recognizing the great scope of nepotism in American society, contended that a "New nepotism" in America was beneficial for the economy and other spheres of social life.[2]

This opinion is widely shared by ordinary Russians, who do not consider the high role of the personal factor and nepotism as a major evil in society. They are much more hostile toward extortion, bribes, and embezzlement than toward the impact of personal relations on the behavior of officials or businesspeople. Asked what they understood by the term "corruption" in the Fund of Public Opinion survey in 2006 (which used open questions), the Russians placed "bribes" (39 percent) in the first place, followed by stealing among the high echelons of power (15 percent), abuse of power (9 percent), and finally nepotism (2 percent).[3] Some Russian intellectuals, such as Andrei Konchalovskii, have lambasted the influence of nepotism in contemporary Russia and compared it with the influence of kinship on political life in the Middle Ages. However, these authors do not find support among the ordinary Russians who consider nepotism an unavoidable development in everyday life.[4]

Marxists and social scientists who incorporated, in one form or another, the idea of "objective" stratification of society were right when they suggested that society is usually divided into classes, groups, or strata on the basis of various objective factors, including economic and social statuses, economic and political interests, demographics, and place of residence.

However, the vision of society based on the feudal model, and particularly of societies with weak states, as in the case of post-Soviet Russia, allows us to see another type of division based on clans, "teams," and "cliques," which unite people who are loyal to the same leader. The members of a clan support each other not because of their common social status or origin, as Marxists like to stress (even if these factors are indeed quite important), but because they share the same fate and will prosper or perish together—the sort of behavior and mentality seen in movies and television shows such as *The Godfather* and *The Sopranos*. In the first decade of the twenty-first century, Russia was divided not only into rich and poor, educated and noneducated, residents of metropolitan areas and small cities, people living in the west and the east, Russians and non-Russians, and citizens and illegal immigrants, but also into different clans, people using different "roofs" and having different patrons.

Among other key areas of social life in which the role of personal relations is especially high is the selection of people for various positions in society, particularly in management, politics, the economy, and culture. In fact, there is little doubt that the magnitude of the personal factor in the selection of cadres and in the character of supervision over their work highly influences the efficiency of all major institutions in the country—economic, political, and military in the first place—as well as the political and social stability of society and the positions of the ruling elites.[5] While in most cases personal preferences and nepotism clearly have a negative effect on the efficiency of social institutions, they also solidify the social and political order in society. For the Russians, personal relations are particularly important for enabling people to solve their problems without help from public institutions. Personal relations are the best way to overcome life's various difficulties.

Mikhail Afanas'ev, a thoughtful Russian historian, described the high role of personal relations in contemporary Russia and compared them with the vassal relations in the Middle Ages. He also connected them, alluding to the title of Milan Kundera's famous novel *The Unbearable Lightness of Being,* directly with "the unbearable weakness of the state" or "the deficit of the state." The high role of personal relations in social life reflected the alienation of the Russian people from the state and the lack of trust in official institutions.[6] Afanas'ev was seconded by Valentin Gefter, director of the Moscow Institute of Human Rights, who also insisted that "personal factors in Russia are more important than law."[7]

The selection of people for various positions in society illustrates the contrast between personal and nonpersonal relations. In general, there are three ways of selecting cadres and controlling their performance. The authoritarian and particularly the totalitarian ones tend to totally ignore the personal factor and suppose that only those who are fully devoted to the supreme leader and the major values of the system (the state, the party, and the dominant ideology or religion) can be members of the nomenklatura. This mechanism also suggests that the performance of apparatchiks is judged by the same criteria. It supposes that the leader does not tolerate any form of divided loyalty (to immediate superiors, the church, or even spouses and friends). He would see loyalty to others as almost state treason. The leader harshly punishes anybody among the ruling elite who is influenced by personal or clannish interests. The consistent hierarchical principle in the selection of cadres and the evaluation of their performance materialized in Stalin's and Hitler's states, to consider only a couple of contemporary examples.

The second principle in the selection of cadres and the supervision over them works in a democratic society. It is based on democratic and market postulates and ultimately on merits, competence, and rationality, as described by Weber and Parsons. It supposes that the people elect the citizen who is best suited for the job and that elected bodies supervise the quality of nonelected officials, while market competition selects the best managers in the economy and several other spheres of social life. In democratic societies, the intrusion of personal relations in the decision-making process in politics is considered as a sort of deviance, often illegal, that challenges the fundamentals of the society.

Unlike the authoritarian and democratic societies, personal relations were the most important basis of feudal societies. In these societies, the selection of cadres was based first of all on their loyalty to those who chose them for the position. The superior's emotional and intellectual trust in the subordinates—beyond the institutional guarantee against treason—was a fundamental factor in the functioning of any organization. The choice of relatives for high positions in government was also dictated by the desire to have as the executors of important decisions people whom the superior could trust. While competence was not ignored in the feudal-like selection of cadres, as was also the case with the totalitarian form of selection (the conflict between "red" and "competent" managers was typical for societies of the Soviet type), it was considered much less important than the cadre's loyalty to the immediate superior. The personal factor significantly diminished the rigidity of the control over the performance of subordinates in so far as they maintained their loyalty to superiors.

FEUDAL PERSONAL RELATIONS IN THE SOCIAL SCIENCES

Meanwhile, political science and sociology in the twentieth century tended to strongly underestimate the role of personal relations in political and social life. Among the social sciences, only anthropology, with its focus on nonmodern societies, was an exception.[8] When social scientists could not avoid the subject, they treated the impact of personal relations on politics or other spheres of social life as "natural," and as implicitly assumed, and therefore undeserving of special attention in the study of macrosocial issues. In textbooks on government or political science, as well as in sociological texts dealing with political matters, it is almost impossible to find a discussion of this crucial social issue.

Even contemporary social psychology, which says a lot about human relations, mostly ignores not only the dominance-submission pattern of behavior in personal relations and its impact on political and economic life in society, but even the interaction of independent actors that are not determined by institutional factors. What is more, social psychologists tend to underestimate the importance of kinship in social life (an important issue not only for Middle Ages societies but also for contemporary societies).[9] Since 1964, after W. D. Hamilton initiated studies on kinship in everyday life, a few scholars began to pay more attention to this issue.[10] The interest in this issue increased after Richard Dawkins' work in the 1970s about helping (or altruistic) behavior and people's willingness to help those who will carry on their genes.[11] However, even these empirically well-founded studies did not push social scientists to make important inferences for social and political life. The major reason for this state of affairs was the belief that the high role of personal relations in political and social life belongs to the past and is incompatible with the contemporary rational and law-abiding society.

The disregard of personal relations as an important political and social factor was typical for macrosocial theories. This was true first of all for the analysis of society as a whole. The influential symbolic interactionist school did not change the high disregard of personal relations in the analysis of major social and political processes in contemporary society. Its champions, such as Herbert Blumer and Erving Goffman, were obsessed with the interaction of independent individuals in small groups and displayed no interest in studying the impact of these interactions on political or social conflicts.

Weber and then Parsons gave a theoretical justification for the disregard of personal relations with the dominance component in contemporary Western society. Weber described the ideal society as based on impersonal relations, rationality, and competence. With his belief in the rationality of contemporary bourgeois society, he described anonymity, as opposed to personal relations, as the main generic feature of contemporary society and opposed it to feudal society. He opposed gemeinschaft, a concept of communities with face-to-face relations, to gesellschaft, a society based on anonymity, which was consonant with Weber's eulogy on nonpersonal relations.

Later, Parsons, with his utopian and idealistic belief in the triumph of rationality and universalism in the world, was confident that the role of "ascription"—when one's social status is determined by factors outside one's efforts and skills—would decline and be replaced by "achievement."

The Marxist and left radical vision of human relations was essentially close to the Weberian-Parsonian belief in the prevalence of the impersonal approach in social relations. It supposed that the class proximity and commonality of all ideologies determine the selection of cadres in a capitalist society. This was one of C. Wright Mills' main ideas on the formation of elites in American society.[12] Both theories—the Weberian-Parsonian and Marxist—depersonalized human relations, making them mostly dependent on external factors, such as class (or group) or social values, both of which are not controlled by individuals.

The concepts of networks and social capital, which became popular by the second half of the twentieth century, challenged the Weberian-Parsonian focus on the anonymity of human relations in contemporary society. The emergence of these concepts in the 1970s partially repaired this flaw, particularly because they paid such close attention to the role of individuals' trust in each other. However, these concepts have been used mostly to analyze microsocial relations, and practically none of the authors who wrote on this issue extended their ideas in high politics.[13] But even more important was that both concepts operate with autonomous and independent individuals who interact with each other on an equal basis, as if none of the participants have any advantage over each other in terms of power (political, economic, or ideological). This was the premise of Marc Granovetter's pioneering work in 1973.[14] Most studies on social capital and networks were devoted to such organizations as school boards, scouting organizations, amateur sports leagues, fraternal organizations, and the Internet. Even such critical sociologists as Pierre Bourdieu, in "The Forms of Capital" (1986), tended to talk about social capital outside the realm of power relations as existing between members of groups and as based on mutual acquaintanceship and recognition.[15] Robert Putnam, author of *Bowling Alone* and a champion of the concept of social capital, also talked about the social networks that unite people and make them ready to do things for each other. It was only natural that Putnam and his followers considered social capital as a crucial factor for building and maintaining democracy.[16] Other authors, such as James Coleman and Francis Fukuyama, who wrote about social capital operated with individuals who deal with other ordinary actors in networks on the basis of equality. Only a few other authors, most of them outside the areas of sociology and social psychology, indulged in a wide narration about nepotism.

There was also weak interest in personal relations and kinship in the mainstream economic literature. Most publications on this issue were related to the early stages of capitalism or to nonmodern societies.[17] Weber discussed the subject of kinship in economic organization only as it related to China in the beginning of the twentieth century.[18] The subject was mostly ignored in the analysis of contemporary developed capitalist societies. An exception was made in the case of special subjects such as family business and discrimination against women in business.[19] In economics textbooks and in texts devoted to capitalism as a system, the subject was treated sporadically and quite superficially.

The neoclassical economists who dominated the discipline in America, and particularly libertarians, would only reluctantly discuss the subject. Sharing the Weberian image of capitalism as a rational, effective system and the Jeffersonian focus on meritocracy, they avoided discussing the obstacles to perfect competition and the most effective use of resources. In any case, it was difficult to expect to find a discussion on the impact of inheritance or nepotism on the efficiency of private business in Milton Friedman's famous work *Capitalism and Democracy*.[20] Rather, it is the authors of great novels about capitalist society who colorfully depict nepotism, such as Thomas Mann, in *Buddenbrooks* (1901), Maxim Gorky, in *The Artamonov Business* (1927), Upton Sinclair, in *The Jungle* (1928), and Theodore Dreiser, in *The Financier* (1940), as well as journalists who describe the history of various private firms and how, with each new generation of owners, their interest in the business of their own companies has declined.[21]

Very few professional economists raised the issue in their publications. Only Bellow, a journalist, as cited above, dealt with the role of personal relations and kinship in the economy. He insisted that the generations of Fords, Coorses, Graces, Sulzbergers, and Goldmans were successful businessmen who carried on traditions of excellence in the auto industry, consumer products, newspapers, and investments, respectively, and also efficient managers who only rarely used the influence of their clans. Other authors such as Loyiso Mbabane, an expert on privatization in South Africa, defended "cronyism," or nepotism, simply because cronyism is a normal feature of capitalism. He wrote that if he were the owner of a multibillion-dollar operation, he would be foolish to appoint a complete stranger to run it. He insisted that typically the heir or any person who gets recruited to the top would be someone very well known either to him or to his top management (the "who you know versus what you know" maxim). Mbabane is sure that this goes for any type of serious enterprise, venture, or institution (including government). When a new political party comes to power in the United States, it changes all the top management, replacing it with people who are loyal to the new dispensation. Loyalty to the new dispensation is in fact viewed as a critical component of one's "competence" for a public service position.[22]

LOYALTY AND TRUST AS THE MAJOR FACTORS OF PERSONAL RELATIONS IN THE MIDDLE AGES

The personal relations between the lord and his vassals and between the members of a family were based on the hierarchical principle, and in this capacity made up an essential part of the social fabric in the Middle Ages. The high importance of personal relations in this period highlighted two social factors: loyalty and trust.

Paul Vinogradoff described the ceremonial establishment of relations between the lord and tenant as a key element of life in the Middle Ages. The tenant had to appear in person before the lord, surrounded by his court, kneel before him, put his folded hands into the hand of the lord, and promise him loyalty. This act of homage corresponded with the "investiture" by the lord, who delivered to his vassal a flag, a staff, a charter, or some other symbol of property ownership.[23]

Loyalty was a leading issue in Shakespeare's plays. For instance, in *King Lear,* Cordelia epitomized loyalty to her father. Loyalty was a leading theme in *Macbeth* and *Much Ado about Nothing* as well. Loyalty was also praised in almost all the plays of the authors of classicism, Racine and Corneille in the first place, but mocked by the authors of the new, bourgeois era such as Molière and Beaumarchais.

Kinship and Personal Relations

Kinship is a particular type of personal relation that has played an important role in societies throughout history. In primitive societies, prior to the formation of the state, and in the Middle Ages in particular, the importance of kinship reached its apex. In fact, kinship was a form of relation that prevailed in many tribes before the formation of the state.[24] Middle Ages societies were based on kinship relations, even if the term kinship has been used quite broadly. People in the Middle Ages talked not about coworkers, but about kinsmen; not about peers, but about brothers; not about associations, but about fraternities.

A critical difference was the medieval perception of reciprocity and kinship. Position, power, and place within society were based not on individual freedoms and impersonal relationships, but on highly personal relationships of the reciprocating type, entered into contractually and described with kinship terminology. In the political realm, kinship, the right to inherit royal power, was the most important phenomenon.[25]

Kinship relations were crucial in Russia in the Middle Ages. As one Russian chronicler discussed, the senior prince of Kiev, Sviatoslav, during his speech to the Russian princes, addressed them in order of kinship status. The social network based on kinship was extremely important in medieval Russia until the time of Ivan the Terrible, according to Vasilii Kliuchevskii.[26]

A TOTALITARIAN SOCIETY: THE SOVIET CASE

In a totalitarian society the role of personal relations, particularly based on kinship, was reduced to a minimal level, even if it never disappeared completely. Stalin was hostile toward the impact of kinship on the selection of cadres and only allowed it in rare cases, such as the active political role of Lazar Kaganovich's family and the role of Yurii Zhdanov, the son of politburo member Andrei Zhdanov, and later the husband of Stalin's daughter Svetlana, as the head of the Department of Science in the Central Committee.[27] Stalin was also against the selection of cadres on the basis of personal loyalty. Stalin publicly lambasted those party apparatchiks who violated this iron postulate of the Soviet system.[28]

Nepotism clearly increased in post-Stalin times, even though the children of leaders were still rather invisible in public life.[29] However, the recruitment of personally loyal people in the party and state apparatus became a typical phenomenon. A new general secretary usually brought to the highest echelon of power people with whom he worked in the provinces. Khrushchev filled many positions with people from Kiev, where he worked for many years. Brezhnev invited his subordinates from Dnepropetrovsk to Moscow, where they formed the so-called Dnepropetrovsk's mafia; Gorbachev recruited for the Central Committee many people from his native region, Stavropol, while Yeltsin brought in people from Sverdlovsk.[30]

Stalin strongly discouraged the members of the politburo meeting each other privately, because he was concerned about them plotting against him. Indeed, the conspiracy against Khrushchev in 1964 happened only because the discontented members of the politburo disregarded the rule and intensively communicated with each other in private. However, in Brezhnev's times, personal and family contacts between the members of the politburo were still strongly discouraged.[31]

The role of semilegal and illegal personal relations in the economy, politics, and other spheres of social life was much greater, as mentioned, in the Caucasian and central Asian republics, where clannish and tribal structures, similar to vassal relations, existed. Each official, minister, or party secretary in these republics had their own network of vassals, many of whom were relatives or people from the leader's tribe or region. The Soviet totalitarian state, with the appointment of ethnic Russians to key positions in national republics and with powerful local supervising agencies directly subordinated to Moscow (the local branches of the KGB, the Ministry of Internal Affairs, the Ministry of Defense, the Central Statistical Board, and several others), was able to restrain somewhat the impact of personal relations and clan-kinship on the life in these republics.[32] However, with the collapse of the empire, most constraints were removed and these relations almost openly became the basis of social organization in central Asia.[33]

Personal relations among people of the same rank, based on the illegal exchange of goods and services, represented another important part of life in Soviet society. These relations existed even under Stalin, but flourished in post-Stalin Russia. Almost everyone, particularly the members of the intelligentsia and the managerial class, had their own network of friends (social capital). The Russian term "blat," which referred to opportunities stemming from personal connections, was used in Russia much earlier than the terms "social capital" and "network." The high role of interpersonal relations in social life was seen in the cult of friendship in the Soviet Union and many other totalitarian societies. This cult evidently resembled the code of honor of medieval knights with its high praise for devotion not only to the suzerain, but also to his comrades in arms and beloved women.[34]

THE COLLAPSE OF THE SOVIET SYSTEM AND THE INCREASED ROLE OF PERSONAL RELATIONS

The collapse of the totalitarian state opened the flood gates for personal relations, including kinship, in economic and political life. The demise of the Soviet system was accompanied by a rapid weakening of the state, and the fall of social order and ideology, which influenced the behavior of officials and even ordinary people. If in central Asian republics the collapse of the empire allowed the traditional social structures to develop on full scale, in Russia and other Slavic republics, personal relations began to play a role they had never played before, excluding in the Middle Ages. If, as mentioned, personal relations in the Soviet times were used as a shield against the state and against the specific character of the state economy, now these relations came up as the replacement for the weakened and corrupt state and discredited social institutions as an antidote to the growing chaos and as a means for adapting to the new society.

Even in the early years of the twenty-first century, 15 years after the fall of the Soviet system, Russia was a country, much more than any other, that mistrusted almost all social institutions in the country and political institutions in the first place. According to data from the Levada-Tsentr, there was, in 2005, no one institution that could garner more than 40–50 percent of the nation's trust. The three most popular institutions (the president, the church, and the army) could garner 47 percent, 41 percent, and 31 percent, respectively. However, most political institutions enjoyed a confidence level of only 10 to 30 percent and some even lower. Only 15 percent of the public trusted the courts and only 10 percent the police. The prestige of the State Duma and political parties was even lower, 10 percent and 5 percent, respectively.[35] Other polling data matched these findings.[36]

Contrary to the mistrust in social institutions, Russians in the post-Soviet period increased their belief in the family as the most important institution. In 2001, two-thirds of the Russians supported the idea that the interests of the family were more important than the interests of society.[37] It is worth noting that the degree of optimism was much higher among people who lived in families than among single individuals. Also, the bigger the family the greater was the optimism. For instance, in 2004, only 30 percent of single people were confident in tomorrow, compared to 46 percent of those whose family contained four people.[38]

Yeltsin's Family

The increased role of personal relations after the collapse of the Soviet system should be attributed to a great degree to the behavior of Yeltsin and "the family." As a matter of fact, the family of the Soviet leaders played practically no role at all in Soviet public life (the one exception was Nadezhda Krupskaia, Lenin's wife, who, as an old Bolshevik, played some modest political role on her own).

In fact, the Soviet public did not even know the names of Stalin's, Brezhnev's, Andropov's, or Chernenko's wives and children.[39] Khrushchev's wife was the only one who, before perestroika, was seen in a photograph of the Soviet leader during one of his trips abroad.[40] The wives of leaders were never involved with their husbands in political life.[41] Gorbachev's wife Raisa was the first wife of a leader to became visible on the political scene. Her frequent appearances beside her husband on various occasions aroused high emotion, mostly negative, in society. However, even Raisa Gorbacheva did not formally take part in the decision-making process in the Kremlin.[42]

Yeltsin's family entered the country's political and economic life almost immediately after 1991. Already in the first years of Yeltsin's rule, "the family" became a leading term in the Russian political vocabulary. In fact, it became so well known that pollsters could include this term without problem in their questionnaires when they asked about who ruled the country. In any case, the Russian public soon considered the family as one of the most powerful actors in the country. Even two years after Yeltsin's resignation in 1999, 22 percent of the Russians (in 2001) were sure that the country was run by "the family."[43]

Yeltsin's youngest daughter, Tatiana, along with her two consecutive husbands, Leonid Diachenko and Valentin Yumashev, and his eldest daughter, Elena, and her husband Valerii Okulov became fabulously rich by the end of his rule. Tatiana's second husband (in fact, it was her third husband if to count the one she divorced before 1991) was the father-in-law of Oleg Deripaska, an aluminum magnate and one of the richest people in Russia. Deripaska had also made his gigantic fortune in the first few years of Yeltsin's regime.[44] The participation of the family in corruption was well known in Russia and abroad. It was known, for example, that Boris Berezovskii, when he belonged to the ruling elite, gave Tatiana two very expensive cars as gifts.[45] Since the corruption at the top of power was difficult to detect, in Russia as well as in any other society, it was not easy to document all cases of corruption in which the family was involved. Among various stories about the enrichment of the family, there was sound evidence that the two daughters of Yeltsin had participated in a financial speculation using inside information that was accessible only to state officials. Their scheme earned gigantic revenues while the rest of the country faced the financial catastrophe of August 1998. This information was provided by Yurii Skuratov, prosecutor general under Yeltsin, who was later fired.[46] The existence of Tatiana's secret accounts in Swiss banks and the two accounts of her husband Diachenko in the Bank of New York was debated in foreign and Russian media and even at the meetings of the American congress.[47] Other sources, including a famous Russian muckraker Yurii Shchekochikhin (according to several Russian journalists, he was poisoned in 2003), brought data about Tatiana's villa in Antibe on the Lazure Coast in the south of France (estimated to be worth $11 million), as well as her castle in the German city of Garmich.[48]

Foreign prosecutors from the United States, Switzerland, and Italy have tried several times to prove the illegal origin of the family's wealth, but due to lack of help from the Russian prosecutor general they did not succeed. The same was true in many other cases of corruption in Russia, such as the case of Pavel Borodin, who, as the manager of Kremlin Properties, was directly involved in the enrichment of the family.[49]

Even more important for Russian society was the active role of the members of the family, Tatiana in the first place, in the political decision-making process. She even held a special position as an adviser to the president. For instance, Tatiana and Yeltsin's wife Naina were behind the ailing Yeltsin's decision to run for a second term as president, which exposed Yeltsin to serious health risks. Tatiana was a major political figure in Yeltsin's Russia and held a high place in the hierarchy among the most influential Russian politicians. Indeed, according to a survey that asked about the most influential politicians in the country (conducted by Boris Grushin's polling firm Vox Populi in December 1999), Putin and Yeltsin filled the first two places with rankings of 7.42 and 6.81, respectively, on a ten-point scale. The third place went to Berezovskii (6.41), while Diachenko scored fourth (6.25).[50]

THE CHOICE OF AN HEIR: RUSSIA'S MONARCHIC PRINCIPLE

Yeltsin's choice of an heir was directed exclusively by his desire to find someone he could trust, someone who would not send him or any member of his family to prison for their unlawful acts, which included violating the constitution, shelling the Parliament building in October 1993, and various other illegal actions and self-enrichment acts. Before choosing Putin, Yeltsin tested several candidates by appointing them temporarily to the position of prime minister. There is no direct evidence, however, that Putin vowed, in one way or another, to protect Yeltsin. The contract between them was purely personal in the spirit of the seignior-vassal contract and was never made public.[51]

In any case, Putin's first edict after his inauguration as president was to declare Yeltsin's immunity and a series of other decisions that guaranteed the former president a generous material living and high status; no one from Yeltsin's family was sued or brought up on charges of illegal activity.[52]

Of course, in a monarchy, the successor to the throne in most cases was someone with kinship ties to the previous monarch. In some post-Soviet republics, such as Azerbaijan, where Geidar Aliev was succeeded in 2003 by his son Ilham, or North Korea, where Kim Il-sung was succeeded in 1994 by his son Kim Jong-il, the succession occurred in accordance with the ideal monarchic principle.

However, the core of the monarchic principle of transition from one leader to another is not so much a succession on a kinship basis, but the power of the current leader to appoint an heir and disregard the will of the people and many elites. This circumstance was of greatest importance for contemporary Russia, where a sort of feudal monarchy emerged, with succession based not on kinship but on the choice of the current leader from a few candidates, a practice that was elaborated in the Roman Empire.[53]

Indeed, as a rule, Roman emperors transferred their power not to their children, but to adopted sons. One of the most well-known cases of the choice of a successor took place during the Roman Empire in the second century A.D. Emperor Hadrian, who himself was a ward of Emperor Trojan, chose as his successor Antonius Pius. Hadrian's successor in turn selected, at the suggestion of Hadrian, two people, Lucius Ceionius Commodus, the son of his wife's brother, and Marcus Aurelius, the famous preacher of stoicism. Finally, Marcus Aurelius became the successor.[54] The monarchic principle of succession in its Roman version is a rather "normal institution," used in order to avoid chaos in a period of transition.

Many Russians regarded the implementation of the monarchic principle in this way. Already in the mid-1990s, the debates about the restoration of monarchy in Russia began to circulate in Moscow.[55] In any case, it became a habit in this period to name Yeltsin "Tsar Boris." What is more, Yeltsin surprised everyone during his visit to Orlov in September 1997 by referring to himself as Tsar Boris and comparing to Peter the Great. One journalist even published a book with the title *The Times of Tsar Boris.*[56] The utopian dreams about the enthronement of Yeltsin did not materialize. However, the circumstances under which Yeltsin transferred his power to Putin stood as evidence of the deeply rooted, if inconspicuous, monarchic tendencies in the political culture. Indeed, Putin's sudden emergence as president showed how deeply "the monarchic factor" was embedded in Russian political mentality.

In 1999, less than 5 percent of the population "trusted" the president and 4 percent regretted his resignation.[57] In mid-May, the Parliament began impeachment proceedings against Yeltsin, accusing the 68-year-old leader of five counts of betrayal, treason, and even murder. When the president emerged from the process unscathed, the public widely attributed his escape to the Kremlin's almost open bribing of Parliament deputies. According to the Fund of Public Opinion, only 12 percent of the Russians were glad that Yeltsin was not ousted from his position, while two-thirds supported his impeachment.[58] However, the fact that Yeltsin, who was held in contempt by so many people, chose Putin as his successor bothered only half the population and did not damage the chances of Putin becoming the new president.[59]

The idea of a smooth transition of power was also much stronger than the public's concern about the rude violation of democratic principles in the campaign for elections to the State Duma in December 1999 (when it was necessary for the Kremlin to destroy the chances of possible rivals to Yeltsin's appointees Yurii Luzhkov and Evgenii Primakov) and the presidential election in March 2000 (when Putin's rivals were in a very unfavorable position).[60] As reasonably noted by Joel Ostrow, it is remarkable that several astute observers of Russian politics, such as McFaul,[61] Donald Barry,[62] and the authors of Vladimir Tikhomirov's noted collection,[63] "call[ed] what happened in March 2000" "a regular democratic presidential election," which, as Ostrow contended, is "patently absurd."[64]

There were several data suggesting that support for monarchy in general grew after Yeltsin's rule. While many supporters of monarchy saw it first of all as a stabilizing factor in the succession process, others yearned for monarchy, mostly an absolutist one, as an alternative to democratic order.[65] Some analysts in Russia supposed that the idea of monarchy was supported by Putin's Kremlin and by the security services.[66]

In any case, in 2000, a fifth of the Russians who answered a question about their attitudes toward restoring "pure" monarchy endorsed it, even if most of these people thought that their wishes could never be materialized.[67] By 2006, this number had not changed much[68]; no less than 40 percent were ready to vote in 2006 for a candidate chosen by Putin.[69]

PUTIN AND HIS NETWORK OF KGB PEOPLE

Under Putin, the role of vassal relations in the country increased enormously. As a Russian journalist noted, "Putin, with his mistrust toward any public institution, liked to solve all problems relying on personal relations."[70] During his stay in power between 2000 and 2006, Putin created a network of people with whom he had worked as a KGB agent in the Soviet Union, along with old acquaintances of other origins (those with whom he worked in Leningrad when he served as a deputy to the mayor and those with whom he lived in a dacha village close to Leningrad). He installed his personal friends, acquaintances, and other KGB people, all of whom he trusted, at the highest positions in the country. These people controlled major positions in the state and led some of the country's richest companies.[71] As the Russian researcher Aleksei Mukhin noted, "Two criteria were the basis for the selection of cadres under Putin: his work in the KGB and his involvement in the local government in Leningrad when he served as vice mayor."[72]

Under Putin, the large network of people from the KGB and the army and the extremely high proportion of security people in the government and economy made the country quite unique in the contemporary world. According to Ol'ga Kryshtanovskaia, the leading Russian expert on elites, one-quarter of the members of the ruling elite had worked for the KGB/FSB or the Main Intelligence Directorate of the army (the GRU).[73] Former KGB members, army generals, and officers were often appointed as governors (for example, General Boris Gromov became the governor of the Moscow Region, General Vladimir Kulakov in the Voronezh Region, Viktor Maslov in the Smolensk Region, and Georgii Shpak in the Riazan Region). Another example can be seen in the leadership of Gazprom, a major state gas company. Among the top managers were 17 former KGB/FSB agents. A vice president of the company, Valerii Golubev, was a former officer of the security service. According to research on Russian banks conducted by *Novaia Gazeta*, "[I]n literally all banks you will find 'silovikov' (people from the FSB or the army) either in the role of founder or in the security service."[74]

The Russians soon grasped the real role of the network of security and army officers as the crucial instrument for running the country. By the middle of 2000, the Russians put this network in the first place among the most powerful actors in the country: 52 percent of the respondents pointed to the KGB and army officers, 40 percent to the "governors and political elite," 25 percent to oligarchs, while only 6 percent mentioned "the people as a whole."[75]

THE CREATION OF CRONY CAPITALISM

Although the role of personal relations in politics was quite important, its role in the economy was even more vital to Russia's future. In fact, the whole social fabric of contemporary society was created through privatization in the 1990s, which was permeated by the dominance of personal relations, including kinship. These relations turned out to be quite similar to those in the early Middle Ages (or even before, in tribal societies). They played a key role in the maintenance of order, given the absence of a strong and efficient Weberian state.

In the early 1990s, the rapid privatization of the gigantic Soviet state economy was the priority for the ruling liberal elite. The pace of privatization had major historical consequences for the future of the country.[76] Those who controlled the Kremlin in the aftermath of the anti-Communist revolution in 1991 were confident that privatization had to be brought about in the quickest way through "shock therapy." This was perceived as important for two reasons: first, to prevent a return of totalitarianism to Russia, which was based on central planning and the state monopoly on economic resources; and second, as the necessary condition for the acceleration of economic growth and the quickest path to increasing the standard of living.[77] The presidential edict on December 29, 1991, only three months after the change of the regime, had a remarkable title: "On the acceleration of privatization of state and municipal enterprises."[78] As a matter of fact, the reformers managed to achieve their goal (at what price was another question). Within three years they privatized up to two-thirds of the state property in the economy.

As in other post-Communist countries, privatization in Russia began with the intention to evenly distribute the wealth among the population using vouchers, which provided each citizen with part of the national wealth (10,000 rubles in 1992). Even if the distribution of vouchers was formally implemented (the population received 146 million rubles of "investment checks"), the operation failed because the vouchers almost immediately lost their value due to hyperinflation (within two years the vouchers declined in value by 60 percent). It was easy to buy them from people at a symbolic price, often for a bottle of vodka (almost immediately, one-quarter of all vouchers were sold). Various other ways were used by officials and criminals to persuade citizens to sell their vouchers, including violence and fear tactics.[79]

Formally, the Parliament endorsed several modes of privatization that differed in the extent to which directors and employees had advantages over outsiders in the acquisition of stocks.[80] However, essentially, the Russian elites implemented their own principles for distributing state property through networks of friends, colleagues, and relatives. According to Marshall Goldman, an American expert on the Russian economy, 80–90 percent of the Russians did not benefit at all from privatization.[81]

Privatization was a complex process that began with the decision of state officials to privatize factories, mines, companies in the oil industry, and research institutes. The people who worked in the offices of privatization decided, at the national and local levels, what would be the objects and methods of privatization. Of course, the decisions regarding the most valuable objects of privatization, first of all oil companies, were made by the Kremlin (Yeltsin, and later Putin).

As a rule, the major beneficiaries of privatization were the high officials themselves, whose "social capital" consisted of friends or at least colleagues and acquaintances of different sorts (for instance, based on communication about hunting or discussions in the public baths) who had access to privatization. As officials mostly contacted other officials, they made up the vanguard of the first owners of the means of production in Russia.[82] Since the directors of the companies were also among those who made decisions about privatization, with the endorsement of the offices of privatization, those who were close to them again had the highest probability of receiving a chunk of state property. Of course, there were many people outside the official establishment who were able to grab state property, but most of them used their connections with official structures as a necessary condition for success.[83]

KINSHIP AND FRIENDSHIP IN PRIVATIZATION AND ECONOMIC LIFE

Kinship was one of the most powerful factors that influenced privatization. In some cases, close relatives were used by bureaucrats for personal enrichment. Those who made the decisions on privatization would give their relatives, usually wives or children, private companies through legal or illegal means. Governors often helped the privatized business of their relatives become a monopoly supplier of various goods and services at exorbitant prices to a region or a city. The classic case was the entrepreneurial activity of Elena Baturina, wife of Moscow mayor Yurii Luzhkov. With $1.3 billion in assets, she became the owner of a construction company in Moscow; in 2006 she made it onto the *Forbes* list of the richest people in the world (number 507 in the world and number 25 in Russia).[84]

The enrichment of their children by the members of the elite was one of the most typical developments in the process of privatization. Let us consider, for example, the role of kinship in Gazprom, the leading gas company in Russia. Viktor Chernomyrdin, the Soviet minister of the gas industry (1985–1989) and later Yeltsin's prime minister (1992–1998), converted Gazprom, in 1989, into a gigantic gas company that operated as a semiprivate firm and was elected as its chairman. His fortune was estimated, by the end of the 1980s, at $5 billion. In his capacity as chairman he could easily enrich his children, using mostly the daughter companies of Gazprom. Chernomyrdin's two sons, Vitalii and Andrei, in 1995 received control over a daughter company of Gazprom named Stroitransgas (it built pipes for Gazprom). They were allowed to purchase 5 percent of Gazprom's stock at a very low price.[85] Often the children of other top managers at Gazprom, such as Rem Viakhirev, who became the chairman of Gazprom in 1992, and his deputy, Viacheslav Sheremet, also received a juicy chunk of the privatized company's assets. Tatiana Dedikova, Viakhirev's daughter, and Elena Dmitrieva, Sheremet's daughter, along with the relatives of other managers also bought, at a symbolic price, a company that supplied Gazprom with imported equipment. The same children of the top managers received a company that exported gas to Hungary. They paid only four marks for this acquisition.[86]

Prime Minister Mikhail Fradkov appointed his 28-year-old son Piotr as a top manager at the State Maritime Company in the Far East and then as a leading manager in the Foreign Trade Bank. His other son, 24-year-old Pavel, received a prestigious position in the Ministry of Foreign Affairs. Sergei Ivanov, the minister of defense, found good jobs in leading banks for his two sons, also at very young ages.[87]

The role of personal relations in economic life did not decrease when the major phase of privatization ended. The state's choice of suppliers and services continued to be deeply influenced by personal connections. The minister of health services and social issues Mikhail Zurabov selected pharmaceutical companies managed by his wife and his friends as the providers of free medicines for retired people. As Moscow media insisted, Zurabov chose the companies without any bidding process and accepted their exorbitant prices. Among these companies was NPO Microgen, headed by Anton Katlinskii, who was formerly Zurabov's deputy. Another company, Medstore, had close connections to Zurabov's wife.[88]

The Case of Non-Russian Republics

The presidents of non-Russian republics were almost completely free to enrich themselves through various illegal means and to help the members of their families and even remote relatives to enrich themselves by appointing them to rule various lucrative businesses. It was well known in Tatarstan that Mintimer Shaimiev's family owned a big chunk of the economy. The same was true for the family of the Bashkir president Murtaza Rakhimov. His son Ural Rakhimov ran two major companies in the republic, named Bashkir kapital and Bashneft.[89] Corrupt officials such as Rishat Iskhakov, the head of Iglinsk District who had ties with Ural Rakhimov, were immune to criminal prosecution.[90]

PERSONAL RELATIONS IN THE RUSSIAN MIND

The high role of personal relations and nepotism in society, and particularly during privatization, had a major influence on Russian society after 1991. The belief that politicians were absorbed only with their private interests, made important decisions based only on their personal interests (and those of their relatives and friends), and ignored the issue of competence when selecting cadres made the majority of Russians deeply cynical and quite indifferent toward public affairs, a phenomenon that was seen in the Middle Ages. There were several indicators that showed how much the Russians were absorbed with their personal life and how little concern they had about social issues. Less than 10 percent of the Russians were involved in the activities of political parties. Often only less than 20 percent participated in local elections, which prompted the State Duma in November 2006 to cancel the requirement of no less than 20 percent voters in a regional election.[91]

According to a VTSIOM survey in 2006, the peculiar character of Russian political culture can be seen in the fact that 68 percent of the respondents thought that the Russians "refused to participate in political life"; 56 percent thought that their countrymen "disrespect the law," and 52 percent thought the Russians "in general mistrust ideals and principles."[92] Besides, most Russians did not believe in the possibility of honest competition in politics or in the economy; 60 percent did not believe in the efficacy of the competition between political parties in the country.[93] Most people were against free prices as regulators of business in a competitive market. In 2006, three-quarters of the population (those who answered the question in the VTSIOM survey) condemned the release of prices at the beginning of the market reforms in 1992.[94]

However, even more important was the widely spread conviction that the enrichment of the country was based not on real achievements that were useful for society, but on people's connections with power holders, and on corruption and the assistance of criminals. Asked in a

2004 survey by the Institute of Complex Social Research, sponsored by the German Ebert Fund, "What is necessary for economic success?" the Russians ranked "connections" (65 percent) in the first place, "abilities" (52 percent) in the second place, "education" (49 percent) in the third place, and "political connections" (48 percent) in the fourth. According to the same study, in 2004, more than two-thirds of the Russians had deeply negative attitudes toward rich people; only 5 percent thought that the rich people achieved their status due to hard work and talent.[95] In another survey conducted by VT-SIOM in 2006, the Russians were asked about the factors that determined "success in life." Those who answered were divided into two equal groups: people who pointed to "personal qualities, abilities and talent" and those who stressed the crucial importance of "personal connections."[96] Other data pointed to an even greater importance of "personal connections" in the life of Russians. According to ROMIR's survey in the 1990s, 84 percent of Russians saw personal relations as the best instrument to solve their problems.[97]

In some ways, given the public's acquiescence to personal relations as the basis for political and economic life, the Russians were not alone in the world. Personal relations and nepotism dominated political life in many countries of Africa, Asia, and Latin America. It is enough to mention contemporary Venezuela, where all five brothers of President Hugo Chavez and his father held various lucrative positions in the country, while being involved in corruption and embezzlement.[98] Western countries were also far from being free of nepotism, which could be found in the United States[99] and particularly in Italy.[100]

CONCLUSION

The role of informal, personal relations in post-Soviet Russia is difficult to overestimate. Challenging formal legal structures, personal relations penetrated literally each cell of society. Quite often, individuals' place in society was determined not so much by their objective characteristics, including their political and economic position, but by the clan that protected them. The high role of personal relations in politics and the economy was accepted by the population as a necessary condition for the organization of life in post-Soviet society. At the same time, the prevalence of personal relations fostered corruption and criminalization in society and weakened the state and social institutions. The flourishing of personal relations has made the functioning of democratic mechanisms practically impossible. It has also instilled a deep distrust of democracy among the people.

CHAPTER 11

PRIVATE SECURITY

A Typical Feudal Phenomenon

INTRODUCTION

Among the various consequences of the weakness of state is the need for private protection on the part of ordinary citizens and particularly big businesses and other major organizations. The high role of private protection represents one of the central aspects of the feudal model. The search for protection was one of the most important elements of Western European societies of the early Middle Ages. After the collapse of the Roman Empire, the central administration was extremely weak and unable to enforce its laws or guarantee the security and property of the people and various social organizations, including guilds and the church. Only after the emergence of absolute monarchy (as in France in the seventeenth century) did the need for private protection decline. However, private protection as an institution never disappeared from Western Europe. In fact, it has remained an important factor of social life until the present day in most countries of the world, including the United States. Only strong authoritarian and totalitarian regimes have reduced the need for private protection to very low levels.

PRIVATE SECURITY IN THE MIDDLE AGES

Marc Bloch described the inability of the state to provide security in the Merovingian period as a main factor that led to the development of a vast network of personal relationships, which eventually evolved into the societies in Western Europe in the Middle Ages.[1] Neither the state nor the family could provide adequate protection. The village community was barely strong enough to maintain order within its boundaries. Everywhere the weak felt vulnerable. On the one hand, there was the urgent quest for a protector. On the other, there were usurpations of authority, often by violent means.

Charles Tilly, a great contemporary expert on the Middle Ages, was right when he wrote that the word "protection" sounds two contrasting tones: With one, protection calls up images of the shelter against danger provided by a powerful friend, a large insurance policy, or a sturdy *roof*. With the other, it evokes the racket in which a local strong man forces merchants to pay tribute in order to avoid damage— damage the strong man himself threatens to deliver. Tilly suggested that someone who produced both the danger and, at a price, the shield against it was a racketeer, while someone who provided the needed shield but had little control over the danger's appearance qualified as a legitimate protector, especially if the price he charged was no higher than the competitor's.[2]

A key institution in the Middle Ages, particularly between the seventh and ninth centuries, was commendation, which supposed the voluntary submission of small landowners to the feudal lord in exchange for protection (commendation was equivalent to "roof" in contemporary Russia). Commendation was one of the factors that accounted for the emergence of the serf class. Those who fell under the protection of the lord paid him regularly in the form of goods, work on the lord's land (the famous corvée), or military service.

In feudal France, the inability of the state to protect its citizens allowed the feudal lords to gain greater power on their territories than could the king. Embroiled in bitter civil wars, the Carolingian Kingdom was unable to protect its citizens from raiders. As the vassals of the sons and grandsons of Louis the Pious fought each other, the local lords used their knights to protect their personal holdings and their subjects. While the king had little ability to enforce laws in the vast territories of the empire, the local lords attacked each other and entered into agreements of mutual protection. In Europe, in the early Middle Ages, there were more armed men and fortified castles than ever before. Between the ninth and twelfth centuries, with the growing population and economic progress, particularly in agriculture, there was more agrarian wealth for the taking.[3]

At the same time, there were threats from foreign enemies. European societies at the close of the Dark Ages were characterized by extreme military insecurity. Paul Vinogradoff wrote that in the Middle Ages it was dangerous for people to be outside the feudal nexus. He added that in a time of fierce struggle for bare existence, it was necessary for everyone to look for support.[4]

Security and military forces were private rather than public goods, and lords and their vassals were the main suppliers. Through the wealth gained from participating in the military market of feudal times, the lords who possessed military power were able to compete for land and eventually grew so powerful that they formed institutions.

The job of mercenary was one of the most popular occupations for young men in the Middle Ages. Hess, a German state, was known as a place that provided mercenaries (Hessians) for many countries in the world. Hessians served in foreign armies and worked as guards. The same was true for Switzerland, which provided guards for the pope, among other things.

PRIVATE PROTECTION IN MODERN SOCIETY

Private protection agencies were common in societies (past or present) with weak and corrupt states, including post-Soviet Russia and some Latin American and African countries. Indeed, even the most efficient modern states were sometimes unable or unwilling, whatever the reason might be (a lack of resources, corruption of law enforcement agencies, the state's lack of legitimacy in the eyes of the population, or conflicts between elites), to fully protect their citizens. Timothy Fry, an active researcher of private protection, suggested that few contemporary societies approached the Weberian ideal, which supposed the efficient state's total monopoly over the use of force in the given territory.[5] The idea that the weakness of the state encouraged private protection was shared by several authors.[6] The relative role of private protection in society changed over time depending on the dynamics of the four factors mentioned above. Of course, the dynamics of each of these factors was determined by the concrete historical context and the dominant social and cultural relations.[7] In the case of Russia, the weakness of the central administration clearly led to an immense expansion of private protection.

Writing about private protection in the contemporary world, several authors, among them Timothy Fry, described the use of private protection agencies with the capitalist model.[8] They presented these organizations as ordinary capitalist enterprises that sell their services. They did not see any difference between criminal organizations that offer protection and "normal capitalist firms." The authors who discussed this subject deemphasized the role of violence and the fact that private protection, in many cases, is not chosen by the businesses. Rather, it was often imposed on them by mafias or private agencies supported by various state agencies and particularly by the police.[9]

The same critique of the market approach to private protection was advanced by Vadim Volkov, an expert on private protection in Russia, who underscored that the use of force (or coercion) constitutes a specific type of social action distinct from the economic action characteristic of the realm of exchange. He added that pure economic relations existed only on paper; in reality, they were closely intertwined with "relations of force."[10]

Those who use the capitalist model for analyzing private security fail to recognize that the managers of companies often see "private protection organizations" as "foes not friends."[11] It would be wrong to idealize the new "order" based on roof. Just as feudal lords of the Middle Ages could not always protect their vassals and peasants against violence, the same was true of criminal structures offering protection to their clients, voluntarily or involuntarily. The redistribution of spheres of influence and places in the criminal hierarchy was a continuous process.

THE NEED FOR PROTECTION
IN POST-SOVIET RUSSIA

Private protection did not exist in the Soviet Union. Only members of the politburo received the services of personal security wardens provided by the state.[12] However, the situation changed radically after 1991. Three interacting processes led to a huge increase in the number of private protection organizations (PPO) in post-Soviet Russia. One of these processes was the weakening of the state and the prevalence of lawlessness in all spheres of social life, including a steep rise in crime. The personal security of people diminished drastically in comparison with the Soviet period. Another process was the privatization of state property, which was carried out in a violent criminal climate in which laws were rudely violated. The most successful grabbers of state property were people with connections to the government (mostly members of the former nomenklatura) or to the criminal world. At the same time, as the third process, there was a major expansion of the informal economy in which illegal transactions were a normal part of life, especially in the area of small business. The informal economy played a key role in Russian society even after privatization peaked in the mid-1990s. By the beginning of the twenty-first century, the informal economy made up roughly 40 percent of the GDP.[13]

Against this economic and political background, private protection became a leading sector of society. Since the collapse of the Soviet state and the beginning of privatization, the political and business landscapes were littered with cases of extortion and blackmail. With the corruption of the police, it became evident that the victims had no hope of gaining help from law enforcement agencies.

After 1991, the murder of businesspeople, political officials, and journalists became a regular phenomenon in Russia and remained a major problem. There are no statistics available on the number of killings of prominent businesspeople in Russia. It suffices to mention only the most known murders. In September 2006, the deputy chairman of the State Bank, Andrei Kozlov, was murdered. The leading Russian businessman Ivan Kivelidi was killed in 1995, and Liudmila Krasnoger, a vice president at the bank Pervoe O.V.K., was murdered in 2001. There were attempts on the lives of Sergei Dubinin, the chairman of the Central Bank, in 1996 and 1997, as well as Andrei Vavilov, the deputy minister of finance, and Anatolii Chubais, the head of the Unified Energy System of Russia.[14]

CRIMINAL PROTECTION OF BUSINESSES IN POST-SOVIET RUSSIA

In the mid-1990s, the term "roof" emerged in Russia.[15] The term conveyed a very important message to the world: the country was deeply corrupt and every active person in the economy, politics, or media needed protection. Roof was used not only for protection, but also for aggressive acts against rivals in business and politics. In other words, roof was a way of life in a society with a weak, corrupt state.[16] According to a survey of 240 small businesses in Poland and Russia conducted at the end of 1990, roughly half the businesspeople in Russia (65 percent in Ulianovsk, 42 percent in Moscow, and 22 percent in Smolensk) and 16 percent of Polish businesspeople had worked with mafias to ensure their protection.[17] A survey of the retail sector in three Russian cities conducted in 1996 showed that private protection had become routine. Over 40 percent of retail shop owners in Moscow, Smolensk, and Ulianovsk admitted to frequent "contact with rackets," but also considered it a relatively minor problem (they rated it on average as 3.13 on a scale of 1 to 10) compared to state taxes and capital shortfalls. The study also revealed that shopkeepers believed that private protection served as a substitute for state-provided police protection and, to a lesser extent, for state-provided courts.[18]

Under the new conditions, people running small businesses, from street vendors to the owners of kiosks or small firms, decided to accept the "offer" of criminals to provide them with a roof against other racketeers. This roof would typically cost 10 to 30 percent of their income. After 1991, criminal organizations extended their activities to medium-size and even big businesses. These organizations were also required to find a roof.

The relationships among various roofs were as complicated as the networks of seigniors and vassals in the Middle Ages. Entities that served as roofs for other people might also look for a roof among more powerful organizations. Roofs represented an extremely important component of social and political life in Russia.

SEMILEGAL PROTECTION OF BUSINESSES

As an alternative to criminal PPOs, businesses, particularly banks, also bought protection from corrupt police officers, members of the FSB (formerly the KGB), and other "power agencies" of the state, such as railway guards who would fend off criminal gangs for roughly the same fee. As Russian folklore suggests, the businesses that enjoyed the state's powerful roof "lived under socialism, while the public lived under capitalism."[19] In the hierarchy of roofs, a state roof was best because no criminal organization could face off against the state's military units.

According to a survey of 634 policemen conducted by the Levada-Tsentr in 2005, roughly two-thirds of them confessed that they moonlighted as security guards.[20] The police and criminal structures usually respected each other's territory and followed the "first-come-first-serve" rule when providing clients with a roof.[21]

OWN PRIVATE PROTECTION OF BUSINESSES

With their growing awareness of the unwillingness or inability of the state to protect them against violence, big businesses created their own private armies, consisting of well-trained and heavily armed security forces.[22] This was especially true for big businesses that were concerned about relying on criminals for protection. In the post-Soviet period, hiring private bodyguards was a normal practice for prominent Russian businesspeople.

According to data provided by Nikolai Kovalev, head of the FSB, each of the 2,000 commercial banks in Russia had their own security services. Some of the private security units were comparable in size and composition to a regional office of the FSB.[23] Large companies spent up to a third of their profits on security and intelligence gathering. Surrounded by armed guards on all sides, the headquarters of some companies were reminiscent of European castles of the Middle Ages. As an eloquent example of the state's inability to provide security to businesses, in 2007, the State Duma endorsed the creation of a special security force that would be controlled by two major oil and gas companies (Gazprom and Transneft). The new security force was given the authority to use firearms not only to defend company property, but also outside the property and, for instance, to attack people who presented a danger to the companies.[24]

LEGAL PRIVATE PROTECTION FIRMS

The history of legal private protection firms in post-Soviet Russia began in March 1992 when the federal law on private detectives and protection activity was adopted. In his study of "violent capitalism," Vadim Volkov noted that the first PPOs, such as Aleks in Moscow and Zashchita in Petersburg, were set up even before 1992, in advance of the new legislation.

Between 1991 and 1996, the overall growth rate of private protection firms was especially dramatic; the number of agencies almost doubled, reaching nearly 8,000. After 1996, the growth continued, but the rate slowed. By the end of 1999, the number of private security agencies reached 11,652 and by 2006, 20,000; the number of licensed security personnel (i.e., those entitled to carry firearms) reached 196,266 and the total number of employees in this industry exceeded 850,000. Private agencies owned 71,400 firearms. In 2006, there were 4,000 private security agencies in Moscow alone.[25] The composition of the workforce in private protection agencies was noticeable: 22.6 percent of all employees had once served in the Ministry of Internal Affairs, 7.9 percent in the KGB/FSB, and 0.8 percent in other security and law enforcement organizations. Many future PPOs started as private guard or informal security services for particular business projects. For example, the Petersburg PPO Severnaya Pal'mira, headed by the former colonel of military counterintelligence Evgenii Kostin, was initially set up as a security service for Muraveinik, the city market for construction materials. Later it became an independent supplier of security for a number of construction companies, such as Business Link Development, Com & Com, and the official Peugeot dealer in Petersburg, Auto-France. In the second half of the 1990s, many private protection companies were organized by former KGB agents and people from the Ministry of Internal Affairs. Such was the origin of the famous Alex Company.[26]

Private protection firms generally maintained close relations with criminal organizations and sometimes used them to find "solutions" to their clients' problems. As a result, the border between the legal and illegal activities of private security agencies was quite vague. What is more, the members of these firms often participated in purely illegal activities, such as robbery and killing.[27]

PRIVATE DETECTIVE ACTIVITY

There were many private agencies that collected information about businesses and politicians at the request of customers, using legal and illegal means. This information was used as a weapon against rivals. In 2005, there were 30 "Pinkerton firms," employing 2,000 private detectives (often former agents from the special services), operating in Moscow alone. Private detectives in Russia used the most sophisticated technology for bugging and watching their targets. Some detective firms looked for information that could discredit prominent people; they often sold these "juicy" products to customers using the Internet. As one Pinkerton firm in Moscow boasted, "Our private detectives could even find compromising material on the Queen of England."[28]

ROOF FOR PEOPLE IN THE MEDIA, SCIENCE, AND ARTS

Feelings of helplessness or a lack of confidence in state institutions compelled people from all walks of life to look for roof. The prestigious newspaper *Segodnia* and the popular television network Independent TV did not hide the fact that the financial giant Most served as their roof. Moreover, it was widely known that each newspaper in Moscow and each well-known journalist had their own roof. Some journalists and cultural figures were directly connected to criminal structures. For instance, Iosif Kobzon, a famous singer, boasted once about his connections with the world of crime. Due to these connections, he was banned from entering the United States.

GATED COMMUNITIES

The weakness of the Russian state, as in the case of societies of the Middle Ages, also led to the emergence of gated communities—large residential areas separated from the rest of the city. There were at least two popular examples located near Moscow, one called "Rublevskoe shosse" and the other "Gorki 8." Russian journalists referred to these communities as "closed cities." In Soviet times, the same term was used for cities with important military installations, such as "Cheliabinsk 8," which produced nuclear weapons. Closed cities now housed some of the richest politicians and oligarchs in the country. The founder of Gorki 8 was Dmitrii Yakubovskii, who spent several years in prison for corruption, and who in the beginning of the twenty-first century ran this community with 94 members gated from the external world. Only people with special passes could enter. The settlement had its own police station, a supermarket, hospital, bank, and church.[29]

CONCLUSION

Weakness of the state in any society forces people to look for private sources of protection. In the Middle Ages, private protection of all sorts flourished. Contemporary Russia, with its corrupt and inefficient state, presents another case of how important private protection (criminal and legal) becomes in societies with weak states. The structure of private protection was always in flux and changed under the impact of a number of political and economic factors. In the first decade of the twenty-first century, criminal organizations yielded their role as protectors to the police and state security agencies working on a private basis. With the high role of private protection, the occupation of security guard became one of the most popular jobs for Russian men.

CONCLUSION

This book attempts to show that it is impossible to describe any society as an integrative system. Each society contains elements that belong to various types of social organization. A vision of society based on only one type of social organization has been elaborated by numerous social scientists, such as Marx, Spencer, Weber, and Parsons, and the economists of the neoclassical school. The integrative-system approach continues to dominate the mainstream of contemporary social sciences, as seen in the textbooks on sociology, political science, and economics. Such an approach tends to underestimate the importance of any social element that is "alien" to the given system, which, in turn, leads to a distorted picture of social reality.

The most fruitful method for studying societies is the segmented approach, which supposes that various types of social organization coexist in each society and that societies are generally heterogeneous, even if one type of organization plays the dominant role. This approach finds support from scholars with a Marxist orientation, as well as from those who defend the multicultural vision of society.

Using post-Soviet Russia as a case study, it is easy to see that the analysis of this country in the last decade has been deeply flawed. Many scholars have attempted to use only one type of macrosocial model (either liberal or totalitarian) for describing it. The wide use of a "transitional model" has not improved the understanding of the nature of post-Communist societies in general.

The disarray in the literature on contemporary Russia reflects the difficulties in theoretically grappling not only post-Soviet developments but also the "objective facts." Russian society is deeply fragmented across many lines: ideological, political, social, economic, ethnic, and cultural. The heterogeneity of contemporary Russia is a perfect case to show the inability of a single model to adequately describe a society. The descriptions of Russia as a "criminal," "oligarchic," or "bureaucratic" society are as problematic as the claim that Russia is a "normal democratic society" or a society steadily moving in that direction. The liberal and authoritarian (or in some cases totalitarian) models, in their various forms, have failed to fully explain the social, political, and economic changes in post-Soviet countries. While these two models remain relevant for the analysis of Russian society, they need to be used in conjunction with a third model, the feudal model, which on its own is probably able to describe more elements of post-Soviet society than the other two.

A clear distinction must be drawn between the nature of societies of Western Europe in the Middle Ages and the feudal model that was invented for the purpose of explaining this period of history. This model cannot explain all aspects of life in the Middle Ages. Rather, it should be seen merely as one of the best models for describing this period, just as the totalitarian model stands out as a model for describing Soviet society and the liberal model is best for analyzing contemporary Western countries.

The weakness of the central administration is the main characteristic of the feudal model. I attempt to show in this book how, under such conditions, social actors decentralize the governing of the country, with focus on smaller social units, such as regions or corporations. This book follows the political interpretation of feudalism as developed by the famous French historian Fustel de Coulanges. My views are also close to those of Marc Bloch and other members of the famous Annales School, which placed vassal relations at the center of their analysis of the Middle Ages. At the same time, I do not share the view that the feudal model is pertinent only to the European Middle Ages and instead assume that it should be seen as a theoretical device of universal application, along with the authoritarian (or in some cases totalitarian) and liberal models. With such a view, I belong to the formal school in sociology founded by Georg Simmel. He also enrolled as allies Weber and a few other contemporary social scientists who advocated universalism in social analysis.

The weakness and inefficiency of the central administration determined most elements of life in the Middle Ages, including the autonomy of regional barons and other actors, such as churches, cities, guilds, and universities; the high level of criminality, corruption, and extortion; the precarious status of private property rights; and the difficulties in interregional commerce. In fact, the feudal model is relevant to any society in which the central administration is weak or ineffective, whatever its major causes (a lack of resources at the disposal of the central administration, or the high level of corruption of the leadership and bureaucracy). In such a society, the state delegates, completely or partially, its major functions (and first of all the maintenance of law and order) to other institutions, such as local barons or private agents.

The main idea of this book is that the use of the feudal model can strongly improve the analysis of contemporary Russian society, an idea that I myself, probably as the first among social scientists in the world, floated in the mid-1990s.

As in the case of societies of the Middle Ages, Russia's major problem was the weakness of the post-Soviet state, mostly a result of the corruption of top politicians and state agencies, along with the limited amount of resources available to the government. Corrupted from the top down, the state machine, the police and courts in particular, was unable to fight all forms of crime, from street crime to white collar crime, which spread in all spheres of society. The fear of criminals and corrupt officials (a typical phenomenon of the Middle Ages) became a "normal" part of Russian life. The fear of losing one's life or property was particularly strong among people active in economy and politics. Indeed, with state agencies often colluding with criminal structures, the regular killing of businesspeople, politicians, and journalists became a fixture in Russian life. At the same time, rich people and officials were usually immune to prosecution, and as a rule the court exonerated them from their criminal acts.

Organized crime also became a powerful actor in Russian society, a big contrast to the Soviet past. The collusion of criminal organizations, big businesses, and political bodies, as well as the police and court system became a normal part of life. At the same time, as in the Middle Ages, the ineptitude of the state and the spread of corruption and crime generated a universal disrespect for law.

Several actors in post-Soviet Russian society are quite similar to those of the Middle Ages. Among them the most important are the head of state, oligarchs (or the heads of corporations), and local governors.

The specific feature of a feudal society lies in the peculiar position of the head of state. It is very different from the position of the head of state in predominantly totalitarian or liberal societies. The ability of the leader in a feudalized society to run the country is very weak compared with that of the leader in a totalitarian society. Compared with the leader in a liberal society (the president or prime minister), the head of a feudalized society, in order to keep his power and extend it beyond legal terms, is permanently in conflict with the law and liberal institutions in his society.

One of the most important characteristics of the head of a feudalized society is his tendency to accumulate personal wealth in order to guarantee a high style of life for himself and his family even after he leaves office; his wealth is also a crucial condition for strengthening and extending his power when in office.

For this reason, a leader's private property (domain) plays an important role in societies with strong feudal elements. The royal domain was a crucial institution in the early Middle Ages. It lost its significance only with the formation of the absolutist monarchies. The leader's domain was a very important factor in politics in contemporary Russia as well as in several other post-Soviet republics. The key role of the leader's domain could also be seen outside the post-Soviet space, particularly in some African and Asian countries.

The creation and expansion of his domain was one of the leading motivations for the activities of the first Russian president Boris Yeltsin, who unceremoniously helped his family accumulate wealth. Yeltsin's choice of an heir, when he became unfit to rule due to his failing health, was influenced by his determination to find a candidate who would guarantee his immunity and the wealth of his family. Without his domain, Yeltsin would not have been able to avoid impeachment.

Putin's domain turned out to be quite different from Yeltsin's. Unlike Yeltsin's times, there was not an open appropriation of state assets. Putin's "family property" played a much smaller role than in the case of Yeltsin. Putin expanded his domain mostly by diminishing the border between his personal property and that of the Kremlin. The most important source of Putin's domain was his personal control over the major oil and gas companies in Russia. For the most part, he expanded his domain through his proxies—people from Petersburg, mostly Chekists, who became members of the boards of directors of leading monopolies in oil, gas, electricity, and railway transportation.

After the head of state, the oligarchs (or corporations) are the most important feudal actors, mostly due to their powerful role in infusing money in political life, a phenomenon that clearly contrasts with its almost nonexistent role in Soviet politics, with some exceptions found in central Asia and the Caucasus. The basis of the oligarchs' position in society is the rent-seeking activity, which fuels the corruption of government and the disregard for law. The oligarchs in Russia could not function without help from high state officials, which they purchased with cash, gifts, and company stock. What is more, almost all fortunes in the country were created with the help of the state. The relationship between oligarchs and the central administration changed over time. In some periods, the oligarchs played an active political role in society, buying offices in order to serve as ministers or governors and almost imposing their will on the Kremlin. At other times, they retreated to the obedient role of faithful vassals, even if they still had autonomy inside their corporations and disregarded the law. After Putin came to power, the oligarchs who tried to play a political role in Russia, such as Mikhail Khodorkovsky, were crushed by the state machine.

The high role of oligarchs in post-Soviet Russian society made it necessary for them to elaborate their own ideology. The oligarchic ideology is deeply hostile toward the authoritarian and liberal ideologies. Oligarchs dislike both the strong state and real democracy. The oligarchic ideology supposes that only successful businesspeople can efficiently run the country. It disregards the conflict between the egotistical interests of the ruling elite and the nation's interests. It also justifies rent-seeking activity and the corruption of the bureaucracy and accepts nepotism as a reasonable phenomenon in society. The oligarchic ideology is permeated with contempt for ordinary people and democratic procedures. Of course, this ideology is deeply hostile toward social equality and indifferent toward social polarization. The characteristics of this ideology can also be seen in the behavior of wealthy people who praise the "glamour life" and are engaged in conspicuous consumption on full scale.

The third set of crucial actors in post-Soviet Russia includes the governors and local elites. As in the case of oligarchs, their relation with the center is unstable and depends on the developments in the capital, including the unity of ruling political elites, the level of corruption, and the ability and desire of the leader to combat the autonomy of the local authorities.

Russia started its move toward a polycentric and decentralized society under the impact of the liberalization of the monocentric Soviet society during perestroika. The withering of the totalitarian state immediately triggered the process of decentralization. The local elites started to expand their power. The clash in the capital among different factions and the emergence of several centers of power only increased the level of decentralization. At the same time, the weak center expanded the power of regional elites, because it could not satisfy the basic needs of the local populations nor maintain order in the regions. These social and political processes were quite similar to those in Europe in the early Middle Ages.

By 2004–2005, a new balance of power emerged between the Kremlin and the local barons. The governors and presidents of non-Russian republics abandoned their previous roles as active politicians in the national policy arena. The Federal Council, with local governors as its members, lost its political importance. However, the governors and republican presidents, as soon as they were appointed by the president, possessed full and almost unlimited control over their respective regions. In this area, the presidential emissaries who overlooked their activities did not restrain their power. The Kremlin, with its inefficient bureaucracy, shifted the major responsibility for the regions onto the local barons and was ready to tolerate, or even encourage, their autonomy as well as their corrupt activities and criminal ties. Ramzan Kadyrov, considered a bandit by many, was supported by Putin because this Chechen warlord guaranteed a sort of pacification of the rebellious republic. Putin was ready to permit the Tatar president to remain in power for four terms in a row, because he could sustain peace in the republic drawing on the strong, local nationalism.

The president, following the feudal tradition, only rarely removed the governors and presidents from their positions; they were allowed to stay in power as long as they showed their loyalty to him, sustained order in their regions, supported his party, and provided him with votes during key elections. The regional leaders were autocratic rulers and almost completely ignored democratic principles. They ran their regions like fiefs, in the same authoritarian fashion in which Putin ran the country. They also stifled the freedom of media and rigged elections.

The weakness of the state deeply influenced various aspects of life in the societies of the Middle Ages and in post-Soviet Russia. This book discusses three developments in post-Soviet Russia that resulted from the weakness of the state and the low respect for law. One of them is the precarious nature of property relations in contemporary Russia. As in the Middle Ages, when the major social actors of the day were always concerned about their property rights, in post-Soviet Russia everyone feared that the state or its rivals might suddenly confiscate their wealth and assets. The highly valued property in Moscow was particularly vulnerable. Even the owners of homes and apartments in the capital were worried that the state, a private firm, or a criminal organization could use many tricks to oust people from their homes. The land owned by peasants might also be threatened by the local bosses, agricultural corporations, or builders of resorts.

The use of physical coercion in the redistribution of property became one of the most important features of post-Soviet social life. At the beginning of the twenty-first century, a series of new battles for the redistribution of property erupted in Russia. Almost everyone supposed that illegal methods and direct violence were being used. The Western term "hostile takeover" does not adequately explain the technologies used in the Russian case. A sophisticated technology called "raiding" was elaborated for the purpose of taking control over various forms of property. The strategies included the use of tax mechanism to set up artificial bankruptcies, various forms of pressure placed on stockholders to sell their stock, falsification of documents, bribing of courts and police, harassment of companies with various government inspections (fire, sanitation, and others), confiscation of commodities sold by companies as counterfactual, physical elimination of owners, and laundering of illegally acquired property by selling it to proxy companies.

The second development described in this book is the high role of informal, personal relations in a feudalized society. In such a society, divisions based on clans, "teams," and "cliques," which unite people who are loyal to the same leader, play an extremely important role. The members of a clan support each other not because of their common social status or origin, as Marxists like to stress, but because they are loyal and trust each other—human qualities so valued in the Middle Ages. Of special importance is the magnitude of the personal factor in the selection of cadres and in the character of supervision over their work, which has a vast influence on the efficiency of all major institutions in the country—economic, political, and military in the first place—as well as on the political and social stability of the society and the position of the ruling elites. In fact, the role of personal relations, including kinship, in politics and the economy has hardly been studied by social scientists.

Meanwhile, in post-Soviet Russia, where society has fragmented across all possible lines, the role of personal relations is difficult to overestimate, a total contrast to the Soviet system, where the role of personal relations and kinship in politics was minimal. These relations served as the structural basis for the privatization of state property in the 1990s, which brought about "crony capitalism." The family of Russian president Yeltsin became a key political institution in the country. The succession of power was based not on democratic procedures, but on monarchic principles, which supposed that the current leader could choose an heir. Putin selected people for top positions from his personal network of friends and colleagues, most of them related to his previous work in the KGB.

The disregard of merits and the high importance given for personal relations in the appointment of people in government or business were accepted as a normal development and did not arouse many grudges. At the same time, the prevalence of personal relations fostered the corruption and criminalization of society and weakened the state and social institutions. The flourishing of personal relations has made the functioning of democratic mechanisms in society practically impossible. It has also instilled a deep distrust of democracy among the population.

The third feudal development in Russia is the high role of private protection. In the Middle Ages, private protection of all sorts flourished. Contemporary Russia, with its corrupt and inefficient state, presents another illustration of how important private protection (criminal and legal) is in a society with a weak state. Private security became a crucial issue for Russian businesses, which are the regular targets of organized criminal structures.

The structure of private protection was always in flux and changed under the impact of a number of factors. In the early years of the twenty-first century, criminal organizations mostly yielded their role as protectors to the police and state security agencies that worked on a private basis and to numerous legal private protection organizations.

At the same time, big businesses in Russia created their own security teams, hiring former KGB people to head them. Almost all relatively prominent people in business and politics had their own personal guards. With the high role of private protection, the occupation of security guard became one of the most popular jobs for Russian men. The spread of gated communities in Russia is another important development generated by the deficit of security in the country.

The feudal model is an important theoretical tool for analyzing post-Soviet Russia. Without looking through the lens offered by this model, it would be impossible to understand the character of the political, social, and economic developments in this country.

As this book shows, these elements are deeply rooted in many parts of Russian society. Given the country's weak liberal institutions, the political passivity of the population, the lack of a unified ideology, and the corruption of bureaucracy, feudal elements in Russia will likely persist over several decades ahead. Those who wish to forecast Russian developments in the future, or the policies of foreign governments toward Russia, should consider the feudal tendencies in this big and very important country.

NOTES

CHAPTER 1

1. See Vladimir Shlapentokh, *A Normal Totalitarian Society* (Armonk, N.Y.: M. E. Sharpe, 2001).
2. Kira Latukhina et al., "Surkov vyshel iz teni," *Vedomosti*, June 29, 2006; see also Aleksandr Tsipko, "Ideologiia suverennoi demokratii," *Izvestiia*, April 21, 2006.
3. Aleksandra Samarina and Sergei Varshavchik, "Suverennuiu demokratiiu— kazhdomu," *Nezavisimaia Gazeta*, August 31, 2006.
4. Such is the view of Valerii Zorkin, the chairman of the Constitutional Court (see Boris Tumanov, "Na proshloi nedele: Kak obustroit Rossiu'," *Novoie Vremia*, September 10, 2006; see also Andranik Migranian, "Zachem Rossii kontseptsiia 'suverennoi demokratii'?" *Izvestiia*, July 27, 2006; Kirill Privalov, "Narod Rossii—samostoiatel'nyi sub'ekt istorii," *Izvestiia*, July 12, 2006; and Ekaterina Zabrodina, "Parad suverennykh demokratii," *Moskovskie Novosti*, September 7, 2006).
5. See political scientist Sergei Markov's interview with *Argumenty i Fakty* ("Chto takoe suverennaia demokratiia?" September 6, 2006).
6. See Andrei Shleifer and Daniel Treisman, "A Normal Country," *Foreign Affairs*, March/April 2004.
7. See Yegor Gaidar, *Dolgoe vremia: Rossiia v mire; Ocherki ekonomicheskoi istorii* (Moscow: Delo, 2005).
8. See T. I. Zaslavskaia, "O roli sotsial'noi struktury v transformatsii rossiskogo obshchestva," in *Kuda idet Rossiia.Vlast': Obshchestvo; Lichnost'*, ed. T. I. Zaslavskaia (Moscow: Vysshaia shkola sotsial'nykh i ekonomicheskikh nauk, 2000, p. 222); see also Zaslavskaia's "Contemporary Russian Society: Problems and Perspectives," *Sociological Research*, July/August 2006, pp. 13–14 (initially in *Obshchestevennye Nauki i Sovremennost'*, No. 5, 2004).
9. V. A. Yadov, "Rossiia kak transformiruiushcheesia obshchestvo: Reziume mnogoletnei diskussii sotsiologov," in Zaslavskaia, *Kuda idet Rossiia.Vlast'*, p. 383.
10. L. A. Beliaeva, "Dinamika sotsial'noi stratifikatsii v period reform," in Zaslavskaia, *Kuda idet Rossiia.Vlast'*, p. 243.
11. L. A. Khakhulina, "Srednii klass v Rossii: Mify i real'nost'," in Zaslavskaia, *Kuda idet Rossiia.Vlast'*, p. 279.

12. See "Puti Rossii: 2007" (the program of the symposium), http://www .msses.ru/win/science/kuda/itogi-puti-2007.html (accessed February 14, 2007).

13. Archie Brown, "Vladimir Putin's Leadership in Comparative Perspective," in *Russian Politics under Putin,* ed. Cameron Ross (Manchester: Manchester University Press, 2004, pp. 4, 12–14); Brown, "Introduction," in *Gorbachev, Yeltsin, and Putin: Political Leadership in Russia's Transition,* ed. A. Brown and L. Shevtsova (Washington, D.C.: Carnegie Endowment for International Peace, 2001, p. 6).

14. David Lane, "The Economic Legacy: What Putin Had to Deal with and the Way Forward," in Ross, *Russian Politics under Putin,* p. 95.

15. James Millar, "Normalization of the Russian Economy: Obstacles and Opportunities for Reform and Sustainable Growth," http://www.nbr .org/publications/article.aspx?ID=183 (accessed April 12, 2007).

16. Thomas Remington, "Putin, the Duma, and Political Parties," in *Putin's Russia: Past Imperfect, Future Uncertain,* ed. Dale Herspring (Lanham, Md.: Rowman, 2003, pp. 56–57).

17. Luke March, "The Putin Paradigm and the Cowering of Russia's Communists," in Ross, *Russian Politics under Putin,* p. 60.

18. R. W. Davies, *Soviet History in the Yeltsin Era* (New York: St. Martin's Press, 1997).

19. William Cocherham, *Health and Social Change in Russia and Eastern Europe* (New York: Routledge, 1999).

20. Timothy Colton and Michael McFaul, "Putin and Democratization," in Herspring, *Putin's Russia,* p. 36.

21. Ibid., p. 35; Masha Lipman and Michael McFaul, "Putin and the Media," in Herspring, *Putin's Russia,* pp. 77–78.

22. Cameron Ross, "Putin's Federal Reforms," in Ross, *Russian Politics under Putin,* pp. 170–71.

23. Eugene Huskey, "Political Leadership and the Center-Periphery Struggle: Putin's Administrative Reforms," in Brown and Shevtsova, *Gorbachev, Yeltsin, and Putin,* pp. 126–34.

24. Liliia Shevtsova, *Putin's Russia* (Washington, D.C.: Carnegie Endowment for International Peace, 2005, pp. 322–51); Shevtsova, "From Yeltsin to Putin: The Evolution of Presidential Power," in Brown and Shevtsova, *Gorbachev, Yeltsin, and Putin,* pp. 67–70.

25. Yurii Levada, "Obshchestvennoe mnenie i obshchestvo na pereput'iakh 1999 goda," in Zaslavskaia, *Kuda idet Rossiia.Vlast',* p. 147.

26. V. V. Shelokhaev, "Osobennosti otnoshenii vlasti i obshchestva v Rossii: Istoriia i sovremennost'," in Zaslavskaia, *Kuda idet Rossiia.Vlast',* p. 10.

27. V. V. Zhuravlev, "Lichnost' kak zalozhnitsa gosudarstva i obshchestva," in Zaslavskaia, *Kuda idet Rossiia.Vlast',* p. 92.

28. V. N. Dakhin, "Nekotorye voprosy analiza rossiiskoi vlasti," in Zaslavskaia, *Kuda idet Rossiia.Vlast',* p. 101.

29. N. G. Shcherbinina, "Mifologicheskii Komponent Regional'nogo

Izbiratel'nogo Prozessa," in Zaslavskaia, *Kuda idet Rossiia. Vlast'*, p. 217.

30. L. V. Poliakov, "Rossiiskii avtoritarnyi sindrom: Anamnez i epikriz," in Zaslavskaia, *Kuda idet Rossiia.Vlast'*, p. 173.

31. Stephen White, "Russia's Disempowered Electorate," in Ross, *Russian Politics under Putin*, pp. 76–92.

32. Nikolai Petrov and Darrell Slider, "Putin and Regions," in Herspring, *Putin's Russia*, p. 35.

33. Radio station *Ekho Moskvy*, "Osoboe Mnenie," June 28, 2006.

34. Stephen Hedlund, *Russia's Market Economy: A Bad Case of Predatory Capitalism* (London: University College London Press, 1999).

35. V. P. Danilov, "Rossiiskaia vlast' v 20 veke," in Zaslavskaia, *Kuda idet Rossiia.Vlast'*, p. 6.

36. A. I. Shcherbinin, "Chelovek vo vlasti (regional'nye politicheskie elity v sovremennom izbiratel'nom protsesse)," in Zaslavskaia, *Kuda idet Rossiia. Vlast'*, p. 209.

37. V. M. Mezhuev, "Traditsiia samovlastiia v sovremennoi Rossii," in Zaslavskaia, *Kuda idet Rossiia.Vlast'*, pp. 81, 86.

38. A. G. Zdravomyslov, "Vlast' i obshchestvo: Krizis 90-x godov," in Zaslavskaia, *Kuda idet Rossiia.Vlast'*, pp. 135, 142.

39. Shevtsova, *Putin's Russia*.

40. Aleksandr Koksharov, "Imperializm: Globalizatsiia nevozmozhna bez imperii," *Expert*, January 31, 2005.

41. Sergei Shapoval, "Aleksei Miller: Kriterii dlia otsenki imperii—chelovecheskaia zhizn'," *Moskovskie Novosti*, July 21, 2006.

42. Aleksandr Prokhanov, "Bitva za 'piatuiu imperiiu," *Zavtra*, June 28, 2006; see Vadim Stepantsov, "Ya liubliu tebia, imperiia," *Zavtra*, July 12, 2006; Mariia Protasova, "Imperiia umerla?" *Zavtra*, June 28, 2006; Prokhanov, "Nimby russkoi kul'tury," *Zavtra*, June 21, 2006.

43. See Aleksandr Dugin, "Natsionalizm: Russkii ili rossiiskii?" *Vremia Novostei*, March 15, 2006; and his article "Vyzovy ksenofobii," *Vremia Novostei*, July 7, 2006.

44. "Dolzhna li Rossiia byt' imperiei?" *Izvestiia*, December 10, 2004.

45. Richard Pipes, *Struve, Liberal on the Left, 1870–1905* (Cambridge, Mass.: Harvard University Press, 1970).

46. Dar'ia Guseva, "Imperiia dobra: Pravye ne otkazalis' ot idei perevospitat' chelovechestvo," *Vremia Novostei*, December 20, 2004.

47. Andrei Konchalovskii, "Verit' ili razmyshliat'," *Moskovskie Novosti*, July 13, 2006.

48. V. Fedotova, *Modernizatsiia drugoi Evropy* (Moscow: IF RAN, 1997).

49. Yadov, "Rossiia kak transformiruiushcheesia obshchestvo," p. 385.

50. Aleksandr Akhiezer, "Rossiia: Nekotorye problemy sotsial'no-kul'turnoi dinamiki," *Mir Rossii*, No. 1, 1995.

51. O. V. Gaman-Golutvina, "Biurokratiia ili oligarkhiia," in Zaslavskaia, *Kuda idet Rossiia.Vlast'*, p. 162.

52. S. P. Peregudov, "Korporativnyi kapital v bor'be za izbiratelia," in Zaslavskaia, *Kuda idet Rossiia.Vlast'*, p. 200.

53. V. I. Il'in, "Metodologicheskie problemy analiza klassovoi struktury," in Zaslavskaia, *Kuda idet Rossiia.Vlast'*, p. 265.

54. E. Z. Maiminas, "Sootnoshenie vlasti, obshchestva i lichnosti," in Zaslavskaia, *Kuda idet Rossiia.Vlast'*, p. 207.

55. William Tompson, "The Russian Economy under Vladimir Putin," in Ross, *Russian Politics under Putin,* p. 126.

56. Andrew Jack, *Inside Putin's Russia* (Oxford: Oxford University Press, 2004, pp. 5, 215).

57. Peter Rutland, "Putin and Oligarchs," in Herspring, *Putin's Russia,* pp. 148–49.

58. Stephen Handelman, *Comrade Criminal: Russia's New Mafia* (New Haven, Conn.: Yale University Press, 1995).

59. Evgenii Chernov, "Meksika mezhdu stabil'nost'iu i buntom," *Novoie Vremia,* June 16, 2006.

60. Aleksandr Sevast'ianov, "Noveishaia istoriia: Politprosvet; Solo partiia," *Literaturnaia Gazeta,* December 28, 2006.

61. Peter Rutland, "Putin and Oligarchs," in Herspring, *Putin's Russia,* pp. 148–49.

62. Joseph Douglas Krouse, *Kremlin Capitalism: The Privatization of Russian Economy* (Ithaca, N.Y.: Cornell University Press, 1997).

63. Grigorii Yavlinsky, "Unizhennyie liudi ne sozdadut ekonomiku 21 veka," *Novaia Gazeta,* November 11, 2002.

64. Vadim Volkov, *Violent Entrepreneurs: The Use of Force in the Making of Russian Capitalism* (Ithaca, N.Y.: Cornell University Press, 2002).

65. William Webster, ed., *Russian Organized Crime and Corruption* (Washington, D.C.: The CSIS Press, 2000, p. 2).

66. Virginie Coulloudon, "Putin's Anticorruption Reforms," in Herspring, *Putin's Russia,* pp. 85–100.

67. For more about the political background of the polemics surrounding the term "sovereign democracy," see Sergei Chugaev, "Spor o terminakh," *Izvestiia,* July 25, 2006.

68. Dmitrii Medvedev, "O suverennoi demokratii i ne tol'ko," *Izvestiia,* July 25, 2006; see also Medvedev's interview with *Moskovskii Komsomolets,* September 14, 2006.

69. Chernov, "Meksika mezhdu stabil'nost'iu i buntom."

70. Russel Ackoff, *Re-creating the Corporation* (New York: Oxford University Press, 1999, p. 8). The author insisted that each part of the system "is necessary . . . for carrying out" a "defining function" of the given system (p. 6).

71. John Horgan, "Einstein Left the Building," *The New York Times Book Review,* January 1, 2006.

72. See such works by Talcott Parsons as *The Social System* (Glencoe, Ill.: Free Press, 1951); *The System of Modern Society* (Englewood Cliffs, N.J.: Prentice Hall, 1971); *Societies: Evolutionary and Comparative Perspectives* (Englewood Cliffs, N.J.: Prentice Hall, 1966, p. 27); and "Evolutionary

Universals in Society," *American Sociological Review* 29, no. 3 (1964): 339–57.

73. See Ruth Benedict, *Patterns of Culture* (New York: Houghton Mifflin, 1934).

74. G. Piers and M. Singer, *Shame and Guilt: A Psychoanalytical and Cultural Study* (New York: Norton, 1953/1971); M. R. Creighton, "Revisiting Shame and Guilt Culture: A Forty Year Pilgrimage," *Ethoc* 18, no. 3 (1990): 279–307.

75. Harry Triandis, *Individualism and Collectivism* (Boulder, Colo.: Westview, 1995); Andrew Michener, John D. DeLamater, and Shalom H. Schwartz, under the general editorship of Robert K. Merton, *Social Psychology* (San Diego, Calif.: Harcourt Brace Jovanovich, 1986).

76. Roy Macridis, *Modern Political Regimes* (Boston: Little, Brown, 1986); John Nagle, *Introduction to Comparative Politics* (Chicago: Nelson-Hall, 1985); Mikhail Curtis et al., *Introduction to Comparative Government* (New York: Harper, 1990, pp. 3–15); S. Berstein, *Démocraties, régimes autoritaires et totalitarismes au XXe siècle* (Paris: Hachette, 1992). Some authors use other typologies of government, but they are not popular typologies in contemporary political science. For example, see Bernard Crick's division of all regimes into autocratic, totalitarian, or republican (*Basic Forms of Government,* London: Macmillan, 1973). Jean Blondel operates with five types of systems: liberal-democratic, egalitarian-authoritarian, traditional inegalitarian, populist, and authoritarian-inegalitarian (*Introduction to Comparative Government,* New York: Harper, 1990, pp. 3–15).

77. Most contemporary economists operate with only two types of economy: market and command. See the following popular textbooks: N. G. Mankiw, *Principles of Micro Economics,* 1st ed. (London: Dryden Press, 1997, p. 9); K. E. Fair and R. C. Fair, *Principles of Micro Economics,* 4th ed. (Upper Saddle River, N.J.: Prentice Hall, 1996, pp. 41–44); Adam Przeworski, *Democracy and Market* (Cambridge: Cambridge University Press, 1991); Morris Bornstein, *Comparative Economic Systems: Models and Cases* (Burr Ridge, Ill.: Irwin, 1994, p. 16); Martin Schnitzer, *Comparative Economic Systems* (Cincinnati, Ohio: South-Western Publishing, 1994, pp. 3–21). Paul Samuelson uses the same position in all editions of his famous textbook. In the 1973 edition, he dealt with "one capitalism" and "several socialist-Communist economies" (British, French "indicative planning," Stalinist, Yugoslav, Maoist, and Soviet). See Paul Samuelson, *Economics,* 9th ed. (New York: McGraw-Hill, 1973, pp. 867–86).

78. Robert Solo, *Economic Organizations and Social Systems* (Ann Arbor: University of Michigan Press, 2000).

79. Ibid., pp. 3–4.

80. Francis Fukuyama, *The End of History and the Last Man* (New York: Free Press, 1992). See the critique of this view in John Gray, *Liberalism Edition,* 2nd ed. (Buckingham: Open University Press, 1995), and his

Enlightenment's Wake: Politics and Culture at the Close of the Modern Age (New York: Routledge, 1995).

81. See Victor Nee, "A Theory of Market Transition: From Redistribution to Markets in State Socialism," *American Sociological Review* 54, no. 1 (1989): 663–81; Mikhail Buravoy and Pavel Krotov, "The Soviet Transition from Socialism to Capitalism," *American Sociological Review* 57, no. 1 (1992): 16–39; Victor Nee and Rebecca Mathews, "Market Transition and Societal Transformation in Reforming State Socialism," *Annual Review of Sociology* 22 (1996): 401–35.

82. See, for example, Martin Malia, "The Haunting Presence of Marxism-Leninism," *Journal of Democracy* 10, no. 2 (1999): 41–46.

CHAPTER 2

1. See the following works by Vladimir Shlapentokh: "Four Russias," *The Tocqueville Review* 19, no. 1 (1998): 9–34; "The Four Faces of Mother Russia," *Transition* 4, no. 5 (1997): 60–61; "'Normal' Russia," *Current History* 212 (1997): 331–36; "Mnogosloinoe obshchestvo," *Sotsiologicheskii Zhurnal* 4 (1997): 5–21.

2. Fernando Cardoso, "The Age of Citizenship," *Foreign Policy* 119 (2000): 40.

3. Moris Ecksteins, "Too Much of the Same," *Times Literary Supplement*, July 28, 2006.

4. The following textbooks were used in the analysis: M. Andersen and H. F. Taylor, *Sociology*, 2nd ed. (Belmont, Calif.: Wadsworth, 2002); Rodney Stark, *Sociology*, 8th ed. (Belmont, Calif.: Wadsworth, 2001); J. Macionis, *Sociology*, 8th ed. (Englewood Cliffs, N.J.: Prentice Hall, 2001); J. M. Henslin, *Essentials of Sociology*, 6th ed. (Belmont, Calif.: Wadsworth, 2006); B. Hess, E. Markson, and P. Stein, *Sociology*, 4th ed. (Boston: Allyn and Bacon, 1993); T. Sullivan, *Sociology*, 6th ed. (Boston: Allyn and Bacon, 2004); W. E. Thomson and J. V. Hickey, *Society in Focus*, 5th ed. (New York: HarperCollins, 2005); D. Stanley Eitzen and Maxine Baca Zinn, *In Conflict and Order: Understanding Society* (Boston: Allyn and Bacon, 1993).

5. Max Weber, *Economy and Society: An Outline of Interpretive Sociology*, vol. 1 (Berkeley: University of California Press, 1978, pp. 20–21).

6. Ibid., pp. 1070–72, 1091.

7. Georg Simmel, *On Individuality and Social Forms: Selected Writings*, ed. Donald N. Levine (Chicago: University of Chicago Press, 1971); Georg Simmel, *Problems in Philosophy of History* (New York: Free Press, 1977); see also G. Oakes, *Introduction to G. Simmel, Essays on Interpretation in Social Science* (Totowa, N.J.: Rowman and Littlefield, 1980, p. 8); David Frisby, "Simmel," in *The Cambridge Dictionary of Sociology*, ed. Bryan Turner (Cambridge: Cambridge University Press, 2006, pp. 551–53).

8. Emile Durkheim, *Les règles de la méthode sociologique* (Paris: Felix Alcan, 1927); Emile Durkheim, *The Division of Labor in Society*, translated from the French by George Simpson (Glencoe, Ill.: Free Press, 1960).

9. There are a host of authors who published books and articles on "two Americas," or "two Englands," including Michael Harrington (*The Other America: Poverty in the United States,* New York: Macmillan, 1969). See Stanley Greenberg, *The Two Americas: Our Current Political Deadlock and How to Break It* (New York: Thomas Dunne Books, 2004); Steven Messner and Richard Rosenfeld, *Crimes and the American Dream* (Belmont, Calif.: Wadsworth, 1997); Leo Kuper, "Plural Societies: Perspectives and Problems," in *Pluralism in Africa,* ed. Leo Kuper and M. G. Smith (Berkeley: University of California Press, 1969, pp. 7–26); Michael Hechter, *Containing Nationalism* (Oxford: Oxford University Press, 2000).

10. Perry Anderson, *Passage from Antiquity to Feudalism* (London: Verso, 1974).

11. See François Furet and Denis Richet, *French Revolution,* trans. Stephen Hardman (New York: Macmillan, 1970); Suzanne Berger, *How We Compete: What Companies around the World Are Doing to Make It Today's Global Economy* (New York: Doubleday, 2006); John Gray, "The Global Delusion," *The New York Review of Books,* April 27, 2006, p. 22.

12. Michael Mann, "The Social Cohesion of Liberal Democracy," *American Sociological Review* 35, no. 3 (1970): 423–39; and his *Sources of Social Power* (Cambridge: Cambridge University Press, 1986).

13. Charles Taylor, *Multiculturalism and the Politics of Recognition* (Princeton, N.J.: Princeton University Press, 1992); Charles Taylor, "Liberal Politics and the Public Sphere," in *New Communitarian Thinking: Persons, Virtues, Institutions, and Communities,* ed. Amitai Etzioni (Charlottesville: University Press of Virginia, 1995, pp. 183–217).

14. Stephen Brooks, ed., *The Challenge of Cultural Pluralism* (Westport, Conn.: Praeger, 2002).

15. Mark P. Orbe, *Constructing Co-cultural Theory: An Explication of Culture, Power, and Communication* (Thousand Oaks, Calif.: Sage Publications, 1998).

16. Carole S. Angell, *Celebrations around the World: A Multicultural Handbook* (Golden, Colo.: Fulcrum, 1996); Ramón Máiz and Ferran Requejo, eds., *Democracy, Nationalism and Multiculturalism* (New York: Frank Cass, 2005).

17. Kenneth Waltz, *The Theory of International Politics* (New York: Random House, 1979, p. 66).

18. See Marcus Fischer, "Feudal Europe, 800–1300: Communal Discourse and Conflictual Practice," *International Organization* 46, no. 2 (1992): 462.

19. Vladimir Lenin, *Sobranie Sochinenii,* 4th ed., vol. 32 (Moscow: Politizdat, 1951, pp. 272–73).

20. See, for instance, Yurii Kukushkin, ed., *Istoriia SSSR: Epokha sotsializma* (Moscow: Vysshaia shkola sotsial'nykh i ekonomicheskikh nauk, 1985, pp. 144–45).

21. Iosif Stalin, *Vorposy Leninizma* (Moscow: Gospolitizdat, 1952).

22. E. P. Ivanov, ed., *Istoriia otechestva: Porblemy, vzgliady, liudi* (Pskov, Russia: Pskov State Pedagogical Institute, 2005, p. 260).

23. A. Martynov, *Transformatsiia makrosotsial'nykh system v postsotsialisticheskom mire: Metodologicheskii aspect* (Moscow: Lenand, 2006, p. 163).

24. O. Fadeeva, "Neformal'naia zaniatost' v sibirskom sele," *Ekonomicheskaia Sotsiologiia* 2, no. 2 (2001): 61–93.

25. Richard Sakwa, *Putin: Russia's Choice* (New York: Routledge, 2004, p. 112).

26. Francois-Lois Ganshof, *Feudalism* (New York: Harper and Row, 1964, p. 15).

27. Gordon Marshall, ed., *The Concise Oxford Dictionary of Sociology* (Oxford: Oxford University Press, 1994, pp. 180–81).

28. H. G. Richardson and G. O. Sayles, "The Governance of Mediaeval England from the Conquest to Magna Carta," *Speculum* 39, no. 3 (1964): 561–65; Elisabeth Brown, "The Tyranny of a Construct: Feudalism and Historians of Medieval Europe," *American Historical Review* 79, no. 4 (1974): 1063–88; Susan Reynolds, *Fiefs and Vassals: The Medieval Evidence Reinterpreted* (Oxford: Oxford University Press, 1994).

29. Clifford Backman, *The Worlds of Medieval Europe* (Oxford: Oxford University Press, 2003, p. 176).

30. In his fourth annual State of the State address in January 2007, Governor Arnold Schwarzenegger called for the transformation of California into a sort of independent entity, like the city-states of Athens, with its "ideas," and Sparta, with its "power." The governor, in fact, wants his state to become a medieval fief. He supposedly forgot that the opposition of any state to the nation, whatever the arguments for it, could have tragic consequences. On the surface, the governor called for decentralization. However, in fact, he called for the feudalization of the United States. Indeed, decentralization in the spirit of the founding fathers' federalism meant that the wealth of the nation, not of any one state, is the aim of the Americans. But Governor Schwarzenegger's proposal is intended only for improving the life of Californians, without mention of the interests of the nation (Gar Alperovitz, "California Split," *New York Times*, February 10, 2007). It was remarkable that a reader of the *New York Times* titled his letter-to-the-editor (February 17, 2007), which supported the California governor's initiative, "Is America Just Too Big for Its Own Good?"

31. Fustel de Coulanges, *Histoire des Institutions Politique de Lncienne* (Paris: Hachette, 1923, p. 703).

32. Oliver Volckart, *Wettbewerb und Wettbewerbsbeschränkung im vormodernen Deutschland, 1000–1800* (Tübingen, Germany: Mohr Siebeck, 2002).

33. Marc Bloch, *Feudal Society* (Chicago: University of Chicago Press, 1961).

34. Barbara Rosenwine, *A Short History of the Middle Age* (Orchard Park, N.Y.: Broadview Press, 2005, p. 147).

35. Pierre Dubuis, *Les vifs, les morts et le temps qui court: Familles valaisannes, 1400–1550* (Lausanne, Switzerland: Section d'histoire, Faculté des lettres, Université de Lausanne, 1995, p. 161).

36. Marjorie Chinball, *Anglo-Norman England, 1066–1166* (Oxford: Blackwell, 1986, p. 125).

37. Jacques Le Goff, *Medieval Civilization, 400–1500,* trans. Julia Barrow (New York: Blackwell, 1988, p. 40).

38. Laurent Théis, *Histoire du Moyen Age français: Chronologie commentée de Clovis à Louis XI, 486–1483* (Paris: Perrin, 1992).

39. Ganshof, *Feudalism.*

40. N. P. Pavlov-Sylvanskii, *Feodalizm v drevnei Rusi* (St. Petersburg: Brokgauz-Efron, 1907).

41. D. Likhachev, B. Romanov, and V. Adrianova-Peretts, eds., *Povest' vremennykh let* (Moscow: Izd-vo Akademii Nauk SSSR, 1950).

42. See among recent works on federalism in various countries: Michael Burgess, *Comparative Federalism: Theory and Practice* (New York: Routledge, 2006); Wilfried Swenden, *Federalism and Regionalism in Western Europe: A Comparative and Thematic Analysis* (New York: Palgrave Macmillan, 2006); G. Alan Tarr, Robert F. Williams, and Josef Marko, eds., *Federalism, Subnational Constitutions, and Minority Rights* (Westport, Conn.: Praeger, 2004); Anand Menon and Martin Schain, *Comparative Federalism: The European Union and the United States in Comparative Perspective* (Oxford: Oxford University Press, 2006).

43. See about the relations between regionalization and the interests of the country in David B. Audretsch and Charles F. Bonser, eds., *Globalization and Regionalization: Challenges for Public Policy* (Boston: Kluwer, 2002).

44. See among recent publications on self-determination, Igor' Primoratz and Aleksandar Pavkovi, eds., *Identity, Self-Determination and Secession* (Aldershot, England: Ashgate, 2006); Stephen Macedo and Allen Buchanan, eds., *Secession and Self-Determination* (New York: New York University Press, 2003).

45. See, for instance, a few texts from the last decade: Irving Horowitz and May Strong, *Sociological Realities* (New York: Harper, 1971); Jonathan Turner, *Sociology: The Science of Human Organization* (Chicago: Nelson-Hall, 1985); Leonard Gordon and Patricia Harvey, *Sociology and American Social Issues* (Dallas, Tex.: Houghton, 1978); Eitzen and Baca Zinn, *In Conflict and Order* (Boston: Allyn and Bacon, 1993); Joseph Fichter, *Sociology* (Chicago: The University of Chicago Press, 1971); Earl Babbies, *Sociology: An Introduction* (Belmont, Calif.: Wadsworth, 1983); Donald Light and Suzanne Keller, *Sociology* (New York: Knopf, 1982).

46. Neil Smelser, *Sociology* (Englewood Cliffs, N.J.: Prentice Hall, 1981).

47. Ibid., pp. 399–400.

48. Neil Smelser, *Sociology* (Cambridge, Mass.: Blackwell, 1994, p. 73).

49. Robert Dahl, "Numerical Democracy and Corporate Pluralism," in *Political Opposition in Western Democracies,* ed. Robert Dahl (New Haven, Conn.: Yale University Press, 1968, p. 106).

50. See Robert Dahl, *Polyarchy: Participation and Opposition* (New Haven, Conn.: Yale University Press, 1971, p. 7).

51. Max Weber, *Economy and Society of Interpretive Sociology,* vol. 2 (Berkeley: University of California Press, 1978, pp. 1070–72, 1091); see about Weber's attitude toward patrimonialism in Susanne Karstedt, "Knights of Crime: The Premodern Structures," in *Social Dynamics of Crime and Control: New Theories for a World in Transition,* ed. Susanne Karstedt and Kai-D Bussmann (Oxford: Hart Publishing, 2000, p. 55).

52. Marc Bloch and Léopold Benjamin, *Feudal Society,* translated from the French by L. A. Manyon, foreword by M. M. Postan (Chicago: University of Chicago Press, 1961, p. 241).

53. Karstedt, "Knights of Crime," p. 58.

54. Karstedt, "Knights of Crime," pp. 56–58; see also use of the feudal model for social analysis in Ulrich Beck and Jane Wiebel, *The Normal Chaos of Love* (Oxford: Polity Press, 1995, p. 25).

55. John Hall, "Feudalism in Japan: A Reassessment," *Comparative Studies in History and Society* 5, no. 1 (1962): 15–51.

56. Peter Duus, *Feudalism in Japan* (New York: McGraw-Hill, 1993).

57. Carolyn Webber and Aaron Wyldavsky, "Feudalism Nothing," in *The Blackwell Dictionary of Twentieth-Century Social Thought,* ed. William Outhwait and Tom Bottomore (Oxford: Blackwell, 1994, p. 228).

58. Ruslan Grinberg, interview with *Moskovskii Komsomolets,* March 31, 2006.

59. Aron Gurevich, *Problemy genezisa feudalizma v zapadnoi Evrope* (Moscow: Vysshaia shkola, 1970).

60. Vladimir Shlapentokh, "Early Feudalism—the Best Parallel for Contemporary Russia," *Europe-Asia Studies* 48, no. 3 (1996): 393–411.

61. Anatolii Lieven, "The Masque of Democracy; Russia's Liberal Capitalist Revolution," *Johnson's List,* July 16, 1998.

62. Richard E. Ericson, *Post-Soviet Russian Economic System—an Industrial Feudalism* (Helsinki: Bank of Finland Institute for Economies in Transition, 2000).

63. Peter J. Stavrakis, *Shadow Politics: The Russian State in the 21st Century* (Carlisle Barracks, Pa.: Strategic Studies Institute, U.S. Army War College, 1997).

64. Stephen Blank, "Russian Democracy: From the Future to the Past," *Demokratizatsiia* 1, no. 3 (1998): 550–77.

65. Andrei Konchalovskii, "Mafiia? Kak eto po-russki," *Argumenty Nedeli,* November 9, 2006; http://www.konchalovsky.ru/sub1.php?razdel=7& id=20 (accessed March 1, 2007).

66. See Ruslan Grinberg's interview with *Moskovskii Komsomolets,* March 31, 2006.

67. Petr Orekhovskii, "Chem samoupravliat' budem," *Izvestiia,* September 6, 2005.

68. V. P. Danilov, "Rossiiskaia vlast' v 20 veke," in *Kuda idet Rossiia.Vlast':*

Obshchestvo; Lichnost', ed. T. I. Zaslavskaia (Moscow: Vysshaia shkola sotsial'nykh i ekonomicheskikh nauk, 2000, p. 6).

69. Yuliia Latynina's talk on radio station *Ekho Moskvy,* May 19, 2000.

70. Yuliia Latynina, *Okhota na Iziubria* (Moscow: Ëksmo, 2005).

71. Yuliia Latynina, "Feodal'nye voiny oligarkhov," *Komsomol'skaia Pravda,*
    December 10, 2002.

72. Yuliia Latynina, "Zakhvat: Segodniashnii peredel sobstvennosti—kak
    ekonomika voiny," *Novaia Gazeta,* March 26 and 28, 2001.

73. Sergei Guriev, "Industrial'nyi feodalizm: Nizkaia geograficheskaia mo-
    bil'nost' trudovykh resursov sderzhivaet restrukturizatsiiu ekonomiki,"
    Ekspert, April 10, 2001.

74. Yuliia Latynina, "Patent na blagorodstvo: Vydast li ego literatura kapi-
    talu?" *Novyi Mir* 11 (1993): 191–95.

75. These institutions allowed feudal barons and bishops to influence the king
    and protect their interests. For examples of these institutions in the Mid-
    dle Ages, let us consider feudal France. According to Fustel de Coulanges,
    in a period of 125 years between Pepin the Short and Charles the Bold in
    the eighth to ninth centuries, there were 125 assemblies. Elections were
    also an important part of political life in the German kingdoms in the
    sixth/seventh centuries. See Robert Fossier, ed., *The Cambridge Illus-
    trated History of the Middle Ages (350–950)* (Cambridge: Cambridge
    University Press, 1990, p. 417). Feudal civil society included bodies that
    represented all major strata of the population, including the third estate
    (comprising the bourgeois, artisans, and peasants), particularly in Italian
    and Dutch cities. King Philip and his sons, in thirteenth/fourteenth
    centuries, convened the three estates of his realm, the clergy, the nobil-
    ity, and the "third Estate." The practice of consultation in the Estates
    General was extended by the development of provincial estates later in
    the fourteenth century. Of course, with the extension of royal power, its
    role was diminishing. It was not convened after 1484, and only the suc-
    cession crisis in 1560 temporarily resuscitated it.

76. For a detailed analysis of the totalitarian model and the real totalitarian
    society, see Vladimir Shlapentokh, *A Normal Totalitarian Society* (Ar-
    monk, N.Y.: M. E. Sharpe, 2001); among recent publication on totalitar-
    ian society, see Jerzy W. Borejsza and Klaus Ziemer, in cooperation with
    Magdalena Huas, *Totalitarian and Authoritarian Regimes in Europe:
    Legacies and Lessons from the Twentieth Century* (New York: Berghahn
    Books, 2006); Juan J. Linz, *Totalitarian and Authoritarian Regimes*
    (Boulder, Colo.: Lynne Rienner Publishers, 2000).

77. For more about the totalitarian tendencies in Russia, see Vladimir
    Shlapentokh's publications: "Two Pictures of Putin's Russia: Both
    Wrong," *World Policy Journal* 22, no. 1 (Spring 2005): 61–72; "Wealth
    versus Political Power: The Russian Case," *Communist and Post-
    Communist Studies* 37, no. 2 (2004): 135–60; "Hobbes and Locke at Odds
    in Putin's Russia," *Europe-Asia* 55, no.7 (2003): 981–1007; "Russia's

De-democratization," *World and I,* December 2006 (available at www
.worldandi.com). See also Regina Smyth, *Candidate Strategies and Electoral Competition in the Russian Federation: Democracy without Foundation* (Cambridge: Cambridge University Press, 2006); Michael McFaul,
Nikolai Petrov, and Andrei Ryabov, with Mikhail Krasnov et al., *Between
Dictatorship and Democracy: Russian Post-Communist Political Reform*
(Washington, D.C.: Carnegie Endowment for International Peace,
2004); United States Senate Committee on Foreign Relations, *Democracy in Retreat in Russia: Hearing before the Committee on Foreign Relations,* 109th Cong., 1st sess., February 17, 2005 (Washington, D.C.:
GPO, 2005); Michael Steven Fish, *Democracy Derailed in Russia: The
Failure of Open Politics* (New York: Cambridge University Press, 2005).

CHAPTER 3

1. For Martin Carnoy, for instance, "the larger the public sector, the
   stronger is the state." Martin Carnoy, *The State and Political Theory*
   (Princeton, N.J.: Princeton University Press, 1984). Several other authors gravitate to the same perception of the "strong state," considering
   other versions of the same indicator, such as the ratio of government expenditures to the GNP. Jackman offers "the autonomy of state" as a cri-
   terion. See Robert Jackman, *Power without Force: The Political Capacity
   of Nation-States* (Ann Arbor: University of Michigan Press, 1993, pp.
   62 65); Stephen Krasner, "United States Commercial and Monetary
   Policy," in *Between Power and Plenty: Foreign Economic Policy of Advanced Industrial States,* ed. Peter Katzenstein (Madison: University of
   Wisconsin Press, 1978, pp. 51–89); Neil Smelser, *Sociology* (Oxford:
   Blackwell, 1994, p. 63).
2. See Aleksandr Sevast'ianov, "Noveishaia istoriia: Politprosvet; Solo partiia," *Literaturnaia Gazeta,* December 28, 2006; Stanislav Govorukhin,
   Velikaia Kriminal'naia Revoliutsiia (Moscow: Andreevskii Flag, 1993).
   Several other authors described Russia in a similar way, including Grigorii
   Yavlinsky, who labeled the society a "corporate-criminal system" (Grigorii Yavlinsky, "Unizhennye liudi ne sozdadut ekonomiku 21 veka," *Novaia Gazeta,* November 11, 2002).
3. See George Breslauer, "Evaluating Gorbachev and Yeltsin as Leaders," in
   Gorbachev, Yeltsin and Putin: Political Leadership in Russia's Transition,
   ed. Archie Brown and Liliia Shevtsova (Washington, D.C.: Carnegie Endowment for International Peace, 2001, p. 47).
4. Michael McFaul, *Russia's Unfinished Revolution: Political Change from
   Gorbachev to Putin* (London: Cornell University Press, 2001, pp.
   122–85).
5. Donald Barry, *Russian Politics: Post-Soviet Phase* (New York: Peter Lang,
   2002, pp. 124–26).
6. It is interesting that several authors talked about "the centrality of
   Yeltsin's personality." See Liliia Shevtsova, *Yeltsin's Russia: Myths and*

Reality (Washington, D.C.: Carnegie Endowment for International Peace, 1999, p. 288); Paul Hollander, *Political Will and Personal Beliefs: The Decline and the Fall of Soviet Communism* (New Haven, Conn.: Yale University Press, 1999); Timothy Colton and Robert Tucker, eds., *Patterns in Post-Soviet Leadership* (Boulder, Colo.: Westview, 1995). However, they all skirted the prosaic motivation of Boris Yeltsin for power and greed.

7. Georges Duby, *Féodalités* (Paris: Presses universitaires de France, 1998).

8. David Charles Douglas, *The Norman Achievement, 1050–1100* (London: Eyre & Spottiswoode, 1969, p. 177).

9. François Louis Ganshof, *Feudalism,* translated by Philip Grierson with a foreword by Sir F. M. Stenton (New York: Harper and Row, 1964).

10. Hunt Janin, *Medieval Justice: Cases and Laws in France, England, and Germany, 500–1500* (Jefferson, N.C.: McFarland, 2004).

11. Barbara A. Hanawalt and David Wallace, eds., *Medieval Crime and Social Control* (Minneapolis: University of Minnesota Press, 1999).

12. Claude Gauvard, "Fear of Crime in Late Medieval France," in Hanawalt and Wallace, *Medieval Crime and Social Control,* pp. 1–48.

13. See Natalie Davis, *The Gift in Sixteenth-Century France* (Madison: University of Wisconsin Press, 2000).

14. James O. Finckenauer and Yuri A. Voronin, *The Threat of Russian Organized Crime* (Washington, D.C.: U.S. Department of Justice, Office of Justice Programs, National Institute of Justice, 2001); see Annelise Anderson, "The Red Mafia: A Legacy of Communism," in *Economic Transtion in Eastern Europe and Russia: Realities of Reform,* ed. Edward Lazear (Stanford, Calif.: Hoover Institution Press, 1995, pp. 340–66).

15. Mikhail Morozov, "Vorovali i budut vorovat'," *Tribuna RT,* December 11, 2005.

16. Dzhavokhir Kabilov, "Chopnutaia Rossiia," *Tribuna RT,* March 17, 2006.

17. G. Smirnov, *Organizovannaia prestupnost' i mery po ee presecheniiu* (Ekaterinburg: MVD RF, 1995).

18. Yakov Gilinskii, *Organizatsionnaia prestupnost' v Rossii: Teoriia i real'nost'* (St. Petersburg: Institut Sotsiologii RAN, 1996, p. 77).

19. Vadim Volkov, *Violent Entrepreneurs: The Use of Force in the Making of Russian Capitalism* (Ithaca, N.Y.: Cornell University Press, 2002, pp. 108–22); see Finckenauer and Voronin, *Threat of Russian Organized Crime*; Tat'iana Kuznetsova, "Mafii ob'iavili voinu, kto pobedit," *Argumenty i Fakty,* May 24, 2006.

20. See Arthur Newton, *Travel and Travelers in the Middle Ages* (Freeport, N.Y.: Books for Libraries Press, 1967); Hanawalt and Wallace, *Medieval Crime and Social Control*; Janin, *Medieval Justice*; Trevor Dean, *Crime in Medieval Europe, 1200–1550* (New York: Longman, 2001).

21. J. E. Tyler, *The Alpine Passes: The Middle Ages (962–1250)* (Oxford: B. Blackwell, 1930).

22. Gauvard, "Fear of Crime in Late Medieval France," pp. 1, 14, 23.

23. "Vse passazhirskie poezda budet konvoirovat' militsiia," *Moskovskii Komsomolets,* February 16, 2000.

24. Anastasiia Berseneva, "Poslednee kitaiskoe preduprezhdenie," *Novye Izvestiia,* May 31, 2006.

25. Gauvard, "Fear of Crime in Late Medieval France," p. 1.

26. See Dmitrii Pisarenko, "Kak izbavit'sia ot strakha," *Argumenty i Fakty,* March 22, 2006.

27. See about these developments in Vladimir Shlapentokh, "Detsentrlizatsiia strakha v post Sovetskom obshchestve," *Nezavisimaia Gazeta,* March 13, 1997.

28. Vladimir Shlapentokh and Eric Shiraev, eds., *Fears in Post-Communist Societies: A Comparative Perspective* (New York: Palgrave, 2002).

29. Ibid.

30. Shlapentokh and Shiraev, *Fears in Post-Communist Societies;* Richard Lotspech, "Crime in the Transition Economies," *East-Asia* 47, no. 4 (1995): 555–89; Tania Frisby, "The Rise of Organized Crime in Russia: Its Roots and Social Significance," *Europe-Asia Studies* 50, no. 1 (1998): 27–49. For more on organized crime in Russia, see Stephan Handelman, *Comrade Criminal* (New Haven, Conn.: Yale University Press, 1997); J. Leitzel, M. Alexeev, and C. Gaddy, "Mafiosi and Matrioshki: Organized Crime and Russian Reform," *The Brookings Review* 13 (Winter 1995): 26–29; Vadim Volkov, "Violent Entrepreneurship in Post-Communist Russia," *Europe-Asia Studies* 51, no. 5 (1999): 751–54; Anton Oleinki, *Organized Crime, Prison, and Post-Soviet Societies* (Burlington, Vt.: Ashgate, 2003); David Satter, *Darkness at Dawn: The Rise of the Russian Criminal State* (New Haven, Conn.: Yale University Press, 2003); Marc Galeotti, *Russian and Post-Soviet Organized Crimes* (Brookfield, Vt.: Ashgate, 2002).

31. See Levada-Tsentr, Bulletin, December 29, 2005.

32. See Dmitrii Slobodianiuk et al., "Smert' Ivana Kivelidi: Neshchastnyi sluchai ili ubiistvo?" *Izvestiia,* August 5, 1995.

33. Volkov, *Violent Entrepreneurs;* James Finckenauer, *The Threat of Russian Organized Crime* (Washington, D.C.: National Institute of Justice, 2001); Federico Varese, *The Russian Mafia: Private Protection in a New Market Economy* (Oxford: Oxford University Press, 2001).

34. Mikhail Lamzov, "Zhiguli na krovi," *Argumenty i Fakty,* September 11, 2002.

35. There have been numerous rumors in Russia about the connection of the Kremlin with criminal organizations, particularly in relation to Aleksandr Korzhakov, the former head of Yeltsin's security, and the Solnstev gang.

36. See Vladimir Vasil'ev's (deputy minister of internal affairs) article on the power criminal structures (*Moskovskie Novosti,* January 4, 1998). See about the Kursk in *Komsomol'skaia Pravda,* August 12, 1997; see about Petersburg and Ekaterinburg in *Moskovskii Komsomolets,* July 12, 1997; and about Sochi in *Literaturnaia Gazeta,* June 25, 1997.

37. Konstantin Simonov, "Krupnyi bizness mozhet nas spasti ot kriminala," *Vek*, November 1, 2002.

38. Volkov, *Violent Entrepreneurs*, p. 97.

39. William Webster, ed., *Russian Organized Crime and Corruption* (Washington, D.C.: The CSIS Press, 2000, p. 2).

40. Dean, *Crime in Medieval Europe*, p. 41.

41. J. C. Waquet, *Corruption: Ethics and Power in Florence, 1660–1770* (University Park: Pennsylvania State University Press, 1991, pp. 1–2).

42. W. Blockmans, "Patronage, Brokerage and Corruption as Symptoms of Incipient State Formation in the Burgundian-Habsburg Netherlands," in *Klientelsysteme im Europa der Frahen Neuzeit,* ed. A. Maczak (Munich: R. Oldenbourg, 1988, pp. 117–26).

43. Davis, *Gift in Sixteenth-Century France*, pp. 4, 15, 142–51; F. Pollock and F. W. Maitland, *The History of English Law before the Time of Edward I,* 2nd ed. (Cambridge: Cambridge University Press, 1968, p. 557).

44. Janin, *Medieval Justice*, pp. 126–27. This author also cites a document that explains how King Henry II tried to deal with the problem of corruption through his "Inquest of Sheriffs." The description of the activities of judges in France in the tenth and eleventh centuries was similar. The court was already out of the control of the king. It often became an institution used by lords to rob ordinary people. See Duby, *Féodalités*, p. 395; Dean, *Crime in Medieval Europe*, pp. 34–41.

45. Pollock and Maitland, *History of English Law.*

46. Dean, *Crime in Medieval Europe*, pp. 31–32.

47. Yurii Chaika, "Korruptsiia pronizyvaet vse urovni vlasti," *Novaia Gazeta*, November 29, 2006.

48. See the report by Transparency International, Global Corruption Barometer, Policy and Research Department, International Secretariat, December 9, 2005.

49. Here and later I will use data collected by the Moscow polling firm Fund INDEM, which conducted a survey of 2,500 Russians in 1999, 2000, 2001, and 2005. The project was headed by Georgii Satarov, a former aid to Yeltsin, and was devoted to the study of corruption in Russia. It was sponsored by the World Bank and resulted in a published book. See Georgii Satarov, ed., *Diagnostika: Rossiiskaia korruptsiia* (Moscow: IN-DEM, 2002), www.anti-corr.ru; K. I. Golovshchinskii et al., *Bizness i korruptsiia: Problemy protivodeistviia; Itogovyi otchet* (Moscow: INDEM, 2004); Georgii Satarov, *Diagnostika rossiskoi korruptsii 2005*, www.indem .ru/Russian.asp. For more about the project, see a series of articles titled "Power and Money" (*vlast i dengi*) in *Novaia Gazeta* (August 5 and 12, 2002); Georgii Satarov, "Otdel'nyi razgovor: Delo o $400 milliardakh," *Novaia Gazeta*, July 29, 2002; Sergei Valianskii and Dmitrii Kaliuzhnyi, "Nuzhna li vlasti bor'ba s korruptsiei," *Literaturnaia Gazeta*, August 2002; Vladislav Vorob'ev, "Tsentr. INDEM—kuda idem . . . ," *Rossiiskaia Gazeta*, June 29, 2002; Irina Rinaeva, "Ni dnia bez vziatki,"

Moskovskii Komsomolets, May 22, 2002; Maria-Luisa Tirmaste, "Rossi-iskoi korruptsii postavlen unikal'nyi diagnoz," *Kommersant-Daily,* May 22, 2002.

50. Transparency International, Global Corruption Barometer, 2005.

51. Igor' Korol'kov, "Spetsial'noe rassledovanie: Chernye diplomy," *Novaia Gazeta,* April 24, 2006.

52. Ibid.; Igor' Korol'kov, "Mesto sobytii: Diplomy pakhnut porokhom," *Novaia Gazeta,* April 20, 2006.

53. Georgii Satarov, *Corruption Process in Russia: Level, Structure, Trends* (Moscow: INDEM, 2006), http://www.indem.ru/en/publicat/2005 diag_engV.htm.

54. See several publications in VTSIOM, *Monitoring Obshchestvennogo Mneniia,* during 1994–2002; Satarov, *Corruption Process in Russia.*

55. Levada-Tsentr, Bulletin, May 5, 2006.

56. Ekaterina Grigor'eva, Svetlana Popova, and Natal'ia Ratiani, "Kulakom po seredniaku," *Izvestiia,* August 17, 2002.

57. See, for instance, Satarov's reflections on Yeltsin's period in "Pred-varitel'nye itogi," *Nezavisimaia Gazeta,* November 1, 2001; and his "Maska dlia prezidenta," *Moskovskii Komsomolets,* January 2, 2002.

58. Putin's TV interview on December 26, 2000 (*Izvestiia,* December 27, 2000); his interview with the editors of *Izvestiia* (April 4, 2001); his interview on ORT (February 7–8, 2002, 9:00 P.M. Moscow time); and par-ticularly his presidential addresses to the Russian parliament in April 2001 and April 2002 (*Izvestiia,* April 4, 2001, and *Izvestiia,* April 19, 2002).

59. Yuliia Latynina, "Krestnye ottsy rossiiskoi ryby," *Obshchaia Gazeta,* March 5, 2001; Elena Dikun, "Voloshinu podsadili bol'shogo spetsial-ista," *Obshchaia Gazeta,* February 8, 2001.

60. See Norman Cantor, *Civilization of the Middle Ages* (New York: Harper-Collins, 1993, p. 485).

61. "Posledniaia vziatka v GIBDD," *Sankt-Peterburgskie Vedomosti,* July 7, 2006.

62. Interview with the editor of *Novaia Gazeta* on *Ekho Moskvy* (a program called "A particular opinion"), August 4, 2006.

63. Sergei Avdeev, "Generala pereveli v koloniiu," *Rossiiskaia Gazeta,* Au-gust 2, 2006; Dmitrii Vasil'ev, "Strategicheskaia posadka," *Rossiiskaia Gazeta,* August 2, 2006.

64. Natalia Aliakrinskaia, "Panskov ne vyderzhal sledstviia," *Moskovskie Novosti,* July 28, 2006.

65. Mikhail Belyi and Anna Semenova, "Vysshaia shkola vziatok," *Novye Izvestiia,* July 10, 2006.

66. Aleksandr Bogdanov, "Na zemle greiut ruki," *Trud,* July 18, 2004.

67. Dean, *Crime in Medieval Europe,* p. 31.

68. Mikhail Morozov, "Vorovali i budut vorovat'," *Tribuna RT,* December 11, 2005.

69. V. G. Solov'ev, "Mur natselen na bor'bu s banditizmom," *Sovetskaia Rossiia,* February 22, 2006.

70. Levada-Tsentr, Bulletin, February 15, 2007.
71. Irina Mandrik, "Moia militsiia menia ne berezhet," *Russkii Kur'er,* March 2, 2005; see also "Kogo berezhet moia militsiia?" *Sankt-Peterburgskie Novosti,* December 9, 2005.
72. See VTSIOM, Bulletin, April 7, 2002.
73. Vladimir Shlapentokh, *Fear in Contemporary Society: Its Positive and Negative Effects* (New York: Palgrave, 2006).
74. See Ol'ga Bobrova, "Ishchut pozharnye, ishchet militsiia," *Novaia Gazeta,* March 12, 2006.
75. Azer Efendiev, "S nadezhdoi na znakomstva," *Izvestiia,* August 23, 2002.
76. See, as a recent example, Boris Reznik, "Mafiia i more," *Izvestiia,* August 18–20, 2002.
77. See Rodionov's interview with Deutsche Welle (*Novoie Russkoe Slovo*), August 24–25, 2002; Leonid Ivashov, "Kavkazskaia strategiia," *Sovietskaia Rossiia,* August 8, 2002.
78. See Valerii Solovei, "Katastrofy b'iut po vlasti: No tol'ko v Rossii," *Vek,* August 2, 2002; Yuliia Latynina, "Plotina ne vyderszhala burnogo potoka vorovstva," *Novaia Gazeta,* August 12, 2002.
79. See Elena Korop, "Kas'ianovskii proryv," *Izvestiia,* July 26, 2002.
80. Borislav Mikhailichenko, "Vanichkin i dvoechniki," *Moskovskie Novosti,* August 19, 2002.

CHAPTER 4

1. See about John Galbraith's heritage in Jeffrey Madrich, "A Mind of His Own," *The New York Review of Books,* May 26, 2005.
2. See, for instance, I. Bulev and N. Briukhovetskaia, "Teoriia i otechestvennaia praktika," *Menedzher,* No. 3, March 2002.
3. Gordon Tullock, "The Welfare Costs of Tariffs, Monopolies, and Theft," *Western Economic Journal* (now *Economic Inquiry*) 5, no. 3 (1967): 224–32.
4. Anne Krueger, "The Political Economy of the Rent-Seeking Society," *American Economic Review* 64, no. 3 (1974): 291–303.
5. For more about rent seeking, see James Buchanan, Robert Tollison, and Gordon Tullock, eds., *Toward a Theory of the Rent Seeking Society* (College Station: Texas A&M University Press, 1980); William Mitchell and Michael Munger, "Economic Models of Interests Groups: An Introductory Survey," *American Journal of Political Science* 35, no. 2 (1991): 512–46.
6. Robert Jackal, "Crimes in the Suites," *Contemporary Sociology* 9, no. 3 (1980): 355.
7. See Veronika Chursina, "Kuda propal zakon o korruptsii," *Novaia Gazeta,* December 7, 2006.
8. See Norman Cantor, *Civilization of the Middle Ages* (New York: Harper-Collins, 1993, p. 464).

9. M. Postan, "The Rise of the Money Economy," *The Economic History Review* 14, no. 2 (1944): 123–34.

10. See Peter Spufford, *Money and Its Use in Medieval Europe* (New York: Cambridge University Press, 1988).

11. Henri Pirenne, *Economic and Social History of Medieval Europe* (New York: Harcourt, Brace, 1937, p. 168).

12. Aron Katseneliboigen, "Color Markets in the Soviet Union," *Soviet Studies* 29, no. 1 (1977): 62–85.

13. For more about the role of money and corruption in Soviet society, see Vladimir Shlapentokh, *Public and Private Life of the Soviet People* (New York: Oxford University Press, 1989), and his *A Normal Totalitarian Society* (Armonk, N.Y.: M. E. Sharpe, 2001); Alaina Lemon, "'Your Eyes Are Green Like Dollars': Counterfeit Cash, National Substance, Currency Apartheid in 1990s Russia," *Cultural Anthropology* 13, no. 1 (1998): 24.

14. See Vladimir Kontorovich and Vladimir Shlapentokh, *Organizational Innovation, the Carl Beck Papers* (Pittsburgh, Pa.: University of Pittsburgh Press, 1986).

15. See William Clark, "Crime and Punishment in Soviet Officialdom, 1965–1990," *Europe-Asia Studies* 45, no. 2 (1993): 269.

16. See Galina Vishnevskaia, *Galina: A Russian Story*, translated from Russian by Guy Daniels (San Diego, Calif.: Harcourt Brace Jovanovich, 1984).

17. Luc Duhamel, "Justice and Politics in Moscow, 1083–1986: Ambartsumyan's Case," *Euro-Asia* 52, no. 7 (2000): 1307–29.

18. See, for instance, Yegor Gaidar, *Dolgoe vremia: Rossiia v mire; Ocherki ekonomicheskoi istorii* (Moscow: Delo, 2005).

19. Leon Aron, "Is Russia Really Lost," *The American Enterprise Institute for Public Policy Research*, January 1, 2000; see also Jeffry Klugman, "The Psychology of Soviet Corruption, Undiscipline and Resistance to Reform," *Political Psychology* 7, no. 1 (1986): 67–82.

20. K. I. Golovshchinskii et al., *Bizness i korruptsiia: Problemy protivodeistviia; Itogovyi otchet* (Moscow: INDEM, 2004).

21. Georgii Satarov, *Corruption Process in Russia: Level, Structure, Trends* (Moscow: INDEM, 2006), see www.indem.ru/en/publicat/2005diag_engV.htm.

22. See the Transparency International Corruption Perception Index 2002 (available at www.transparency.org).

23. Department of Investigations, "Glava—vsemu khleb," *Nezavisimaia Gazeta*, April 23, 2006.

24. "Anatolii Chubais stremitsia," *Nezavisimaia Gazeta*, September 13, 1997.

25. See Petr Surazhskii, "Chernaia piatnitsa ONEKSIMbanka," *Segodnia*, July 12, 1997; Ulian Kerzonov, "Rossiia, rynok i Chubais," *Nezavisimaia Gazeta*, November 20, 1997; "Anatolii Chubais stremitsia," *Nezavisimaia Gazeta*.

26. Yuliia Latynina, "Konets legendy," *Izvestiia*, July 15, 1997.

27. Aleksandr Khinshtein, "Shef prezidentskogo protokola . . . i drugie ofit-sial'nye litsa," *Moskovskii Komsomolets,* December 9, 1997.

28. "Chernomyrdin imeet sostoianie v 5 milliardov dollarov?" *Izvestiia,* April 1, 1997.

29. Department of Economics, "Kassovyi apparat," *Novaia Gazeta,* March 2, 2005.

30. Boris Vishnevsky, "Medvedi zaviduiut Medvedevu," *Novaia Gazeta,* March 5, 2006.

31. Anna Lebedeva, "General Kazantsev privlekaet svoiu zhenu," *Novaia Gazeta,* February 19, 2006; Anna Lebedeva, "Velikii miasokombinator," *Novaia Gazeta,* July 19, 2006.

32. See the minutes of the closed meeting of the Committee on National Security in the State Duma in *Novaia Gazeta,* July 29, 2002.

33. Yurii Shchekochikhin, "Prokuratura dlia mebeli," *Novaia Gazeta,* July 29, 2002.

34. Russian TV station RTVI, "Investigation," September 2, 2006.

35. Andrei Uglanov, for instance, wrote that Russians should be grateful to oligarchs, even if "they are no angels," simply because they are Russian citizens and prevented the grabbing of state property by foreigners. The accumulation of Russian money in their foreign accounts is not a big problem because "the money has a considerable chance of returning to the motherland and our economy." Of course, the author brings no evidence in favor of this typical example of wishful thinking (see Andrei Uglanov, "Bol'shaia kremlevskaia neft'," *Argumenty i Fakty,* July 24, 2002). Another author, Yuliia Latynina, found it necessary to soften the image of Berezovskii by praising his managerial skills as the head of Aeroflot, brushing aside the accusation that he embezzled a lot of money from this formerly state-owned enterprise (see Yuliia Latynina, "Praviteli i zalozhniki," *Novaia Gazeta,* June 24, 2002).

36. See, for instance, "Dvizhenie vpered," *Izvestiia,* July 24, 2002; Kirsan Il-iumzhinov, "Obeshchaesh' vypolniai," *Izvestiia,* June 28, 2002.

37. Guy Fourquin, *Lordship and Feudalism in the Middle Ages* (London: G. Allen & Unwin, 1976).

38. See Ol'ga Kryshtanovskaia, *Anatomiia rossiĭskoĭ ëlity* (Moscow: Zakharov, 2005).

39. See the description of the stock auction in favor of Aven in "Korruptsiia," *Moskovskii Komsomolets,* July 17, 1997. The article directly accused Anatolii Chubais and his lieutenants of rigging the auction in favor of Aven, the head of the Alpha financial empire.

40. Yuliia Latynina, "Mikhail Khodorkovsky: Khimiia i zhizn'," *Sovershenno Sekretno,* August 10, 1999.

41. See Khodorkovsky's biography, available at www.mediapoliis.com.ru.

42. In 1996, on the eve of the presidential election, I interviewed Khodorkovsky in his personal office inside his bank, which looked like a fortress (it was guarded by soldiers with machine guns). I proposed a game to the young oligarch, and it pleased me that he was willing to play. I would

play the role of a rude American senator and ask him pointed questions as though he was on trial. I first said, "Mr. Khodorkovsky, you know, of course, the name Bill Gates and how he became so rich and what he did for the American economy?" "Certainly," he replied. "So," I continued, "what was your contribution to the Russian economy?" His answer: "I am creating an infrastructure for boosting the Russian economy." "Well, how much time will you need to do your job, and to see a prosperous Russian economy?" "Some 5–10 years." "Well, Mr. Khodorkovsky, the Bolsheviks asked for no more than 10 years, Gorbachev for much less, and the young reformers only asked for 500 days. Why should your compatriots believe in your promises?" I did not get a reply and decided to stop the game and move to a more traditional interview.

43. Paul Khlebnikov, *The Godfather of the Kremlin: Boris Berezovsky and the Looting of Russia* (New York: Harcourt Trade Publishers, 2000).

44. Roy Medvedev, "Konets oligarkhata, ili chego boiatsia bogatye v Rossii?" *Vecherniaia Moskva*, September 18, 2003.

45. Mikhail Khodorkovsky, "Serzhantov khvatit na vsekh," *Moskovskie Novosti*, July 27, 2003.

46. Ekaterina Grigor'eva, " 'Putin' v kletochku," *Izvestiia*, June 26, 2003.

47. See Sergei Markov, "Pravila oligarkhov," *Moskovskii Komsomolets*, February 4, 2003; Andrei Piontkovskii, "Eshche odin god velikogo pereloma," *Novaia Gazeta*, February 3, 2003.

48. Grigorii Yavlinsky, "Unizhennye liudi ne sozdadut ekonomiku 21 veka," *Novaia Gazeta*, November 11, 2002.

49. For the reflections of a famous Russian economist, see Nikolai Petrakov, "Blesk i nishcheta oligarkhov," *Literaturnaia Gazeta*, November 26, 2002.

50. Aristotle, *The Politics and the Constitution of Athens* (Cambridge: Cambridge University Press, 1884, p. 57).

51. "Stanet li Potanin prezidentom . . . ," *Nezavisimaia Gazeta*, July 29, 1997.

52. Paul Khlebnikov, "The Godfather of the Kremlin," *Forbes*, December 1996.

53. Boris Tupolev, "V sviazi s perekhodom na druguiu rabotu," *Kommersant-Daily*, November 6, 1997.

54. As an educator from Chukotka wrote in a letter to the editor published in *Izvestiia*, "If we put a different oligarch in charge of each of the 89 regions, and put one in the Kremlin, life in Russia would be better" (S. Vozchikov, "90-yi oligarkh dlia Kremlia," *Izvestiia*, August 16, 2003).

55. Ol'ga Bobrova, "Neftianniki kachaiut prava," *Novaia Gazeta*, November 1, 2006.

56. Ol'ga Bobrova, "Sibiriaki osvobozhdaiut goroda," *Novaia Gazeta*, November 8, 2006.

57. Igor' Korol'kov, "Gubernator i Vinni Pukh," *Moskovskie Novosti*, July 9, 2001; "Uvolen sobesednik Putina," *Kommersant-Daily*, July 3, 2002;

Sergei Alekhin, Dmitrii Doroshenko, and Andrei Murashev, "Kuda propal gubernator Butov," *Rossiiskaia Gazeta,* June 29, 2002.

58. See Aleksandr Lebed's letter to the president published in *Nezavisimaia Gazeta,* April 4, 2002.

59. Yurii Chuvashev, "Belyi kon' dlia Anatoliia Bykova," *Nezavisimaia Gazeta,* June 24, 2002.

60. Russian TV station NTV, "News," September 2, 2002.

61. See Mikhail Berger, "Bitva za 'Sviaz'neft': Vaterloo ili Austerlits pravitel'stva?" *Izvestiia,* July 31, 1997; "O svoei otstavke Anatolii Chubais ob'iavit sam," *Izvestiia,* December 24, 1997.

62. See Nemtsov's interviews with *Moskovskii Komsomolets* (August 19, 1997, and December 20, 1997) and with *Izvestiia* (December 24, 1997).

63. Khodorkovsky, "Serzhantov khvatit na vsekh."

64. See these unusual polemics in Yuliia Latynina, "Khodoki u Putina," *Novaia Gazeta,* February 24, 2003.

65. See Yuliia Latynina, "Esli v Rossii peredel sobstvennosti—eto k vyboram," *Novaia Gazeta,* May 15, 2003; see also Ol'ga Kryshtanovskaia, "Operativniki plokhie strategi," *Moskovskie Novosti,* July 14, 2003.

66. See Khlebnikov, *Godfather of the Kremlin.*

67. Khodorkovsky, "Serzhantov khvatit na vsekh."

68. Anna Rudnitskaia, "On gotov otsidet', no ne uekhat'," *Moskovskie Novosti,* July 14, 2003.

69. See Mariia Ignatova, "Aktsii 'Yukosa' snova rastut," *Izvestiia,* October 7, 2003.

70. According to VTSIOM's July survey, which posed the question "What is the cause of the criminal prosecution of Yukos' managers?" 6 percent of those who responded said, "To constrain the non-Russian capital in Russia." The chats on various Russian Web sites about the Khodorkovsky case revealed an outburst of anti-Semitism (see, for instance, Victor Ivanov, "Jew Huner," *The Exile,* November 3, 2006).

71. Aleksandr Arkhangel'skii, "Ne bachu logiki," *Izvestiia,* August 12, 2003.

72. Mariia Kakturskaia, "Smolenskii prodal imperiiu na tri bukvy," *Argumenty i Fakty,* August 6, 2003.

73. See the editorial, "Pedaling Backward," *Washington Post,* October 28, 2003.

74. See Steven Weisman, "Powell Displays Tough U.S. Stance toward Russians," *New York Times,* January 27, 2004.

75. See www.gzt.ru (accessed September 28, 2003) for the full text of Putin's speech before the students of Columbia University; see also "Putin Turns On the Charm to Ease Bankers' Worries," *Financial Times* (UK), October 31, 2003.

76. For instance, see Putin's speech in Malaysia in October 2005 (available at www.kremlin.ru/text/appears/2003/10/54103.html).

77. Larisa Kaftan, "Kogo oligarkhi gotoviat v prezidenty?" *Komsomol'skaia Pravda,* April 20, 2006.

78. See the description of this struggle in ethnic terms by Vladimir Vinogradov in his interview with *Nezavisimaia Gazeta*, December 25, 1997.

79. For more about the battle between the alliance of Berezovskii and Gusinskii (in the past, ardent enemies) and Potanin's group, see Denis Babich, "Privatizatsiia kak zerkalo rossiiskoi blagogluposti," *Nezavisimaia Gazeta*, August 15, 1997.

80. However, several other Russian politicians and journalists recognized, in 1997, that an all-out war between the oligarchs could threaten the existence of Russian statehood. The conflicts involved almost every political actor in the country (see Vitalii Tret'iakov, "1997 nastol'ko plokh, chto etim i khorosh," *Nezavisimaia Gazeta*, December 31, 1997).

81. See about the battle over this company in Dmitrii Travin, "1997: Vkus krovi," http://idelo.ru/376/20.html (accessed February 25, 2007); George Soros, "Berezovsky: Putin. Zapad," *Moskovskie Novosti*, February 28, 2000.

82. See Ol'ga Kryshtanovskaia, "V ch'ikh rukakh sobstvennost'," *Argumenty i Fakty*, April 12, 1995. For several observers from the nationalist and Communist camps, some of these conflicts had a significant ethnic character. They would argue, for instance, that a Jewish coalition of bankers, which included Berezovskii, Gusinskii, and Smolenskii, was in a mortal struggle with an equally influential group of Russian bankers headed by Potanin.

83. See Yuliia Kalinina, "Soiuz iz poslednikh," *Moskovskii Komsomolets*, January 10, 2006.

84. Oligarchs are evidently against politicians who have the ability to install strict order in the country. At the same time, Russian oligarchs favor order to ensure the safety of their interests. It seems oligarchs want a sort of order in which they themselves are exempt.

85. Khodorkovsky, "Serzhantov khvatit na vsekh."

86. A. I. Volskii, S. Borisov, and L. Alekseeva, "Otkrytoe pis'mo obshchestvennykh organizatsii rossiiskikh predprinimatelei i institutov grazhdanskogo obshchestva prezidentu V.V. Putinu," *Izvestiia*, July 25, 2003; see also Valeriia Korchagina and Caroline McGregor, "Oligarchs to Appeal to Putin," *Moscow Times*, July 10, 2003.

87. See Ekaterina Gurkina, "Bizness-soobshchestvo obratilos' k prezidentu," www.gazeta.ru/2003/10/25/biznessoobse.shtml (accessed October 25, 2003).

88. Pavel Voshchanov, "Tainyi zagovor oligarkhov—khit politicheskogo sezona," *Novaia Gazeta*, July 21, 2003.

89. See Aleksandr Golts, "Kontrevoliutsionnaia situatsiia," *Ezhenedel'nyi Zhurnal*, August 18, 2003.

90. Medvedev, "Konets oligarkhata, ili chego boiatsia bogatye v Rossii?"

91. See Maksim Sokolov, "Vykhod iz getto," *Izvestiia*, October 2, 2003; Valeriia Korchagina, "The Elite Demand Some Answers," *Moscow Times*, October 27, 2003.

CHAPTER 5

1. Josiah Ober, *Political Dissent in Democratic Athens: Intellectual Critic of Popular Rule* (Princeton, N.J.: Princeton University Press, 1998).
2. Gilbert Geis and Robert Meier, *White Collar Crime* (New York: Free Press, 1977).
3. Deirdre McCloskey, *The Bourgeois Virtues: Ethics for an Age of Commerce* (Chicago: University of Chicago Press, 2006).
4. Maurice Punch, "Suite Violence: Why Managers Murder and Corporations Kill," *Crime and Social Change* 33, no. 3 (2000): 243–80.
5. Yulii Dubov, *Bol'shaia paika* (Moscow: Vagrius, 2002); Yuliia Latynina, *Stal'noi korol'* (Moscow: Olma Press Ekslibris, 2002); Yuliia Latynina, *Okhota na iziubria* (Moscow: Ëksmo, 2003).
6. Theodore Dreiser, *The Financier* (Cleveland, Ohio: World Publishing, 1967); Theodore Dreiser, *The Titan* (Cleveland, Ohio: World Publishing, 1925); Theodore Dreiser, *The Stoic* (Cleveland, Ohio: World Publishing, 1952); F. Scott Fitzgerald, *The Great Gatsby* (New York: Columbia University Press, 1999); Tom Wolfe, *The Bonfire of the Vanities* (New York: Farrar, Straus, 1987); Tom Wolfe, *A Man in Full* (New York: Farrar, Straus and Giroux, 1998).
7. The prominent Soviet economist Aleksandr Matlin expressed the dominant view among his colleagues when he wrote: "The state cannot be trusted with the management of the economy because the combination of political and economic power leads unavoidably toward monopoly and the war of the state against its own people" (*Izvestiia,* September 21, 1991).
8. See Larisa Piiasheva, "Kontury radikal'noi sotsial'noi reformy," in *Postizhenie,* ed. Fridrikh Borodkin et al. (Moscow: Progress, 1989, pp. 266–67, 271).
9. See Larisa Piiasheva, "V korzinke i koshelke," *Literaturnaia Gazeta,* September 5, 1990; Larisa Piiasheva, "Son o trekh ukazakh," *Literaturnaia Gazeta,* March 13, 1991.
10. Vladimir Perekrest, "Za chto sidit Khodorkovsky," *Izvestiia,* June 9, 2006.
11. Yegor Gaidar, "Revoliutsiia ostalas' v 20 veke, reformy prodolzhaiutsia v 21," *Izvestiia,* January 17, 2001; Yegor Gaidar, "Svoiu povinnost' otbyl," *Moskovskie Novosti,* July 23, 2001.
12. "Corruption," said Chubais, "depends very little on the authorities. It depends on the people" (see Anatolii Chubais' interview with *Moskovskie Novosti,* July 29, 2002; see also Lev Gudkov, "O negativnoi identifikatsii," *Monitoring Obshchestvennogo Mneniia,* No. 5, 2000).
13. See Boris Kagarlitsky, " 'Political Capitalism' and Corruption in Russia," *Links,* May/August 2002; Viktor Polterovich, "Faktory korruptsii," *Ekonomika i Matematicheskie Metody* 34, no. 3 (1998): 30–39.
14. See Oleg Deripaska's interview with VIP-bulletin *Vremia Evrazii,* No. 2, 2006.

15. Viktor Polterovich, "Institutsional'nye lovushki i ekonomicheskie reformy," *Ekonomika i Matematicheskie Metody* 2, no. 35 (1999): 3–19.

16. For the recent debates on the influence of big money on democracy, see William Domhoffiam, *Who Rules America? Power and Politics* (Boston: McGraw-Hill, 2002); Thomas Rye, *Who Is Running America? The Bush Restoration* (Upper Saddle River, N.J.: Prentice Hall, 2002).

17. Robert Dahl, *On Political Equality* (New Haven, Conn.: Yale University Press, 2006); see also Stein Ringen, "Going Soft," *Times Literary Supplement*, November 3, 2006.

18. Lev Gudkov, "O negativnoi identifikatsii," *Monitoring Obshchestvennogo Mneniia*, VTSIOM 5, no. 49 (2000): 25–34.

19. Ibid.

20. Ibid.

21. Boris Dubin, "Zapad, granitsa, osobyi put': Simvolika 'drugogo' v politicheskoi mifologii sovremennoi Rossii," *Monitoring Obshchestvennogo Mneniia*, VTSIOM 6, no. 50 (2000): 35–44.

22. Having recognized this incongruity, a number of "liberal-minded" individuals from the educational establishment proposed that the teachers of Russian "literary arts" reinterpret the Russian classics. For instance, they suggested that readers of Radishchev should not "dwell" on the diatribes of the author, who was exiled by Catherine the Great, on the brazen inequality, and the need for revolution. The same people also advocated a "reserved" presentation of Gorky and Mayakovsky and wanted to abandon the study of Block's poem "Twelve," an ode to revolution (see Benedict Sarnov's interview with *Izvestiia*, October 24, 1997).

23. Gaidar failed to address social inequality in his many thick books on the social problems facing Russia. See his *Gosudarstvo i evoliutsiia* (Moscow: Eurasiia, 1995); *Dni porazhenii i pobed* (Moscow: Vagrius, 1996); *Anomaliia Ekonomichsekogo Rosta* (Moscow: Eurasiia, 1997); *Dolgoe vremia: Rossiia v mire* (Moscow: Delo, 2005); *Gibel' imperii: Uroki dlia sovremennoĭ Rossii* (Moscow: ROSSPĖN, 2006).

24. Gaidar, "Revoliutsiia ostalas' v 20 veke"; Gaidar, "Svoiu povinnost' otbyl."

25. The case of Pavel Borodin, a corrupt official who worked as the head of Kremlin property and was very close to both Yeltsin and Putin, clearly demonstrates the attitudes of Russian elites toward corruption. Borodin was arrested in New York in late 2000 at the request of a Swiss court for stealing money from the Russian state and laundering it in Switzerland. He was kept for a few months in a New York jail and then fined by the Swiss court. Because of lack of cooperation from the Moscow Office of the Prosecutor General, the Swiss court could not mete out a harsher sentence. Russian elites, including prominent cultural figures and famous liberals such as poet Andrei Voznesenskii, theater directors Oleg Tabakov and Galina Volchek, as well as the famous TV journalist Aleksandr Liubimov, without speaking of businesspeople and officials, almost unanimously supported Borodin and refused to recognize his complicity.

26. See Anatolii Chubais' interview with *Moskovskie Novosti,* July 29, 2002. For more about Chubais' views on social equality, see Vladimir Shlapentokh, "Sotsial'noe raventstvo i spravedlivost' v Rossii i Amerike," *Sotsiologicheskii Zhurnal,* No. 3–4, 1998.

27. See, for instance, A. N. Yakovlev's *Gor'kaia chasha* (Yaroslavl': Verkhnevolzhskoe Knizhnoe Izdatel'stvo, 1994). At the beginning of the book, the author touches upon the problems of social inequity, but only in connection with the French Revolution, and limits the discussion to political facets of the problem (p. 42). Further on in the book, this issue comes up only in the context of the author's cursory criticism of *uravnilovka*— wage equalization—which the author seems to equate with social equality and which he blames for "the bolshevism . . . that made the majority of the people dirt poor" (p. 281).

28. Aleksei Uliukaev, "Ne slushali Gaidara—poluchili krizis," *Izvestiia,* August 21, 1998. Viktor Loshak, the editor of *Moscow News,* a liberal weekly, seconding Uliukaev, accused the Russian people of blaming others to justify their inability to work (Viktor Loshak, "Ne pliui v kolodets," *Moskovskie Novosti,* September 15, 1998). In another article, Viacheslav Kostikov, formerly Yeltsin's press secretary, blasted the public for its limited vision of the past as "historical mythology with the images of heroes and scoundrels." He thoughtfully noted that "the people may be seduced and scared, but to think that the people have historical memory is as naive as to think that an agile rural accordion player can execute a passage from Schnittke" (a sophisticated postmodern composer) (Viacheslav Kostikov, "Soblazny i vyzovy natsional'noi diktatury," *Moskovskie Novosti,* September 8, 1998).

29. Koch was blunt in his assessment of the Russian people: "This long suffering people suffers for their own guilt. Nobody occupied them, nobody subjugated them. They tattled on each other (in the Soviet times) and nobody herded them into prisons and they shot each other at the firing squad." He claimed that the Russians had turned into "homo soveticus who does not want to work but keeps his mouth all the time open and wants bread and entertainment." See the text of this unusually revealing speech in Aleksandr Minkin, "Vlast' i sovest'," *Novaia Gazeta,* November 2, 1998.

30. See Boris Yeltsin, *Zapiski prezidenta* (Moscow: Ogonek, 1994).

31. Aside from Gaidar and his subordinates in his Institute of Transitional Economy (see, for instance, Viktor Mau, "Politicheskaia ekonomiia populizma," *Nezavisimaia Gazeta,* March 28, 1998; Aleksei Illarionov, "Tol'ko ekonomika obespechit liudiam dostoinuiu zhizn,'" *Izvestiia,* November 16, 1995), libertarian ideas were also supported by Larisa Piiasheva (see her article "Zhizn' vzaimy," *Izvestiia,* September 25, 1990).

32. Boris Nemtzov, "Sud'ba Rossii," *Nezavisimaia Gazeta,* March 17, 1998; see Nemtzov's interview with *Komsomol'skaia Pravda,* July 29, 1997, and with *Segodnia,* July 30, 1997; Andrei Denisov, "Korotkoe zamykanie," *Moskovskie Novosti,* February 3, 1998.

33. Nataliia Rostova, "Glamur kak natsional'naia ideia," *Novaia Gazeta*, May 17, 2006.

34. In 1990, Piiasheva wrote that she failed to comprehend why "the greater wealth of the new entrepreneurial class" should "lead to deteriorating material conditions of the low-income groups." Piiasheva apparently presumed that the standard of living of the "needy stratum" would automatically grow with the advent of a market economy (Larisa Piiasheva, "Zhizn' na zaemnoe vremia," *Izvestiia*, September 25, 1990).

35. See Aleksandr Yakovlev's interview with *Nezavisimaia Gazeta*, June 10, 1998.

36. See the following works by Vladimir Shlapentokh: "Four Russias," *The Tocqueville Review* 19, no. 1 (1998): 9–34; "Russian Patience: A Reasonable Behavior and a Social Strategy," *Archives Europeene de Sociologie* (*European Journal of Sociology*) 36, no. 2 (1995): 247–80; and "Social Inequality in Post Communist Russia: The Attitudes of the Political Elite and the Masses (1991–1998)," *Europe-Asia Studies* 51, no. 7 (1999): 1167–81.

37. For more on the deep-seated jealousy felt by the Russian elite toward the West, see Vladimir Shlapentokh, "Foreign Countries in the Russian Mind," *Communist and Post-Communist Studies* 31, no. 3 (1998): 119–216.

38. Nataliia Rostova, "Glamur kak natsional'naia ideia," *Novaia Gazeta*, May 17, 2006.

39. See, for instance, an article about the extremely lavish wedding of the daughter of the "Russian Sinatra" Iosif Kobzon, a financial mogul, singer, and politician who is notorious for his connections with the mafia (Vitalii Brodskii, "800 znatnykh gostei guliali na svad'be Kobzona," *Komsomol'skaia Pravda*, September 8, 1998).

40. See Rostova, "Glamur kak natsional'naia ideia."

41. Viacheslav Kostikov, "Otkachka zhira," *Argumenty i Fakty*, June 2, 2006.

42. Bozhena Rynska, "Pochem liubovnitsy oligarkhov," *Izvestiia, Nedelia,* September 1, 2006.

43. Mila Kuzina, "Kak otdykhaiut oligarkhi," *Moskovskii Komsomolets,* November 16, 2006.

44. Dmitrii Loginov and Alina Travina, "Intim s privkusom nikelia," *Moskovskie Novosti*, January 25, 2007.

45. Steven Lee Myers, "Russia's Extended Winter Holidays: A Binge of Drinking and Spending," *New York Times,* January 8, 2006.

46. Irina Lyshchitskaia, "Obruchal'nye kol'tsa okhrany," *Moskovskii Komsomolets,* March 20, 2006.

47. After the financial catastrophe of August 17, 1998, a journalist from the liberal Russian newspaper *Moskovskie Novosti* dared to suggest that the "New Russians" should move toward "voluntary self-restraint" in their consumption and "introduce a moratorium on feasts and luxury" and stop indulging in "scoundrel binges" (Dmitrii Radyshevskii, "Samoograniche-

nie kak programma—minimum," *Moskovskie Novosti,* September 27, 1998).

CHAPTER 6

1. See Department of Economics, "Kassovyi apparat," *Novaia Gazeta,* March 2, 2005; Yuliia Kalinina, "Chelovek s ogon'kom," *Moskovskii Komsomolets,* July 22, 2005; "Vek XXI: Ideologicheskie zametki," *Krasnaia Zvezda,* June 1, 2005.
2. Philippe Aries and George Dubuis, eds., *L'histoire de la vie privee* (Paris: Seuil, 1985, pp. 405–6).
3. Martin Wolfe, "French Views on Wealth and Taxes in the Middle Ages to the Old Regime," *The Journal of Economic History* 26, no. 4 (1966): 467, 470; John Heineman, *Royal Taxes in the Fourteenth Century France: The Development of War Financing, 1322–1356* (Princeton, N.J.: Princeton University Press, 1971).
4. Norman Cantor, *Civilization of the Middle Ages* (New York: Harper-Collins, 1993, p. 266).
5. Guy Fourquin, *Lordship and Feudalism in the Middle Ages* (London: G. Allen & Unwin, 1976, p. 25).
6. See Wolfe, "French Views on Wealth and Taxes," p. 470.
7. Vasilii Kliuchevskii, *Sochineniia v deviati tomakh,* vol. 2 (Moscow: Mysl', 1988, pp. 15–16); see also Sergei Solov'ev, *Istoriia Rossii s drevneishikh vremen* (St. Petersburg: Tovarishchestvo "Obshchestvennaia Pol'za," 1902).
8. Sergei Platonov, *Lektsii po Russkoi istorii* (Moscow: Vysshaia shkola, 1993, p. 160).
9. For Braudel's statement, see Pavel Lukin, *Narodnye predstavleniia o gosudarstvennoi vlasti v Rossii XVII veka* (Moscow: Nauka, 2000, p. 294).
10. Roughly two dozen luxurious country houses served Stalin before his death. Each house was on permanent alert, expecting a sudden visit from Stalin, yet he never even visited some of them (see Oksana Gerasimova, "Skromnoe obaianie generalissimusa," *Moskovskii Komsomolets,* September 4, 2006).
11. The Russian TV program "Vremia," ORT, January 4, 2000.
12. The luxurious lifestyle that Putin promised Yeltsin contrasted with the meager allowances meted out by Yeltsin to Gorbachev. After being humiliated by Yeltsin, Gorbachev was literally ousted from his home and residence the day after his resignation (see Elena Afanas'eva, "Kremlevskaia avos'ka," *Novaia Gazeta,* January 10, 2000; Igor' Domnikov, "Kak provozhaiut demokraty: Strana byla skupa, rasstavaias' s Gorbachevym," *Novaia Gazeta,* January 10, 2000).
13. Two articles in the Russian press predicted great success for this firm because, among other things, it had a reliable "roof" against rackets (see "Under the 'Roof' of Boris Nikolaevich: Warm and Clean," *Moskovskii*

Komsomolets, August 11, 1995; "The Kremlin Is Now a Very Profitable Place," *Komsomol'skaia Pravda,* August 15, 1995).

14. He had tremendous power and influence on the president. Such power had never been wielded by an individual holding such a position in the past, including the notorious general Nikolai Vlasik, who was the chief of Stalin's guard. According to surveys, Korzhakov was the fifth most influential person in Russian politics; see Aleksandr Korzhakov, *Boris Yel'tsin: Ot Rassveta Do Zakata* (Moscow: Interbuk, 1997).

15. See Aron Leon, *Yeltsin: A Revolutionary Life* (New York: Thomas Dunne Books/St. Martin's Press, 2000); Liliia Shevtsova, *Yeltsin's Russia: Myths and Reality* (Washington, D.C.: Carnegie Endowment for International Peace, 1999); Vladimir Solovyov and Elena Klepikova, *Boris Yeltsin: A Political Biography* (New York: Putnam, 1992); George W. Breslauer, *Gorbachev and Yeltsin as Leaders* (Cambridge: Cambridge University Press, 2002).

16. Vitalii Tret'iakov, "Instinkt vlasti," *Moskovskie Novosti,* March 2, 2006.

17. Dar'a Pyl'nova and Dmitrii Shkrylev, "Yakhty dlia prezidenta," *Novaia Gazeta,* May 30 (continued on June 2), 2005.

18. Yuliia Latynina, "Auktsion kak spetsoperatsiia," *Novaia Gazeta,* December 23, 2004; Viktor Gerashchenko's interview with *Novaia Gazeta,* December 27, 2004; Yuliia Latynina, "Esli v Rossii peredel sobstvennosti—eto k vyboram," *Novaia Gazeta,* May 15, 2003.

19. Garry Kasparov, "Say It in Russian: 'Caveat Emptor,'" *The Wall Street Journal,* December 21, 2004.

20. An interview with Sergei Dorenko on radio station *Ekho Moskvy,* August 29, 2005.

21. Stanislav Belkovskii, "Ukhod Putina ili mirnyi perevorot kak al'ternativa krovavoi revoliutsii," *Zavtra,* May 20, 2005.

22. Andrei Illarionov, "Drugaia strana," *Kommersant-Daily,* January 23, 2006.

23. "Kassovyi apparat," *Novaia Gazeta.*

24. Ibid.; Andrew Kramer and Steven Lee Myers, "The Business of Russia: Putin's Long Reach; Workers' Paradise Is Rebranded as Kremlin Inc.," *New York Times,* April 24, 2006.

25. Andrei Illarionov, "Avgust—2006," *Novaia Gazeta,* August 2, 2006.

26. See about Niiazov's obsession with wealth in Yegor Ligachev's interview with *Moskovskii Komsomolets,* July 12, 2005.

27. Latynina, "Auktsion kak spetsoperatsiia"; Latynina, "Ozhidaetsia padenie VVP," *Novaia Gazeta,* June 26, 2006.

Chapter 7

1. Nicholas V. Riasanovsky and Mark D. Steinberg, *A History of Russia,* 7th ed. (Oxford: Oxford University Press, 2004).

2. Aman Tuleev, a populist in Kuzbass, wrote that "regional isolationism is

perceived by local authorities, political leaders and industrialists as the single means of the salvation and defense of their interests" (Aman Tuleev, "Ne ver'te v ostrova protsvetaniia," *Pravda,* November 22, 1992).

3. Aleksei Titkov, "Umret li Moskva," *Nezavisimaia Gazeta,* July 10, 1993.

4. See Vladimir Shlapentokh, Roman Levita, and Mikhail Loiberg, *From Submission to Rebellion: The Province versus the Center in Russia* (Boulder, Colo.: Westview, 1997).

5. Ibid.

6. Lev Freinkman and Stepan Titov, *The Transformation of the Fiscal System in Russia: The Case of Iaroslavl* (Washington, D.C.: World Bank, 1994, pp. 6, 17); Radik Batyrshin, "Nalogovaia voina tsentra i regionov," *Nezavisimaia Gazeta,* September 1, 1993.

7. M. Sabirov, "My vnosim nalogi v federalnuiu kaznu," *Nezavisimaia Gazeta,* October 10, 1993.

8. Goskomstat, *Sotsial'noe polozhenie regionov Rossiiskoi Federatsii* (Moscow: Statistika Rossii, 1994, pp. 578–80); see Mikhail Nikolaev, "Vozvrata k proshlomu net," *Rossiiskaia Gazeta,* December 8, 1992.

9. See Sergei Glaz'ev, *Ekonomika i politika: Epizody bor'by* (Moscow: Gnosis, 1994, pp. 240–41); Vladimir Todres, "Sibir' voiuet za prava exportera," *Nezavisimaia Gazeta,* January 14, 1993.

10. For more on the Association of Eastern Territories, see L. Vardomskii, "Problemy i protivorechiia regional'nogo razvitiia Rossii," in *Rossiia i SNG: Dezintegratsionnye i integratsionnye protsessy,* ed. G. Kostinskii (Moscow: Institut Geografii, 1995, p. 55). For more on the Great Volga organization, see Aleksei Chirkin, "Povolzhskaia respublika: Plany i real'nost'," *Moe,* August 11, 1993.

11. See Artem Tarasov, "Pochemu kazhdyi tretii krasnoiarets golosoval za Zhirinovskogo," *Izvestiia,* December 18, 1993.

12. Alexander Afanas'ev, "Gubernator Sakhalina," *Komsomol'skaia Pravda,* October 23, 1992.

13. Nikolai Troitskii, "Brounovskoe dvizhenie v Rossii," *Moe,* July 21, 1993.

14. The draft, however, was rejected by the local Soviets (Radik Batyrshin, "Krai i oblasti trebuiut sebe prava respublik," *Nezavisimaia Gazeta,* March 20, 1993).

15. See Sergei Gutnik, "Sibiri ne po puti dazhe s 'demokraticheskoi: Rossiei,' " *Sibirskaia Gazeta,* No. 8, 1993.

16. Sergei Alekseev, "Provintsiia khochet svobody," *Izvestiia,* July 9, 1993.

17. A national survey conducted by the Agency of Regional Political Research (ARPI) in October 1999 asked respondents to list the most corrupt politicians in the country. Luzhkov ranked fourth behind Boris Yeltsin, Boris Berezovskii, and Anatolii Chubais (A. Milekhin and N. Popov, *Obshchestvennoe mnenie Rossii,* Moscow: ARPI, 2000, p. 673).

18. See Timothy Harper, *Moscow Madness: Crime, Corruption, and One Man's Pursuit of Profit in the New Russia* (New York: McGraw-Hill,

1999); Peter Reddaway and Dmitri Glinski, *The Tragedy of Russia's Reforms* (Washington, D.C.: United States Institute of Peace Press, 2000, pp. 469–71, 483).

19. Many governors followed the same line. In 2000–2001, the amalgamation of political power and wealth became obvious when Roman Abramovich, a notorious oligarch, was elected as the governor of Chukotka (Roman Orshanskii, "Chukotskie trilliony," *Moskovskii Komsomolets,* May 15, 2001), and Aleksandr Khloponin, another oligarch, became the governor of Taymyr (Valerii Konovalov, "Nachal'nik Taimyra," *Izvestiia,* May 18, 2001).

20. See the interview with Nikolai Travkin in *Literaturnaia Gazeta,* November 11, 1992.

21. A. Uglanov, "Razvalitsia li Rossiia," *Argumenty i Fakty,* January 13, 1993.

22. See Leonid Shebarshin, "Vopros o granites—eto vopros o vlasti," *Ogoniok,* June 25, 1993.

23. Andranik Migranian, "Bitva na rel'sakh v tupike," *Literaturnaia Gazeta,* October 28, 1992.

24. As suggested by Yurii Skokov, a prominent conservative politician, "The Russian people began to lose their place in history. They did not feel responsible for the state and became absorbed with their own private issues." He also deplored the connection with "the strengthening of political tendencies toward closed regional enclaves" (Yurii Skokov, "Strana u kriticheskoi cherty," *Nezavisimaia Gazeta,* April 22, 1995); see also Vladimir Shlapentokh, "Russia: Privatization and Illegalization of Social and Political Life," *Washington Quarterly* 19, no. 1 (1996): 65–85; Vladimir Shlapentokh, "Russian Patience: A Reasonable Behavior and a Social Strategy," *Archives Europeene de Sociologie* (European Journal of Sociology) 36, no. 2 (1995): 247–80.

25. Vox Populi, "Naibolee populiarnye politiki v Rossii v noiabre 1993," *Nezavisimaia Gazeta,* January 12, 1994.

26. VTSIOM, *Ekonomicheskie i sotsial'nye peremeny: monitoring obshchestvennogo mneniia. Informatsionnyi biulleten',* No. 1–6, 1994.

27. See, for instance, Yurii Levada, *Ot mnenii k ponimaniiu* (Moscow: VTSIOM, 2000); see also http://www.medialaw.ru/publications/books/war/1–4.html (accessed January 8, 2007).

28. Conversely, according to VTSIOM data, 74 percent were against keeping Chechnya in Russia (VTSIOM, Bulletin, April 1995).

29. Here are some examples of the headlines in the local press in January 1995: "Today Blood in Chechnya, Tomorrow in Briansk"; "If You Have Power You Do Not Need Brains"; "The March to Chechnya—The Last March" (see Nikolai Petrov, "Regiony ne bezmolvstvuiut," *Nezavisimaia Gazeta,* January 20, 1985).

30. See Vladimir Shlapentokh, "Moscow's Values: Masses and the Elite," in *Nation Building and Common Values in Russia,* ed. P. Kolst (Lanham, Md.: Rowman and Littlefield, 2003, pp. 217–38).

CHAPTER 8

1. Robert Fossier, ed., *The Cambridge Illustrated History of the Middle Ages* (*350–950*) (Cambridge: Cambridge University Press, 1990, p. 422).
2. Kira Latukhina, "Po gubernatoram udarila vertikal'," *Vedomosti*, August 11, 2006.
3. See Stanislav Belkovskii, "Posle tragedii," *Zavtra*, September 24, 2004.
4. Aleksandr Sevast'ianov, "Solo partiia," *Literaturnaia Gazeta*, December 31, 2005.
5. Sergei Surzhenko, Liliia Maikova, and Alla Barakhova, "Kreml' predlozhil Khazretu Sovmenu dorabotat' do otstavki," *Kommersant-Daily*, April 18, 2006.
6. Sevast'ianov, "Solo partiia."
7. Ibid.
8. Aleksandr Bugai, "Osobye otnosheniia: Novye realii," *Krasnaia Zvezda*, November 3, 2005; Elena Rudneva, Svetlana Ivanova, and Anastasiia Kornia, "Suverenitet za NDPI," *Vedomosti*, October 28, 2005.
9. Vera Postnova, "Tatarstan v ob'iatiiakh vakhkhabizma," *Nezavisimaia Gazeta*, November 30, 2004.
10. Svetlana Aleksandrova, "Eto nuzhno ne tol'ko Tatarstanu, no i vsei Rossii," *Gazeta*, March 28, 2005.
11. Sergei Ivlev, "Sam sebe Tatarstan," *Novye Izvestiia*, December 2, 2005.
12. See Vladimir Shlapentokh, Roman Levita, and Mikhail Loiberg, *From Submission to Rebellion: The Provinces versus the Center in Russia* (Boulder, Colo.: Westview, 1997).
13. Oleg Kashin, "Prikliucheniia russkikh v Rossii: Real'nye i mnimye," *Izvestiia*, February 1, 2007; Gul'chachak Khannanova and Il'shat Gainullin, "Bashkirskii iazyk stal obiazatel'nym," *Kommersant-Daily*, September 2, 2006.
14. Il'shat Gainullin, "Bor'ba za vlast': Bashkirskuiu oppozitsiiu zaderzhali dlia besedy," *Kommersant-Daily*, April 4, 2006.
15. Yurii Nikolaev and Nataliia Alekseeva, "Shaimievu dobavili srok: Samyi iz nepokornykh iz glav regionov stanovitsia naznachentsem," *Izvestiia*, March 14, 2005.
16. The Russian TV program "Osoboe Mnenie" on RTVI, July 3, 2006.
17. Yuliia Latynina, "Odin den' s khoziainom Chechni," *Novaia Gazeta*, September 27, 2006.
18. See an interview of the independent member of the State Duma Mikhail Zadornov with *Novaia Gazeta*, July 12, 2004; Vladimir Shlapentokh and Joshua Woods, "Cash Benefits Hazardous to Russia's Health," *The Moscow Times*, January 18, 2005.
19. Andrei Riabov, "Belye slobody i vertikal' vlasti," *Gazeta*, October 3, 2005.
20. Ibid.
21. See A. Sobianin and V. Sukhovol'skii, "Peizazh posle bitvy," *Otkrytaia Politika*, No. 1/2 (1996); Valentin Mikhailov, "Demoktatizatsiia Rossii:

Razlichnaia skorost' v regionakh (Analyz vyborov 1996 i 2000 gg)," *Democracy.ru,* November 11, 2006.

22. See Shlapentokh, Levita, and Loiberg, *Province versus Center in Russia.*

23. Sergei Dorenko's interview with *Ekho Moskvy,* January 30, 2007.

24. "Kak vozbuzhdali ugolovnye dela protiv gubernatorov," *Kommersant-Daily,* May 20, 2006.

25. Vladimir Terletskii, "Mer poskol'znulsia na zemle," *Nezavisimaia Gazeta,* July 16, 2006.

26. Mariia Rogacheva, Aleksandr Sazanov, and Valerii Kornev, "Voina ili spetsoperatsiia," *Izvestiia,* June 7, 2006; Aleksei Osipov, "Korruptsiia—tozhe business," *Novaia Gazeta,* July 9, 2006.

27. Yuliia Latynina, "Zakhvat: Segodniashnii peredel sobstvennosti—kak ekonomika voiny," *Novaia Gazeta,* March 26, 2001.

28. Raj Desai, Lev Freinkman, and Itzhak Golberg, "Fiscal Federalism in Regional Growth: Evidence from Russia," *Journal of Comparative Economics* 33, no. 4 (2005): 814–43.

29. Aleksei Tarasov, "Perpendikuliarnyie liudi," *Novaia Gazeta,* February 19, 2006.

30. Liudmila Butusova, "Zhiv'em brat' demonov!" *Moskovskie Novosti,* August 3, 2006.

31. Aleksandr Yagodkin, "Vesa Orel siadet v kletku," *Novaia Gazeta,* May 10, 2006.

32. See Liudmila Butusova, "Rabochaia dinastiia," *Moskovskie Novosti,* June 3, 2004.

33. Tat'iana Netreba and Tat'iana Bogdanova, "Chukotka—krai alchnykh chinovnikov," *Argumenty i Fakty,* August 9, 2006.

34. Ol'ga Kitova, "Gubernatorskie fondy," *Novaia Gazeta,* June 21, 2006.

35. Viacheslav Nikolaev, "Gubernator, kotoryi poet," *Rossiskie Vesti,* December 12, 2005.

36. Among the recent publications on the arbitrariness of governors, see an article about Krasnodar governor Aleksandr Tkachev (Irina Kirianova, "Naslednik po krivoi," *Literaturnaia Gazeta,* July 17, 2001).

37. Aleksei Chernyshev, "Zhurnalist Karaulov budet chest' znat'," *Kommersant-Daily,* October 9, 2003; Elena Sirotina, "Sud da delo: Gubernator Primor'ia otsudil u Kraulova $10 tysiach," *Komsomol'skaia Pravda,* October 9, 2003.

38. Tat'iana Skorobagat'ko, "Zasada na korruptsionerov: Stan', ministr, nevyezdnym," *Moskovskie Novosti,* May 28, 2004; "Sotrudnichat' s vlast'iu i davit' na nee," *Gazeta,* April 9, 2004; Aleksei Chernyshev, "Yurii," *Kommersant-Daily,* November 29, 2006.

39. Liudmila Butusova, "Ubiistvo obiavlennoe politicheskim," *Moskovskie Novosti,* November 30, 2006.

40. See Ol'ga Lazareva, "Sergei Ivanov ne otvechaet za syna," *Utro.ru,* March 28, 2006 (available at http://www.utro.ru/articles/2006/03/28/534654.shtml).

41. Michael Specter, "Planet Kirsan," *The New Yorker,* April 24, 2006.

42. See Sergei Riabinin, "V N'iu-Vasiukakh uzhe golodaiut," *Argumenty i Fakty,* June 23, 2004.

43. Anastasiia Matveeva, "Oni shli na dva sroka, a im govoryat: Vse, rebiata!" *Gazeta,* March 13, 2003.

44. In Orel and Kemerovo, for example, Governors Yegor Stroev and Aman Tuleev were elected without serious opposition, gaining about 95–97 percent of the votes.

45. See Svetlana Il'ina, "Stolichnyi mer i demokraty prazdnuiut kazhdyi svoiu pobedu," *Nezavisimaia Gazeta,* December 19, 1997.

46. The elections to 27 local parliaments in 1997 were indicative of this tendency. Almost everywhere the majority of the deputies turned out to be local directors and businesspeople. Representatives of political parties (with the exception of the Communists) in most cases could not get elected (Mikhail Afanas'ev, "Golos grazhdanskogo obshchestva stanovitsia vse tishe," *Izvestiia,* December 25, 1997).

47. Elena Rudneva and Kira Latukhina, "Spisok Dar'kina," *Vedomosti,* August 1, 2006.

48. Kira Vasil'eva, "Tvoriat nastoiashchii bespredel," *Novye Izvestiia,* September 7, 2006.

49. Natal'ia Rostova, "Svobody popugaiam," *Novaia Gazeta,* November 19, 2006.

50. Ol'ga Kondreva, "Tri zveta nashego vremeni," *Rossiiskaia Gazeta,* November 21, 2006.

51. Gul'chak Khannanova and Il'shat Gainullin, "Bor'ba za vlast'. Bashkirskomu zhurnalistu grozit desiat' let tiur'my za 'prizyvy k ekstremistskoi deiatel'nosti,'" *Kommersant-Daily,* May 10, 2006; Natal'ia Rostova, "Svideteli sniaty s plenki," *Novaia Gazeta,* November 19, 2006.

52. Pavel Gusev's interview with *Ekho Moskvy,* November 29, 2006.

53. See Shaimiev's interview with *Moskovskii Komsomolets,* January 19, 2007.

54. Boris Bronstein, "Shaimiev—dobryi angel mira," *Novaia Gazeta,* March 5, 2006.

CHAPTER 9

1. Vladimir Shlapentokh, *The Public and Private Life of the Soviet People* (New York: Oxford University Press, 1989).

2. Private plots accounted for 90 percent of potatoes, 77 percent of other vegetables, 52 percent of meat and poultry, and 45 percent of milk produced in Russia. On the whole, in 1996, private plots in Russia produced 46 percent of the agricultural products, against 26 percent in 1990. See Goskomstat Rossii, *Rossiyskii statisticheskii ezhegonik, 1997* (Moscow: Goskomstat Rossii, 1997, pp. 379–80); Caleb Southworth, "The Dacha Debate: Household Agriculture and Labor Markets in Post-Socialist Russia," *Rural Sociology* 71, no. 3 (2006): 451–78.

3. William Kingston, "Property Rights and the Making of Christendom," *Journal of Law and Religion* 9, no. 2 (1992): 372–73.

4. Paul Vinogradoff, "Feudalism," in *The Cambridge Medieval History,* vol. 3, ed. H. M. Gwatkin et al. (Cambridge: Cambridge University Press, 1957, pp. 458–84).

5. Robert Fossier, ed., *The Cambridge Illustrated History of the Middle Ages,* vol. 1 (Cambridge: Cambridge University Press, 1990, p. 445).

6. Kingston, "Property Rights and the Making of Christendom," pp. 379–81.

7. Christopher Dawson, *Religion and the Rise of Western Culture* (New York: Sheed & Ward, 1950, pp. 102, 170).

8. David Herlihy, *The History of Feudalism* (New York: Walker, 1971, p. 251).

9. Frederic Cheyette, "Suum cuique tribuere," *French Historical Studies* 6, no. 3 (1970): 287–99; Stephen White, "The Settlement of Dispute by Compromise in Eleventh Century Western France," *The American Journal of Legal History* 22, no. 4 (1978): 293.

10. Markus Fischer, "Feudal Europe, 800–1300: Communal Discourse and Conflictual Practices," *International Organization* 46, no. 2 (1992): 427–66.

11. T. I. Zaslavskaia, ed., *Kuda idet Rossiia.Vlast': Obshchestvo; Lichnost'* (Moscow: Vysshaia shkola sotsial'nykh i ekonomicheskikh nauk, 2000, pp. 307–9).

12. Goskomstat, *Sotsial'noe polozhenie regionov Rossiiskoi Federatsii* (Moscow: Goskomstat, 1994, pp. 578–80).

13. Yurii Levada, ed., *Est' mnenie* (Moscow: Progress, 1990, p. 282).

14. Yurii Levada, ed., *Prostoi Sovietskii chelovek* (Moscow: Intertsentr, 1993, p. 69).

15. VTSIOM, *Monitoring Obshchestvennogo Mneniia,* Bulletin No. 2, 1997.

16. Shlapentokh, *Public and Private Life of the Soviet People.*

17. Asked in 1998 about the cause of the Soviet collapse, only 20 percent of the Russian people pointed to the "inefficacy of the socialist system" (in 1995, the figure was 23 percent); 63 percent blamed the Soviet leaders (VTSIOM, *Monitoring Obshchestvennogo Mneniia,* No. 6, 1998, p. 14). The November 1998 survey conducted by the Fund of Public Opinion found that 48 percent of the Russians rejected capitalism as a good system for Russia and only 30 percent favored it (see Fund of Public Opinion, Bulletin, November 27, 1998, available at http://www.fom.ru/).

18. Vladimir Shlapentokh, *Soviet Public Opinion and Ideology: The Interaction between Mythology and Pragmatism* (New York: Praeger, 1986).

19. Yegor Gaidar, who was among those who advanced this theory, confounded the two periods (before 1985 and perestroika). Indeed, when Soviet society was in a state of collapse, the holders of power began grabbing state property. However, nothing like this happened before 1989. Gaidar's statements in *The State and Revolution* that "communist oligarchies were the grave diggers of the system" and that between 1953 and 1985 there were "invisible processes of preliminary privatization of property" (pp. 103, 107) were not supported by any empirical data and were fully fictitious. Numerous officials took bribes, but it had nothing to

do with their intentions to privatize state property, even if in "a preliminary form." What is more, most of the nomenklatura were hostile toward
privatization until 1989–1990. Gorbachev himself did not dare to use
the term "private property" until 1990 because of his fear of the nomenklatura. In fact, perestroika was orchestrated by one group of people and
benefited a different one. In any case, among the most notorious Russian
oligarchs, we do not know even one who, before 1989, was a member of
the high echelon of the Soviet bureaucracy. Ol'ga Kryshtanovskaia, the
best Russian expert on elites, in several publications, most notably her
brilliant book *The Anatomy of the Russian Elite* [*Anatomiia rossiiskoi
elity*] (Moscow: Zakharov, 2004), convincingly showed that privatization
with the participation of the nomenklatura started only in 1989.

20. After 1991, Gorbachev reminisced about "what a noisy reaction there
    was in the country when we uttered for the first time the words 'individ-
    ual property' and 'private property'" (see his interview with *Argumenty
    i Fakty*, September 3, 1997). There was no empirical evidence about the
    existence of the "pro capitalist coalition" (David Kotz and Fred Weir,
    Revolution from Above: The Demise of the Soviet System, London: Rout-
    ledge, 1997) inside the nomenklatura before 1985. As noted by Peter
    Rutland, the advocates of this theory tried to prove their case by identify-
    ing the beneficiaries of the transition, implying that they generated pere-
    stroika to further their material interests (Peter Rutland, "Explaining the
    Soviet Collapse," *Transition*, February 1998).

21. See the official description of the new cooperatives in the period of glas-
    nost in Valentin Kuznetsov, *Novye formy kooperatsii v SSSR* (Moscow:
    Mysl', 1990).

22. Peter Reddaway and Dmitri Glinski, *The Tragedy of Russia's Reforms:
    Market Bolshevism against Democracy* (Washington, D.C.: United States
    Institute of Peace Press, 2001).

23. Kupriianova Zoia and Liudmila Khakhulina, "Predprinimatel'skaia
    deiatel'nost' kak osnovnaia i dopolnitel'naia rabota," VTSIOM, *Moni-
    toring Obshchestvennogo Mneniia*, No. 2, 1998, p. 22.

24. Nataliia Zorkaia, ed., *Obshchestvennoe Mnenie, Ezhegodnik, 2003*
    (Moscow: VTSIOM, 2003, p. 42).

25. Zorkaia, *Obshchestvennoe Mnenie, Ezhegodnik, 2003*, p. 41.

26. Fund of Public Opinion, Bulletin, August 9, 2000 (available at http://
    www.fom.ru).

27. Yurii Borisov, "Istoki i smysl rossiiskogo reida," *Rossiiskaia Gazeta*, July
    25, 2006; see also Yurii Borisov, "Reiderstvo—eto kupit' na grosh pi-
    atakov," *Izvestiia*, July 21, 2006.

28. Borisov, "Reiderstvo—eto kupit' na grosh piatakov."

29. Andrew Hacker, *The Corporation Take-Over* (Garden City, N.Y.: Anchor
    Books, 1965).

30. Daniil Dondurei, "Kommentarii," *Novaia Gazeta*, April 16, 2006.

31. El'vira Goriukhina, "Tovarishchestvo moshennikov na paiakh?" *Novaia
    Gazeta*, June 3, 2006.

32. El'vira Goriukhina, "Prokuror obedal u linii 'Fronta,'" *Novaia Gazeta,* October 22, 2006.
33. Viacheslav Shugaev, "Zalivnoe po-sibirski," *Novaia Gazeta,* December 13, 2006.
34. See an article by an expert on Russian raiding: Borisov, "Reiderstvo—eto kupit' na grosh piatokov."
35. Ibid.; see Sabrina Tavernise, "Handful of Corporate Raiders Transform Russia's Economy," *New York Times,* August 13, 2002.
36. Aleksandr Travin, "Reidery: Kak eto delaetsia," *Novaia Gazeta,* April 23, 2006.
37. See Neil Buckley and Arkady Ostrovsky, "Back in Business—How Putin's Allies Are Turning Russia into a Corporate State," *Financial Times,* June 19, 2006.
38. Owen Matthews and Anna Nemtsova, "The New Feudalism: Forget Corruption. In Putin's Russia, the Nexus of Payoffs and Patronage Is Almost Medieval, Touching Every Aspect of Life," *Newsweek International,* October 23, 2006.
39. Shugaev, "Zalivnoe po-sibirski."
40. Nikolai Donskov, "Zachem na miasokombinate golovorezy," *Novaia Gazeta,* September 24, 2006.
41. Aleksandr Dobrovinskii, "Seti vystavleny na shchetchik," *Novaia Gazeta,* April 20, 2006; Anton Gus'kov, "Reiderskie naezdy," *Novaia Gazeta,* April 23, 2006.
42. Mikhail Agarkov, "Konfiskatsiia kak natsional'nyi vid sporta," *Novaia Gazeta,* June 14, 2006.
43. Konstantin Poleskov, "V cul'ture dazhe ne zastoi, a nedvizhimost'," *Novaia Gazeta,* April 16, 2006.
44. Matthews and Nemtsova, "The New Feudalism."
45. Ibid.
46. Ivan Bystrov, "Zloe Butovo," *Moskovskaia Pravda,* October 18, 2006.
47. Andrew E. Kramer and Steven Lee Myers, "The Business of Russia: Putin's Long Reach; Workers' Paradise Is Rebranded as Kremlin Inc.," *New York Times,* April 24, 2006.
48. Aleksei Polukhin, "Rodnoe gosudarstvennoe," *Novaia Gazeta,* March 15, 2006.
49. Ibid.
50. Grigorii Yavlinsky's interview with *Izvestiia,* January 23, 2007.
51. See, for instance, Viacheslav Nikonov, "Kto budet sleduiushchim prezidentom: Original'nyi prognoz," *Izvestiia,* January 25, 2007.

Chapter 10

1. For a similar view, see Mikhail Afanas'ev, "Nevynosimaia slabost' gosudarstva," *Otechestvennye Zapiski,* No. 2, 2004, p.4; Jacques Godbout, *Le Don, la Dette et l'Identité: Homo Donator vs Homo Oeconomicus* (Paris: La Découverte/MAUSS, 2000).

2. Adam Bellow, *In Praise of Nepotism: A Natural History* (New York: Doubleday, 2003); see Brendan Conway, "The New Nepotism," *Public Interest,* Winter 2004.

3. Fund of Public Opinion, Bulletin, November 30, 2006.

4. Andrei Konchalovskii, "Mafiia? Kak eto po–russki," *Argumenty Nedeli,* November 9, 2006.

5. The evolution in the selection of cadres in the USSR had a tremendous impact on life in Soviet society. In the first period of Soviet history, in the aftermath of the revolution (1920s), the selection of cadres was based on devotion to the cause of the revolution, and the apparatchiks considered themselves as shareholders in a common business. In the next period, with the installation of Stalin's cruel totalitarianism, it depended on their loyalty to the leader and whether they looked like "soldiers of the party." After Stalin's death and during the softening of the regime, the selection of cadres became influenced by personal loyalty to the individual party bosses, which lowered the quality of cadres and their performance and opened the way for corruption. The rise in the education level of cadres somewhat countervailed the negative effect of the "personalization" of cadres policy; see Vladimir Shlapentokh, *Soviet Ideologies in the Period of Glasnost: Responses to Brezhnev's Stagnation* (New York: Praeger, 1988).

6. Afanas'ev, "Nevynosimaia slabost' gosudarstva," p. 3.

7. See Maksim Glikin, "Yukosizatsiia rossiiskoi politiki," *Nezavisimaia Gazeta,* July 15, 2005.

8. See the most recent anthropological publications on kinship: J. Carsten, *After Kinship* (Cambridge: Cambridge University Press, 2004); L. Holy, *Anthropological Perspectives on Kinship* (Chicago: Pluto Press, 1996); R. Parkin, *Kinship: An Introduction to Basic Concepts* (Oxford: Blackwell, 1997).

9. See David Buss and Douglas Kenrik, "Evolutionary Social Psychology," in *Handbook of Social Psychology,* vol. 2, ed. Daniel T. Gilbert, Susan T. Fiske, and Gardner Lindzey (Oxford: Oxford University Press, 1989, p. 985); Douglas Kenrik, Josh Ackerman, and Suzan Ledlow, "Evolutionary Social Psychology: Adaptive Predisposition and Human Culture," in *Handbook of Social Psychology,* vol. 1, ed. John Delamater (New York: Springer, 2006, pp. 105–97).

10. W. D. Hamilton, "Genetical Evolution of Social Behavior," *Journal of Theoretical Biology* 7, no. 1 (1962): 1–16.

11. Richard Dawkins, *The Selfish Gene* (New York: Oxford University Press, 1976).

12. C. Wright Mills, *The Power Elite* (New York: Oxford University Press, 1956).

13. Ben Fine, *Social Capital versus Social Theory: Political Economy and Social Science at the Turn of the Millennium* (London: Routledge, 2001).

14. Mark Granovetter, "The Strength of Weak Ties," *American Journal of Sociology* 78, no. 6 (1973): 1360–80.

15. He defines social capital as the aggregate of the actual or potential

resources that are linked to the possession of a durable network of more or less institutionalized relationships, underscoring, at the same time, that these relations are based on mutual acquaintance and recognition. See Pierre Bourdieu, "The Forms of Capital," in *Handbook of Theory and Research for the Sociology of Education,* ed. J. G. Richardson (New York: Greenwood Press, 1986, pp. 241–58).

16. Robert Putnam, *Bowling Alone: The Collapse and Revival of American Community* (New York: Simon and Schuster, 2000).

17. See, for instance, Richard Grassby, *Kinship and Capitalism: Marriage, Family, and Business in the English-Speaking World, 1580–1740* (New York: Woodrow Wilson Center Press and Cambridge University Press, 2001); Naomi Tadmor, *Family & Friends in Eighteenth-Century England: Household, Kinship, Patronage* (New York: Cambridge University Press, 2001); P. Fleming, *Family and Household in Medieval England* (New York: Palgrave Macmillan, 2000).

18. Max Weber, *Essays in Economic Sociology,* ed. Richard Swedberg (Princeton, N.J.: Princeton University Press, 1999, p. 179).

19. See, for instance, Heidi Hartman, "Capitalism, Patriarchy and Job Segregation by Sex," *Signs* 1, no. 3 (1976): 137–69.

20. Milton Friedman, *Capitalism and Democracy* (Chicago: University of Chicago Press, 1962).

21. See among recent publications, Jeff Bailey, "Family Hands Off Its Business and Its Philosophy," *New York Times,* February 24, 2007.

22. Loyiso Mbabane, "Crony Capitalism and Black Economic Empowerment," *Mail and Guardian,* March 26, 2004.

23. Paul Vinogradoff, "Feudalism," in *The Cambridge Medieval History,* vol. 3, ed. H. M. Gwatkin et al. (Cambridge: Cambridge University Press, 1957, pp. 458–84).

24. For more about the role of kinship in tribal society, see Lewis Henry Morgan, *Systems of Consanguinity and Affinity of the Human Family* (Washington, D.C.: Smithsonian Institution, 1870). For a structuralist perspective, see Claude Lévi-Strauss, *Structural Anthropology,* translated from the French by Claire Jacobson and Brooke Grundfest Schoepf (New York: Basic Books, 1963); Miriam Glucksmann, *Structuralist Analysis in Contemporary Social Thought: A Comparison of the Theories of Claude Lévi-Strauss and Louis Althusser* (London: Routledge & K. Paul, 1974).

25. Meyer Fortes, *Kinship and the Social Order* (Chicago: Aldine, 1969).

26. Vasilii Kliuchevskii, *Sochineniia v deviati tomakh,* vol. 2 (Moscow: Mysl', 1988, pp. 112–30).

27. Stalin did this, for instance, with respect to the Kaganovich family in the 1930s-1940s, when three of the brothers held high positions in the Soviet hierarchy (Lazar was a member of the politburo, Mikhail, a minister in the air industry, and Yulii, the deputy of the minister of foreign trade). The fourth brother, Aron, held a lower position as the head of a trust that united leather factories in Kiev, while Lazar's wife Mariia was the

head of a trade union in the textile industry (Stuart Kahan, *The Wolf of the Kremlin*, New York: W. Morrow, 1987).

28. See Stalin's speech at the Seventeenth Party Congress in 1934 (*Voprosy Leninizma*, Moscow: Politizdat, 1952).

29. Among the most known cases was the high role of Aleksandr Adzhubei, Khrushchev's son-in-law, as the editor of a leading newspaper (see R. Adzhubei, V. Akhlomov, and V. Belikov, *Aleksei Adzhubei v korridorakh chetvertoi vlasti*, Moscow: Izvestiia, 2003) and of Yurii Churbanov, Brezhnev's son-in-law, as deputy minister of internal affairs and his son as deputy minister of foreign trade (Sergei Nikolaevich Semanov, *Brezhnev: Pravitel' "zolotogo veka,"* Moscow: Veche, 2004).

30. Sergei Morozov, *Zagovor protiv narodov Rossii segodnia* (Moscow: Algoritm, 1999). Golutvina Oksana Gaman, "Svoi sredi svoikh," *Literaturnaia Gazeta*, July 4, 2006.

31. Nikolai Ryzhkov, *Desiat' let velikikh potriasenii* (Moscow: Assotsiatsiia "Kniga, prosveshchenie, miloserdie," 1995).

32. Boris Z. Rumer, *Soviet Central Asia: "A Tragic Experiment"* (Boston: Unwin Hyman, 1989); Eric McGlinchey, *Paying for Patronage: Regime Change in Post-Soviet Central Asia* (Princeton, N.J.: Princeton University Press, 2003). For more about the role of clans in Turkmenistan, see Adrienne Lynn Edgar, *Tribal Nation: The Making of Soviet Turkmenistan* (Princeton, N.J.: Princeton University Press, 2004).

33. Kathleen Collins, *Clan Politics and Regime Transition in Central Asia* (New York: Cambridge University Press, 2006); Edward Schatz, *Modern Clan Politics: The Power of "Blood" in Kazakhstan and Beyond* (Seattle: University of Washington Press, 2004); Olivier Roy, *New Central Asia: The Creation of Nations* (New York: New York University Press, 2000); Pauline Jones Luong, ed., *The Transformation of Central Asia: States and Societies from Soviet Rule to Independence* (Ithaca, N.Y.: Cornell University Press, 2004); Boris Rumer, ed., *Central Asia in Transition: Dilemmas of Political and Economic Development* (Armonk, N.Y.: M. E. Sharpe, 1996).

34. Among recent publications on honor in the Middle Ages and in contemporary society, see James Bowman, *Honor: A History* (New York: Encounter Books, 2006); Vladimir Shlapentokh, *Love, Marriage, and Friendship in the Soviet Union: Ideals and Practice* (New York: Praeger, 1984); Vladimir Shlapentokh, *Public and Private Life of the Soviet People: Changing Values in Post-Stalin Russia* (New York: Oxford University Press, 1989).

35. Levada-Tsentr, *Press-vypusk*, May 1, 2005; Nina Zorkaia, ed., *Obshchestvennoe mnenie: Ezhegodnik* (Moscow: Levada-Tsentr, 2004, pp. 41–42).

36. ROMIR's survey in February 2005 suggested that 43 percent of the public trusted the president; 16 percent, the church; 14 percent, the army; 8 percent, the government; 7 percent, trade unions; 7 percent, the media; 5 percent, law enforcement agencies; 4 percent, the State

Duma; 4 percent, local authorities; 2 percent, the Council of the Federation; 2 percent, political parties; 33 percent, nobody. See ROMIR, Bulletin, March 17, 2005; see also data from the World Values Survey in Ronald Inglehart et al., eds., *Human Beliefs and Values* (Buenos Aires: Siglo Veintiuno Editors, 2004).

37. VTSIOM, *Press-vypusk,* March 3, 2001.

38. A. Golov, "Uverennost' v zavtrashnem dne: 2000–2004," Levada-Tsentr, *Press-vypusk,* July 13, 2004.

39. Katy Marton, *Hidden Power* (New York: Pantheon, 2001).

40. See the interview of Khrushchev's daughter Rada with *Argumenty i Fakty,* January 18, 2007 (available at http://www.peoples.ru/state/politics/hruschov).

41. With regard to Brezhnev's wife Viktoriia, see Aleksei Bukin, "Dobryi chelovek iz Politbiuro," *RIA Novosti,* January 19, 2007.

42. See Raisa Gorbacheva, *I Hope* (New York: HarperCollins, 1991).

43. Leonid Sedov, "Sostoianie obshchestvennogo soznaniia," Levada-Tsentr, March 6, 2001.

44. Aleksandr Khinstein, *Yeltsin: Kreml'; Istoriia bolezni* (Moscow: OLMA, 2006); Aleksandr Korzhakov, *Boris Yel'tsin: Ot rassveta do zakata* (Moscow: Interbuk, 1997).

45. See "Nekotorye podrobnosti iz zhizni pervogo prezidenta Rossii," www.corruption.ru (accessed May 16, 2001).

46. Aleksandr Khinshtein, "Milliony D'iachenko," *Moskvoskii Komsomolets,* December 16, 1999.

47. Dmitrii Gornostaev, "Klinton sprosil Yel'tsina, bral li on vziatki," *Nezavisimaia Gazeta,* September 9, 1999; see "Sledovateli izuchaiut bankovskie shcheta docheri Yel'tsina," *Lenta.ru,* September 21, 1999.

48. Yurii Shchekochikhin, "U dochki—dachka?" *Novaia Gazeta,* October 11, 1999.

49. See, for instance, "Sem'iu Yel'tsina privlekut k rasseldovaniiu po delu Mabeteks," *Lenta.ru,* October 5, 1999.

50. See Aleksandr Komozin, "100 vedushchikh politikov Rossii v dekabre 1999," *Nezavisimaia Gazeta,* December 31, 1999.

51. Khinstein, *Yel'tsin: Kreml'; Istoriia bolezni*; Korzhakov, *Boris Yel'tsin.*

52. See more about the circumstances of Putin's ascension to power in Richard Sakwa, *Putin: Russia's Choice* (London: Routledge, 2004); Peter Baker and Susan Glasser, *Kremlin Rising: Vladimir Putin's Russia and the End of Revolution* (New York: Scribner, 2005).

53. In the last months of 2006 and in the first months of 2007, several analysts predicted that Putin would choose as his successor, if he decided not to violate the constitutional rule of two terms and leave the Kremlin in 2008, two or even three candidates for his position. In this case, it would be the electorate that supposedly made the choice. But even if this prediction came true (75 percent of the listeners of radio station *Ekho Moskvy* thought so on January 20, 2007), it was the consensus that

none of the other candidates would have the opportunity for honest competition. See Leonid Tomin, "2008: Snova 'moment istiny,'" http://centurion-center.narod.ru/preem.html (accessed January 21, 2007); Evgenii Kisilev's radio program "Power," *Ekho Moskvy*, January 20, 2007.

54. Marguerite Yourcenar, *Memoirs of Hadrian*, translated from the French by Grace Frick in collaboration with the author (New York: Farrar, Straus and Young, 1954).

55. Kisilev, "Power," January 21, 2006.

56. Oleg Poptsov, *Khronika vremen "tsaria Borisa"* (Moscow: Sovershenno Sekretno, 1995).

57. See Levada-Tsentr, *Press-vypusk,* January 19, 2000.

58. Fund of Public Opinion, Bulletin, May 26, 1999.

59. Levada-Tsentr, Bulletin, July 24, 2000.

60. The Kremlin elaborated a malicious election strategy through the media. During the campaign, two major Russian TV stations (ORT and RTR) literally spent hours each day denigrating two of Putin's rivals, Primakov and Luzhkov, in the most aggressive ways. As a rule, the stations never gave the two politicians a chance to answer the allegations. ORT and RTR not only destroyed Putin's enemies but also promoted the progovernmental block "Unity" along with its leaders and other blocks that proclaimed their support for Putin and the Chechen War. The Kremlin also relied on law enforcement agencies to demoralize and intimidate its enemies. Several governors who advocated the Primakov-Luzhkov block succumbed to the Kremlin's weakly veiled threats to cut off financial aid for their reelection campaign if they did not change sides and support Putin (see Nadia Kevorkova, "Za chto Boris Yel'tsin prosil proshchenia u rossiian," *Nezavisimaia Gazeta,* January 11, 2000; see also the interview with Viktor Minin, a Moscow political scientist, in *Novaia Gazeta,* January 17, 2000; Boris Krotkov, "Dve versii otstavki Yel'tsina," *APN,* January 12, 2000).

61. Michael McFaul, *Russia's Unfinished Revolution: Political Change from Gorbachev to Putin* (London: Cornell University Press, 2001, pp. 335–37).

62. Donald Barry, *Russian Politics: Post-Soviet Phase* (New York: Peter Lang, 2002, pp. 124–26).

63. See Graeme Gill's "Vladimir Putin and the Future of Presidency" (pp. 24–26), Leslie Holmes' "Introduction" (pp. 1–2), and Peter Shearman's "Personality, Policies and Power: Foreign Policy under Putin" (p. 223) in *Russia after Yeltsin,* ed. Vladimir Tikhomirov (Aldershot, England: Ashgate, 2001).

64. Joel Ostrow, "Leadership, Democracy and Society: Books about Russia 10 Years after the Fall," *Europe-Asia Studies* 54, no. 8 (2002): 1342.

65. See "Proekt Rossiia," *Glavnaia Tema,* November 2005.

66. See Andrei Zolotov, Jr., "Monarchist Past and Future," *Russia Profile,*

September 28, 2006; political scientist Georgii Satarov's interview with radio station *Ekho Moskvy,* January 20, 2007.

67. Fund of Public Opinion, Bulletin, September 14, 2000.

68. VTSIOM, *Press-vypusk,* September 25, 2006.

69. See Yuliia Kalinina, "Ritual'noe opuskanie," *Moskovskii Komsomolets,* October 24, 2006.

70. Aleksandr Budberg, "Geroi momenta," *Moskovskii Komsomolets,* October 20, 2006.

71. Ol'ga Kryshtanovskaia, *Anatomiia rossiĭskoĭ ëlity* (Moscow: Zakharov, 2005).

72. Aleksei Mukhin, *Putin: Blizhnii krug prezidenta* (Moscow: Algoritm, 2005); Aleksei Mukhin, *Kto est' mister Putin i kto s nim prishel? Dos'e na prezidenta Rossii i ego spetssluzhby* (Moscow: Izd-vo "Gnom i D," 2002).

73. Kryshtanovskaia, *Anatomiia rossiĭskoĭ ëlity.*

74. The Department of Economics, "Ozhidaetsia nastuplenie na fondy i banki 'veteranov' spetssluzhb," *Novaia Gazeta,* September 20, 2006.

75. Levada-Tsentr, Bulletin, July 24, 2000.

76. Marshall Goldman, *Lost Opportunity: Why Economic Reforms in Russia Have Not Worked* (New York: W. W. Norton, 1994); Marshall Goldman, "Kapitalizm insaiderov: Uspekh ili neudacha," *Problemy Teorii i Prakitiki Upravleniia,* No. 3, 1997.

77. Yegor Gaidar, *Days of Defeat and Victory* (Seattle: University of Washington Press, 1999); Yegor Gaidar, *Gosudarstvo i evoliutsiia: Kak otdelit' sobstvennost' ot vlasti i povysit' blagosostoianie rossiian* (St. Petersburg: Izd-vo Norma, 1997); Yegor Gaidar, *Gibel' imperii: Uroki dlia sovremennoi Rossii* (Moscow: ROSSPĖN, 2006).

78. See *Privatizatsiia v Rossii: Sbornik normativnykh dokumentov i materialov,* vol. 1 (Moscow: Yuridicheskaia Literatura, 1993); A. Radygin, *Rossiiskaia privatizatsiia kak protsess formirovaniia institutsional'noi bazy ekonomicheskikh reform* (Moscow: Institut ekonomicheskikh problem perekhodnogo perioda, 1998).

79. Vladimir Shlapentokh, "Privatization Debates in Russia: 1989–1992," *Comparative Economic Studies* 35, no. 2 (1993): 19–32; Peter Reddaway and Dmitri Glinski, *The Tragedy of Russia's Reforms: Market Bolshevism against Democracy* (Washington, D.C.: United States Institute of Peace Press, 2001).

80. There were three main ways of privatization: selling stocks on the open market, selling stocks only or mostly to employees, or leave the enterprise in the collective property of employees (see more in *Privatizatsiia v Rossii,* vol. 1).

81. Goldman, "Kapitalizm insaiderov."

82. Reddaway and Glinski, *Tragedy of Russia's Reforms;* Andrew Scott Barnes, *Owning Russia: The Struggle over Factories, Farms, and Power* (Ithaca, N.Y.: Cornell University Press, 2006).

83. Roy Medvedev, *Chubaĭs i vaucher: Iz istorii rossiĭskoĭ privatizatsii* (Moscow: Izd-vo "Impëto," 1997); for more about the role of private

connections in the formation of the fortune of Boris Berezovskii, see Yulii Dubov's novel *Bolshaia paika* (Moscow: Vagrius, 1999).

84. See Frank Hornig et al., "Western Companies Fight for Press Freedom in Moscow," *Spiegel*, December 14, 2006.

85. Florian Hassel, "Vse ostaetsia v sem'e," *Frankfurter Rundschau*, May 21, 2001 (translated by the online source www.inopressa.ru).

86. "Chernomyrdin i synov'ia," *Itogi*, January 30, 2001.

87. Aleksei Polukhin, "Den'gi khodiat kak poteriannye," *Nezavisimaia Gazeta*, February 2, 2006; "Elitnye deti," *Izvestiia*, *Nedelia*, September 22, 2006. For more about the positions of the relatives of other Russian politicians, such as Boris Gryzlov, the Speaker of the State Duma, Mikhail Zurabov, the minister of health services and social issues, and Liubov' Sliska, the Deputy Speaker of the State Duma, see "Kto oni, brat'ia politikov?" *Argumenty i Fakty*, November 10, 2006.

88. Aleksandr Khinstein, "Glavnei vsego—dokhody v dome," *Moskovskii Komsomolets*, November 29, 2006.

89. Gul'chak Khannanova and Anna Skorniakova, "Bashneft' vernulas' v sem'iu," *Kommersant-Daily*, May 25, 2006; Oleg Rubnikovich, "Bash na neft'," *Gazeta*, August 15, 2006.

90. Marat Musoev, "Vorovstvo na doverii," *Nasha Versiia*, August 14, 2006.

91. Danila Galperovich, "Otmena poroga: Chinovniki budut golosovat' za sebia," *Svoboda*, November 9, 2006.

92. VTSIOM, *Press-vypusk*, June 23, 2006.

93. Fund of Public Opinion, Bulletin, June 29, 2006.

94. Fund of Public Opinion, Bulletin, December 28, 2006.

95. See data from Ebert's Fund at http://www.fesmos.ru/Pubikat/13_Elita%20economics2004/elita_econom_5.html (accessed January 25, 2007).

96. VTSIOM, Bulletin, July 28, 2006.

97. See Afanas'ev, "Nevynosimaia slabost' gosudarstva"; Liliia Shevtsova, ed., *Rossiia politicheskaia* (Moscow: Moscow Carnegie Center, 1988, p. 149); E. Avraamova, "Vliianie sotsial'no-politicheskikh faktorov na formirovanie politicheskogo soznaniia," in *Obshchestvo: Stanovlenie demokraticheskikh tsennostei?* ed. M. Maklol and A. Raibovm Rossiiakoe (Moscow: Moscow Carnegie Center, 1999, p. 23).

98. Simon Romero, "Expanding Power Puts Family of Venezuelan President under Increasing Scrutiny," *New York Times*, February 18, 2007.

99. See Bellow, *In Praise of Nepotism*; also see *Corporate Affairs: Nepotism, Office Romance, and Sexual Harassment* (Washington, D.C.: Bureau of National Affairs, 1988).

100. Paul Ginsborg, *Italy and Its Discontents: Family, Civil Society, State, 1980–2001* (New York: Palgrave Macmillan, 2003); Alexander Stille, "Italy: The Family Business," *The New York Review of Books*, October 9, 2003.

CHAPTER 11

1. Marc Bloch, *Feudal Society* (Chicago: University of Chicago Press, 1964).
2. Charles Tilly, "War-Making and State-Making as Organized Crime," in *Bringing the State Back*, ed. Peter Evans, Trich Reuschmeyer, and Theda Skocpol (Cambridge: Cambridge University Press, 1985, pp. 170–71); Tilly's text was also cited in Timothy Fry, "Private Protection Organizations in Russia and Poland," *American Journal of Political Science* 46, no. 3 (2002): 575.
3. Bisson Jones, *Cultures of Power: Lordship, Status and Process in Twelfth-Century Europe* (Philadelphia: University of Pennsylvania Press, 1995).
4. Paul Vinogradoff, "Feudalism," in *The Cambridge Medieval History*, vol. 3, ed. Henry Gwatkin et al. (Cambridge: Cambridge University Press, 1957, pp. 458–84).
5. Fry, "Private Protection Organizations in Russia and Poland," pp. 574–82; Max Weber, *Theory of Social Organization* (New York: Free Press, 1964, p. 154).
6. Jonathan Hay and Andrei Shleifer, "Private Enforcement of Public Law: A Theory of Legal Reform," *American Economic Review* 88, no. 2 (1998): 398–403; Vadim Volkov, "Violent Entrepreneurship in Post-Communist Russia," *Europe-Asia Studies* 51, no. 5 (1999): 751–54; Curtis J. Milhaupt and Mark D. West, "The Dark Side of Private Ordering: An Institutional and Empirical Analysis of Organized Crime," *The University of Chicago Law Review* 67, no. 1 (2000): 41–98; Federico Varese, *The Russian Mafia: Private Protection in a New Market Economy* (Oxford: Oxford University Press, 2001, p. 55).
7. See the history of private protection in Frederick Lane, *Profit from Power: Reading in Protection Rent and Violence-Controlling Enterprise* (Albany: State University of New York Press, 1963). Lane talked about the protection rent from a monopoly, even if it was temporary and local, which was enjoyed by the protector as well as the protected.
8. Fry, "Private Protection Organizations in Russia and Poland," pp. 574–82.
9. Ibid.; Peter Reuter, *Disorganized Crimes: The Economics of the Visible Hand* (Cambridge: MIT Press, 1983); Varese, *Russian Mafia*; Simon Johnson, Daniel Kaufmann, and Andrei Shleifer, "The Unofficial Economy in Transition," *Brookings Papers on Economic Activity* 1997, no. 2 (1998): 159–239; Timothy Fry and Ekaterina Zhuravskaya, "Rackets, Regulation and the Rule of Law," *Journal of Law, Economics, and Organization* 16, no. 2 (2000): 478–502; Simon Johnson et al., "Why Do Firms Hide? Bribes and Unofficial Activity after Communism," *Journal of Public Economics* 76, no. 3 (2000): 495–520; Jim Leitzel, Clifford Gaddy, and Michael Alexeev, "Mafiosi and Matrioshki: Organized Crime and Russian Reform," *Brookings Review* 13 (Winter 1995): 26; Andrei Shleifer and Robert W. Vishny, "Corruption," *Quarterly Journal of Economics* 108, no. 3 (1993): 602.

10. Vadim Volkov, *Violent Entrepreneurs: The Use of Force in the Making of Russian Capitalism* (Ithaca, N.Y.: Cornell University Press, 2002, pp. 18–21, 25).

11. Fry, "Private Protection Organizations in Russia and Poland," p. 582.

12. According to Vladimir Semichastnyi, former head of the KGB, in the 1960s and 1970s, personal guards had only been used for the members of the politburo—no more than 11 or 12 people (see Vladimir Semichastnyi, "Mne nesterpimo bol'no," *Zavtra,* June 28, 1997).

13. The European Bank for Reconstruction and Development, *Annual Report,* 1997, p. 74, available at http://www.ebrd.org/.

14. Oleg Gladunov, Igor' Veletminskii, and Tat'iana Konishcheva, "Pokushenie na bankovskuiu tainu," *Rossiiskaia Gazeta,* September 15, 2006.

15. A foreigner in the middle of the 1990s who did not know the meaning of such terms as "affirmative action" or "political correctness" had no chance of understanding life in contemporary America. It was the same in Bolshevik Russia after the revolution. Without knowing the meaning of such important political terms as "kulak," "class enemy," or "capitalist encirclement," one would have had no idea about what was going on in Russia through the decades. Post-Communist Russia had its own lexicon, which, in contrast to the past, came not from new politicians, but from underground slang. Among these phrases, the most popular was *krysha,* best translated into English as "roof." This term became widespread in post-Communist Russia and could be found in all Russian newspapers and broadcasting media, central and local. It would be difficult to explain many of the important developments in contemporary Russia without it.

16. Varese, *Russian Mafia.*

17. Fry, "Private Protection Organizations in Russia and Poland," p. 577.

18. Frye and Zhuravskaya, "Rackets, Regulation, and the Rule of Law."

19. The government serves as a roof for Gazprom, a gigantic company that has a monopoly on the extraction and sale of oil and gas. Another case of a roof being offered by the state was the financial complex Most headed by Vladimir Gusinskii. The roof of this company was Moscow mayor Luzhkov, who used city resources for his private gains. As also happens in the underground world, another powerful body, the presidential guard headed by Aleksandr Korzhakov, tried to demonstrate to Most that the roof offered by Luzhkov was not strong enough to protect it. An armed struggle took place in the spring of 1995 between Most and the Moscow police on the one hand and Korzhakov's people on the other hand. The conflict captured the public's attention and stood as an evident example of the struggle between two roofs.

20. Lev Gudkov and Boris Dubin, "Privatizatsiia politsii," *Vestnik Obshchestvennogo Mneniia* 1, no. 81 (2006): 69; see O. Kolennikova, L. Kosals, and R. Ryvkina, "Kommertsialitsiia sluzhebnoi deiatel'nosti militsii," *Sotsiologicheskie Issledovaniia* 1 (2004): 73–83.

21. A successful doctor with a private office in central Moscow once told me a typical story about roof. When several members of an organized crime

family visited him offering roof, he gave them two telephone numbers. One was that of the city police captain and the other was of the leader of another criminal gang in the area, the so-called Solntsevo Gang. His unwanted guests were given the opportunity to choose between retreat or challenging their rivals in providing roof. They later returned to his office with an apology.

22. In 1997, Igor' Sundiev, vice president of the Russian Criminological Association, contended that "in Russia, it is difficult to find banks which do not have criminal roofs" (Igor' Sundiev, "Krov' i nerv kriminal'nogo mira," *Literaturnaia Gazeta,* August 27, 1997).

23. As Kovalev said, one of the biggest banks in Russia almost completely imitated the composition of the Moscow regional branch of the FSB (Nikolai Kovalev, "My otbrosili britanskuiu razvedku na 20 let nazad," *Nezavisimaia Gazeta,* December 19, 1997).

24. In order to hide this new move in the process of privatization of security services, the Duma deputies treated the new security bodies not as private protective agencies but as the units known in the Soviet times as "external services of the Ministry of Internal Affairs," which were subordinate not only to this ministry but also to the heads of the enterprises that these armed guards protected. However, the judicial subterfuge hardly could hide the feudal tendencies in security in Russia. For this reason, several experts, among them Emil Pain, indicated that the decision to "arm" corporations will have many nefarious consequences for the country (see Ivan Rodin and Mikhail Moshkin, "Gazprom i Transneft' vooruzhaiutsia," *Nezavisimaia Gazeta,* March 2, 2007).

25. Rodin and Moshkin, "Gazprom i Transneft' vooruzhaiutsia"; Russian TV, TVC, "The News," August 29, 2006; Steven Myers and Mark Landler, "Intrigues over Spy's Death Spreads to Germany," *New York Times,* December 11, 2006.

26. Volkov, *Violent Entrepreneurs,* p. 135.

27. TVC, "The News."

28. Nadezhda Popova, "U nas vse s 'shikom,'" *Moskovskii Komsomolets,* June 15, 2005.

29. Mikhail Kazakov, "Za zemliu rublevskuiu," *Rossiia,* June 15, 2006.

BIBLIOGRAPHY

Ackoff, Russel. *Re-creating the Corporation*. New York: Oxford University Press, 1999.

Adzhubei, R., V. Akhlomov, and V. Belikov. *Aleksei Adzhubei v korridorakh chetvertoi vlasti*. Moscow: Izvestiia, 2003.

Anderson, Annelise. "The Red Mafia: A Legacy of Communism." In *Economic Transition in Eastern Europe and Russia: Realities of Reform,* edited by Edward Lazear, pp. 340–66. Stanford, Calif.: Hoover Institution Press, 1995.

Anderson, Perry. *Passage from Antiquity to Feudalism*. London: Verso, 1974.

Angell, Carole S. *Celebrations around the World: A Multicultural Handbook*. Golden, Colo.: Fulcrum, 1996.

Aries, Philippe, and George Dubuis, eds. *L'histoire de la vie privee*. Paris: Seuil, 1985.

Aristotle. *The Politics and the Constitution of Athens*. Cambridge: Cambridge University Press, 1884.

Audretsch, David B., and Charles F. Bonser, eds. *Globalization and Regionalization: Challenges for Public Policy*. Boston: Kluwer, 2002.

Avraamova, E. "Vliianie sotsial'no-politicheskikh faktorov na formirovanie politicheskogo soznaniia." In *Obshchestvo: Stanovlenie demokraticheskikh tsennostei?* edited by M. Maklol and A. Raibovm Rossiiakoe. Moscow: Moscow Carnegie Center, 1999.

Babbies, Earl. *Sociology: An Introduction*. Belmont, CA: Wadsworth, 1983.

Backman, Clifford. *The Worlds of Medieval Europe*. Oxford: Oxford University Press, 2003.

Baker, Peter, and Susan Glasser. *Kremlin Rising: Vladimir Putin's Russia and the End of Revolution*. New York: Scribner, 2005.

Barnes, Andrew Scott. *Owning Russia: The Struggle over Factories, Farms, and Power*. Ithaca, N.Y.: Cornell University Press, 2006.

Barry, Donald. *Russian Politics: Post-Soviet Phase*. New York: Peter Lang, 2002.

Beck, Ulrich, and Jane Wiebel. *The Normal Chaos of Love*. Oxford: Polity Press, 1995.

Bellow, Adam. *In Praise of Nepotism: A Natural History*. New York: Doubleday, 2003.

Belyaeva, L. A. "Dinamika sotsialnoi stratifikatsii v period reform." In Zaslavskaia, *Kuda idet Rossiia.Vlast'*, pp. 243–53.

Benedict, Ruth. *Patterns of Culture*. New York: Houghton Mifflin, 1934.

Berger, Suzanne. *How We Compete: What Companies around the World Are Doing to Make It Today's Global Economy.* New York: Doubleday, 2006.

Berstein, S. *Démocraties, régimes autoritaires et totalitarismes au XXe siècle.* Paris: Hachette, 1992.

Blank, Stephen. "Russian Democracy: From the Future to the Past." *Demokratizatsiia* 1, no. 3 (1998): 550–77.

Bloch, Marc. *Feudal Society.* Chicago: University of Chicago Press, 1961.

Bloch, Marc, and Léopold Benjamin. *Feudal Society.* Translated from the French by L. A. Manyon. Foreword by M. M. Postan. Chicago: University of Chicago Press, 1961.

Blockmans, W. "Patronage, Brokerage and Corruption as Symptoms of Incipient State Formation in the Burgundian-Habsburg Netherlands." In *Klientelsysteme im Europa der Frahen Neuzeit,* edited by A. Maczak, pp. 117–26. Munich: R. Oldenbourg, 1988.

Blondel, Jean. *Introduction to Comparative Government.* New York: Harper, 1990.

Borejsza, Jerzy W., and Klaus Ziemer. In cooperation with Magdalena Huas. *Totalitarian and Authoritarian Regimes in Europe: Legacies and Lessons from the Twentieth Century.* New York: Berghahn Books, 2006.

Bornstein, Morris. *Comparative Economic Systems: Models and Cases.* Burr Ridge, Ill.: Irwin, 1994.

Bourdieu, Pierre. "The Forms of Capital." In *Handbook of Theory and Research for the Sociology of Education,* edited by J. G. Richardson, pp. 241–58. New York: Greenwood Press, 1986.

Braginski, Serge Vladimirovich. *Incentives and Institutions: The Transition to a Market Economy in Russia.* Princeton, N.J.: Princeton University Press, 2000.

Breslauer, George. "Evaluating Gorbachev and Yeltsin as Leaders." In Brown and Shevtsova, *Gorbachev, Yeltsin and Putin,* pp. 45–66.

———. *Gorbachev and Yeltsin as Leaders.* Cambridge: Cambridge University Press, 2002.

Brooks, Stephen, ed. *The Challenge of Cultural Pluralism.* Westport, Conn.: Praeger, 2002.

Brown, Archie. "Introduction." In Brown and Shevtsova, *Gorbachev, Yeltsin, and Putin,* pp. 6–8.

———. "Vladimir Putin's Leadership in Comparative Perspective." In Ross, *Russian Politics under Putin,* pp. 4–14.

Brown, Archie, and Liliia Shevtsova, eds. *Gorbachev, Yeltsin and Putin: Political Leadership in Russia's Transition.* Washington, D.C.: Carnegie Endowment for International Peace, 2001.

Brown, Elisabeth. "The Tyranny of a Construct: Feudalism and Historians of Medieval Europe." *American Historical Review* 79, no. 4 (1974): 1063–88.

Buchanan, James, Robert Tollison, and Gordon Tullock, eds. *Toward a Theory of the Rent Seeking Society.* College Station: Texas A&M University Press, 1980.

Buravoy, Mikhail, and Pavel Krotov. "The Soviet Transition from Socialism to Capitalism." *American Sociological Review* 57, no. 1 (1992): 16–38.

Burgess, Michael. *Comparative Federalism: Theory and Practice*. London: Routledge, 2006.

Buss, David, and Douglas Kenrik. "Evolutionary Social Psychology." Chap. 9 in *Handbook of Social Psychology*, vol. 2, edited by Daniel T. Gilbert, Susan T. Fiske, and Gardner Lindzey. Oxford: Oxford University Press, 1989.

Cantor, Norman. *Civilization of the Middle Ages*. New York: HarperCollins, 1993.

Carnoy, Martin. *The State and Political Theory*. Princeton, N.J.: Princeton University Press, 1984.

Carsten, J. *After Kinship*. Cambridge: Cambridge University Press, 2004.

Cheyette, Frederic. "Suum cuique tribuere." *French Historical Studies* 6, no. 3 (1970): 287–99.

Chinball, Marjorie. *Anglo-Norman England, 1066–1166*. Oxford: Blackwell, 1986.

Clark, William. "Crime and Punishment in Soviet Officialdom, 1965–1990." *Europe-Asia Studies* 45, no. 2 (1993): 257–77.

Cocherham, William. *Health and Social Change in Russia and Eastern Europe*. New York: Routledge, 1999.

Collins, Kathleen. *Clan Politics and Regime Transition in Central Asia*. New York: Cambridge University Press, 2006.

Colton, Timothy, and Michael McFaul. "Putin and Democratization." In Herspring, *Putin's Russia*, pp. 13–38.

Colton, Timothy, and Robert Tucker, eds. *Patterns in Post-Soviet Leadership*. Boulder, Colo.: Westview, 1995.

Coulanges, Fustel de. *Histoire des Institutions Politique de Lncienne*. Paris: Hachette, 1923.

Coulloudon, Virginie. "Putin's Anticorruption Reforms." In Herspring, *Putin's Russia*, pp. 85–100.

Cramer, John. "Political Corruption in the USSR." *Western Political Quarterly* 30, no. 2 (1977): 213–24.

Crick, Bernard. *Basic Forms of Government*. London: Macmillan, 1973.

Curtis, Mikhail, Jean Blondel, and Bernard E. Brown. *Introduction to Comparative Government*. New York: Harper, 1990.

Dahl, Robert, ed. *On Political Equality*. New Haven, Conn.: Yale University Press, 2006.

———. *Political Opposition in Western Democracies*. New Haven, Conn.: Yale University Press, 1968.

———. *Polyarchy: Participation and Opposition*. New Haven, Conn.: Yale University Press, 1971.

Dakhin, V. N. "Nekotorye voprosy analiza rossiiskoi vlasti." In Zaslavskaia, *Kuda idet Rossiia.Vlast'*, pp. 101–5.

Danilov, V. P. "Rossiiskaia vlast' v 20 veke." In Zaslavskaia, *Kuda idet Rossiia.Vlast'*, pp. 6–10.

Davies, R. W. *Soviet History in the Yeltsin Era*. New York: St. Martin's Press, 1997.

Davis, Natalie. *The Gift in Sixteenth-Century France*. Madison: University of Wisconsin Press, 2000.

Dawkins, Richard. *The Selfish Gene*. New York: Oxford University Press, 1976.

Dawson, Christopher. *Religion and the Rise of Western Culture*. New York: Sheed & Ward, 1950.

Dean, Trevor. *Crime in Medieval Europe, 1200–1550*. New York: Longman, 2001.

Desai, Raj, Lev Freinkman, and Itzhak Golberg. "Fiscal Federalism in Regional Growth: Evidence from Russia." *Journal of Comparative Economics* 33, no. 4 (2005): 814–43.

Domhoffiam, William. *Who Rules America? Power and Politics*. Boston: McGraw-Hill, 2002.

Domrin, Alexander N. *The Limits of Russian Democratisation: Emergency Powers and States of Emergency*. London: Routledge, 2006.

Douglas, David Charles. *The Norman Achievement, 1050–1100*. London: Eyre & Spottiswoode, 1969.

Dreiser, Theodore. *The Financier*. Cleveland, Ohio: World Publishing, 1967.

———. *The Stoic*. Cleveland, Ohio: World Publishing, 1952.

———. *The Titan*. Cleveland, Ohio: World Publishing, 1925.

Dubov, Yulii. *Bol'shaia paika*. Moscow: Vagrius, 2002.

Dubuis, Pierre. *Les vifs, les morts et le temps qui court: Familles valaisannes, 1400–1550*. Lausanne, Switzerland: Section d'histoire, Faculté des lettres, Université de Lausanne, 1995.

Duby, Georges. *Féodalités*. Paris: Presses universitaires de France, 1998.

Duhamel, Luc. "Justice and Politics in Moscow, 1083–1986: Ambartsumyan's Case." *Euro-Asia* 52, no. 7 (2000): 1307–29.

Durkheim, Emile. *The Division of Labor in Society*. Translated from the French by George Simpson. Glencoe, Ill.: Free Press, 1960.

———. *Les règles de la méthode sociologique*. Paris: Felix Alcan, 1927.

Duus, Peter. *Feudalism in Japan*. New York: McGraw-Hill, 1993.

Eitzen, Stanley, and Maxine Baca Zinn. *In Conflict and Order: Understanding Society*. Boston: Allyn and Bacon, 1993.

Ericson, Richard E. *Post-Soviet Russian Economic System—an Industrial Feudalism*. Helsinki: Bank of Finland Institute for Economies in Transition, 2000.

Fadeeva, O. "Neformal'naia zaniatost' v sibirskom sele." *Ekonomicheskaia Sotsiologiia* 2 (2001): 61–93.

Fair, K. E., and R. C. Fair. *Principles of Micro Economics*, 4th ed. Upper Saddle River, N.J.: Prentice Hall, 1996.

Federico, Varese. *The Russian Mafia: In a New Market Economy*. Oxford: Oxford University Press, 2001.

Fedotova, V. *Modernizatsiia Drugoi Evropy*. Moscow: IF RAN, 1997.

Fichter, Joseph. *Sociology*. Chicago: The University of Chicago Press, 1971.

Finckenauer, James O., and Yuri A. Voronin. *The Threat of Russian Organized Crime*. Washington, D.C.: U.S. Dept. of Justice, Office of Justice Programs, National Institute of Justice, 2001.

Fine, Ben. *Social Capital versus Social Theory: Political Economy and Social Science at the Turn of the Millennium*. London: Routledge, 2001.

Fish, Michael Steven. *Democracy Derailed in Russia: The Failure of Open Politics*. New York: Cambridge University Press, 2005.

Fitzgerald, F. Scott. *The Great Gatsby*. New York: Columbia University Press, 1999.

Fleming, P. *Family and Household in Medieval England*. New York: Palgrave Macmillan, 2000.

Fortes, Meyer. *Kinship and the Social Order*. Chicago: Aldine, 1969.

Fossier, Robert, ed. *The Cambridge Illustrated History of the Middle Ages*. Vol. 1. Cambridge: Cambridge University Press, 1990.

Fourquin, Guy. *Lordship and Feudalism in the Middle Ages*. London: G. Allen & Unwin, 1976.

Freinkman, Lev, and Stepan Titov. *The Transformation of the Fiscal System in Russia: The Case of Iaroslavl*. Washington, D.C.: World Bank, 1994.

Friedman, Milton. *Capitalism and Democracy*. Chicago: University of Chicago Press, 1962.

———. *Free to Choose: A Personal Statement*. New York: Harcourt Brace Jovanovich, 1980.

Frisby, David. "Simmel." In *The Cambridge Dictionary of Sociology*, edited by Bryan Turner, pp. 551–53. Cambridge: Cambridge University Press, 2006.

Frisby, Tania. "The Rise of Organized Crime in Russia: Its Roots and Social Significance." *Europe-Asia Studies* 50, no. 1 (1998): 27–49.

Fry, Timothy. "Private Protection Organizations in Russia and Poland." *American Journal of Political Science* 46, no. 3 (2002): 574–82.

Fry, Timothy, and Ekaterina Zhuravskaya. "Rackets, Regulation and the Rule of Law." *Journal of Law, Economics, and Organization* 16, no. 2 (2000): 478–502.

Fukuyama, Francis. *The End of History and the Last Man*. New York: Free Press, 1992.

Furet, François, and Denis Richet. *French Revolution*. Translated by Stephen Hardman. New York: Macmillan, 1970.

Gaidar, Egor. *Anomaliia Ekonomichsekogo Rosta*. Moscow: Eurasiia, 1997.

———. *Days of Defeat and Victory*. Seattle: University of Washington Press, 1999.

———. *Dolgoe vremia: Rossiia v mire; Ocherki ekonomicheskoi istorii*. Moscow: Delo, 2005.

———. *Gibel' imperii: Uroki dlia sovremennoĭ Rossii*. Moscow: ROSSPĖN (Rossiĭskaia politicheskaia ėntsiklopediia), 2006.

———. *Gosudarstvo i evoliutsiia*. Moscow: Eurasiia, 1995.

———. *Gosudarstvo i evoliutsiia: Kak otdelit' sobstvennost' ot vlasti i povysit' blagosostoianie rossiian*. St. Petersburg: Izd-vo Norma, 1997.

———. *Time of Turmoil and Defeat*. Moscow: Vagrius, 1996.

Galeotti, Marc. *Russian and Post-Soviet Organized Crimes.* Brookfield, Vt.: Ashgate, 2002.

Gaman-Golutvina, O. V. "Biurokratiia ili oligarkhiia." In Zaslavskaia, *Kuda idet Rossiia.Vlast'*, pp. 162–72.

Ganshof, François-Lois. *Feudalism.* New York: Harper and Row, 1964.

Gauvard, Claude. "Fear of Crime in Late Medieval France." In Hanawalt and Wallace, *Medieval Crime and Social Control,* pp. 1–48.

Geis, Gilbert, and Robert Meier. *White Collar Crime.* New York: Free Press, 1977.

Gilinskii, Yakov. *Organizatsionnaia prestupnost' v Rossii: Teoriia i real'nost'.* St. Petersburg: Institut Sotsiologii RAN, 1996.

Ginsborg, Paul. *Italy and Its Discontents: Family, Civil Society, State, 1980–2001.* New York: Palgrave Macmillan, 2003.

Glucksmann, Miriam. *Structuralist Analysis in Contemporary Social Thought: A Comparison of the Theories of Claude Lévi-Strauss and Louis Althusser.* London: Routledge & K. Paul, 1974.

Godbout, Jacques. *Le Don, la Dette et l'Identité: Homo Donator vs Homo Oeconomicus.* Paris: La Découverte / MAUSS, 2000.

Goldman, Marshall. *Lost Opportunity: Why Economic Reforms in Russia Have Not Worked.* New York: W. W. Norton, 1994.

Golovshchinskii, K. I., S. A. Parkhomenko, V. L. Rimskii, and G. A. Satarov. *Bizness i korruptsiia: Problemy protivodeistviia; Itogovyi otchet.* Moscow: INDEM, 2004.

Gorbacheva, Raisa. *I Hope.* New York: HarperCollins, 1991.

Gordon, Leonard, and Patricia Harvey. *Sociology and American Social Issues.* Dallas, Tex.: Houghton, 1978.

Granovetter, Mark. "The Strength of Weak Ties." *American Journal of Sociology* 78, no. 6 (1973): 1360–80.

Grassby, Richard. *Kinship and Capitalism: Marriage, Family, and Business in the English-Speaking World, 1580–1740.* New York: Woodrow Wilson Center Press and Cambridge University Press, 2001.

Gray, John. *Enlightenment's Wake: Politics and Culture at the Close of the Modern Age.* London: Routledge, 1995.

———. *Liberalism Edition,* 2nd ed. Buckingham: Open University Press, 1995.

Greenberg, Stanley. *The Two Americas: Our Current Political Deadlock and How to Break It.* New York: Thomas Dunne Books, 2004.

Gurevich, Aron. *Genesis feudalisma v zapadanoi Evrope.* Moscow: Vysshaia shkola, 1970.

Hall, John. "Feudalism in Japan: Reassessment." *Comparative Studies in History and Society* 5, no. 1 (1962): 15–51.

Hamilton, W. D. "Genetical Evolution of Social Behavior." *Journal of Theoretical Biology* 7, no. 1 (1962): 1–16.

Hanawalt, Barbara A., and David Wallace, eds. *Medieval Crime and Social Control.* Minneapolis: University of Minnesota Press, 1999.

Handelman, Stephen. *Comrade Criminal: Russia's New Mafia.* New Haven, Conn.: Yale University Press, 1995.

Harper, Timothy. *Moscow Madness: Crime, Corruption, and One Man's Pursuit of Profit in the New Russia.* New York: McGraw-Hill, 1999.

Harrington, Michael. *The Other America: Poverty in the United States.* New York: Macmillan, 1969.

Hayek, Friedrich A. *The Constitution of Liberty.* Chicago: University of Chicago Press, 1978.

Hechter, Michael. *Containing Nationalism.* Oxford: Oxford University Press, 2000.

Hedlund, Stephen. *Russia's Market Economy: A Bad Case of Predatory Capitalism.* London: University College London Press, 1999.

Heilbroner, Robert L. *The Nature and Logic of Capitalism.* New York: Norton, 1985.

Heineman, John. *Royal Taxes in the Fourteenth Century France: The Development of War Financing, 1322–1356.* Princeton, N.J.: Princeton University Press, 1971.

Herlihy, David. *The History of Feudalism.* New York: Walker, 1971.

Herspring, Dale, ed. *Putin's Russia: Past Imperfect, Future Uncertain.* Lanham, Md.: Rowman, 2003.

Hollander, Paul. *Political Will and Personal Beliefs: The Decline and the Fall of Soviet Communism.* New Haven, Conn.: Yale University Press, 1999.

Holy, L. *Anthropological Perspectives on Kinship.* Chicago: Pluto Press, 1996.

Horowitz, Irving, and May Strong. *Sociological Realities.* New York: Harper, 1971.

Huskey, Eugene. "Political Leadership and the Center-Periphery Struggle: Putin's Administrative Reforms." In Brown and Shevtsova, *Gorbachev, Yeltsin, and Putin,* pp. 126–34.

Il'in, V. I. "Metodologicheskie problemy analiza klassovoi struktury." In Zaslavskaia, *Kuda idet Rossiia.Vlast',* pp. 265–71.

Inglehart, Ronald, Miguel Basanez, and Alejandro Moreno, eds. *Human Beliefs and Values.* Buenos Aires: Siglo Veintiuno Editors, 2004.

Ivanov, E. P., ed. *Istoriia otechestva: Porblemy, vzgliady, liudi.* Pskov, Russia: Pskov State Pedagogical Institute, 2005.

Ivanovich Ryzhkov, Nikola. *Desiat let velikikh potriaseniĭ.* Moscow: Assotsiatsiia "Kniga, prosveshchenie, miloserdie," 1995.

Jack, Andrew. *Inside Putin's Russia.* Oxford: Oxford University Press, 2004.

Jackal, Robert. "Crimes in the Suites." *Contemporary Sociology* 9, no. 3 (1980): 354–71.

Jackman, Robert. *Power without Force: The Political Capacity of Nation-States.* Ann Arbor: University of Michigan Press, 1993.

Janin, Hunt. *Medieval Justice: Cases and Law in France, England, and Germany, 500–1500.* Jefferson, N.C.: McFarland, 2004.

Johnson, Simon, Daniel Kaufmann, John McMillan, and Christopher

Woodruff. "Why Do Firms Hide? Bribes and Unofficial Activity after Communism." *Journal of Public Economics* 76, no. 3 (2000): 495–520.

Johnson, Simon, Daniel Kaufmann, and Andrei Shleifer. "The Unofficial Economy in Transition." *Brookings Papers on Economic Activity* 1997, no. 2 (1998): 163–69.

Jonathan, Hay, and Andrei Shleifer. "Private Enforcement of Public Law: A Theory of Legal Reform." *American Review Papers and Proceedings* 88, no. 2 (1998): 398–403.

Jones, Bisson. *Cultures of Power: Lordship, Status and Process in Twelfth-Century Europe.* Philadelphia: University of Pennsylvania Press, 1995.

Kahan, Stuart. *The Wolf of the Kremlin.* New York: W. Morrow, 1987.

Karstedt, Susanne. "Knights of Crime: The Premodern Structures." In *Social Dynamics of Crime and Control: New Theories for a World in Transition,* edited by Susanne Karstedt and Kai-D Bussmann, pp. 53–68. Oxford: Hart Publishing, 2000.

Katseneliboigen, Aron. "Color Markets in the Soviet Union." *Soviet Studies* 29, no. 1 (1977): 62–85.

Kenrik, Douglas, Josh Ackerman, and Suzan Ledlow. "Evolutionary Social Psychology: Adaptive Predisposition and Human Culture." In *Handbook of Social Psychology,* edited by John Delamater. New York: Springer, 2006.

Khakhulina, L. A. "Srednii klass v Rossii: Mify i real'nost'." In Zaslavskaia, *Kuda idet Rossiia.Vlast',* pp. 79–93.

Khinstein, Aleksandr. *Yeltsin: Kreml'; Istoriia bolezni.* Moscow: OLMA, 2006.

Khlebnikov, Paul. *The Godfather of the Kremlin: Boris Berezovsky and the Looting of Russia.* New York: Harcourt, 2000.

Kingston, William. "Property Rights and the Making of Christendom." *Journal of Law and Religion* 9, no. 2 (1992): 372–81.

Kliuchevskii, Vasilii. *Sochineniia v deviati tomakh.* Vol. 2. Moscow: Mysl', 1988.

Klugman, Jeffry. "The Psychology of Soviet Corruption, Undiscipline and Resistance to Reform." *Political Psychology* 7, no. 1 (1986): 67–82.

Kolesnikov, Andre. *Vladimir Vladimirovich Putin: Mezhdu Evropoĭ i Azieĭ.* Moscow: Ëksmo, 2005.

Kontorovich, Vladimir, and Vladimir Shlapentokh. *Organizational Innovation, the Carl Beck Papers.* Pittsburgh, Pa.: University of Pittsburgh Press, 1986.

Korzhakov, Alexander. *Boris Yeltsin: Ot Rassveta Do Zakata.* Moscow: Interbuk, 1997.

Kotz, David, and Fred Weir. *Revolution from Above: The Demise of the Soviet System.* London: Routledge, 1997.

Krouse, Joseph Douglas. *Kremlin Capitalism: The Privatization of Russian Economy.* Ithaca, N.Y.: Cornell University Press, 1997.

Krueger, Anne. "The Political Economy of the Rent-Seeking Society." *American Economic Review* 64, no. 3 (1974): 291–303.

Kryshtanovskaia, Ol'ga. *Anatomiia rossiĭskoĭ ėlity.* Moscow: Zakharov, 2005.

———. *The Anatomy of the Russian Elite.* Moscow: Zakharov, 2004.

Kukushkin, Yurii, ed. *Istoriia SSSR: Epokha sotsializma.* Moscow: Vysshaia shkola, 1985.

Kuper, Leo, and M. G. Smith, eds. *Pluralism in Africa.* Berkeley: University of California Press, 1969.

Kuznetsov, Valentin. *Novye formy kooperatsii v SSSR.* Moscow: Mysl', 1990.

Lane, David. "The Economic Legacy: What Putin Had to Deal with and the Way Forward." In Ross, *Russian Politics under Putin,* pp. 95–113.

Lane, Frederick. *Profit from Power: Reading in Protection Rent and Violence-Controlling Enterprise.* Albany: State University of New York Press, 1963.

Latynina, Yuliia. *Hunting Manchurian Deer.* Moscow: Ėksmo, 2003.

———. *Okhota na Iziubria.* Moscow: Ėksmo, 2005.

———. *Steel King.* Moscow: Olma Press Ekslibris, 2002.

Le Goff, Jacques. *Medieval Civilization, 400–1500.* Translated by Julia Barrow. Oxford: Blackwell, 1988.

Leitzel, Jim, Clifford Gaddy, and Michael Alexeev. "Mafiosi and Matrioshki: Organized Crime and Russian Reform." *The Brookings Review* 13 (Winter 1995): 26–29.

Lemon, Alaina. " 'Your Eyes Are Green Like Dollars': Counterfeit Cash, National Substance, Currency Apartheid in 1990s Russia." *Cultural Anthropology* 13, no. 1 (1998): 22–55.

Lenin, Vladimir. *Sobranie Sochinenii,* 4th ed. Vol. 32. Moscow: Politizdat, 1951.

Leon, Aron. *Yeltsin: A Revolutionary Life.* New York: Thomas Dunne Books / St. Martin's Press, 2000.

Levada, Yurii, ed. *Est' mnenie.* Moscow: Progress, 1990.

———. "Obshchestvennoe mnenie i obshchestvo na pereput'iakh 1999 goda." In Zaslavskaia, *Kuda idet Rossiia.Vlast',* pp. 147–62.

———, ed. *Prostoi Sovietskii chelovek.* Moscow: Intertsentr, 1993.

Lévi-Strauss, Claude. *Structural Anthropology.* Translated from the French by Claire Jacobson and Brooke Grundfest Schoepf. New York: Basic Books, 1963.

Light, Donald, and Suzanne Keller. *Sociology.* New York: Knopf, 1982.

Likhachev, D., B. Romanov, and V. Adrianova-Peretts, eds. *Povest' vremennykh let.* Moscow: Izd-vo Akademii Nauk SSSR, 1950.

Linz, Juan J. *Totalitarian and Authoritarian Regimes.* Boulder, Colo.: Lynne Rienner Publishers, 2000.

Lipman, Masha, and Michael McFaul. "Putin and the Media." In Herspring, *Putin's Russia,* pp. 77–78.

Lotspech, Richard. "Crime in the Transition Economies." *East-Asia* 47, no. 4 (1995): 555–89.

Lukin, Pavel. *Narodnye predstavleniia o gosudarstvennoi vlasti v Rossii XVII veka.* Moscow: Nauka, 2000.

Luong, Pauline Jones, ed. *The Transformation of Central Asia: States and*

Societies from Soviet Rule to Independence. Ithaca, N.Y.: Cornell University Press, 2004.

Lynn Edgar, Adrienne. *Tribal Nation: The Making of Soviet Turkmenistan*. Princeton, N.J.: Princeton University Press, 2004.

Macedo, Stephen, and Allen Buchanan, eds. *Secession and Self-Determination*. New York: New York University Press, 2003.

Macridis, Roy. *Modern Political Regimes*. Boston: Little, Brown, 1986.

Maiminas, E. Z. "Sootnoshenie vlasti, obshchestva i lichnosti." In Zaslavskaia, *Kuda idet Rossiia.Vlast'*, pp. 207–9.

Máiz, Ramón, and Ferran Requejo, eds. *Democracy, Nationalism and Multiculturalism*. New York: Frank Cass, 2005.

Mann, Michael. "The Social Cohesion of Liberal Democracy." *American Sociological Review* 35, no. 3 (1970): 423–39.

———. *The Sources of Social Power*. Cambridge: Cambridge University Press, 1986.

March, Luke. "The Putin Paradigm and the Cowering of Russia's Communists." In Ross, *Russian Politics under Putin*, pp. 53–75.

Marshall, Gordon, ed. *The Concise Oxford Dictionary of Sociology*. Oxford: Oxford University Press, 1994.

Marton, Katy. *Hidden Power*. New York: Pantheon, 2001.

Martynov, A. *Transformatsiia makrosotsial'nykh system v postsotsialisticheskom mire: Metodologicheskii aspekt*. Moscow: Lenand, 2006.

McCloskey, Deirdre. *The Bourgeois Virtues: Ethics for an Age of Commerce*. Chicago: University of Chicago Press, 2006.

McFaul, Michael. *Russia's Unfinished Revolution: Political Change from Gorbachev to Putin*. London: Cornell University Press, 2001.

McFaul, Michael, Nikolai Petrov, and Andrei Ryabov. *Between Dictatorship and Democracy: Russian Post-Communist Political Reform*. Washington, D.C.: Carnegie Endowment for International Peace, 2004.

McGlinchey, Eric. *Paying for Patronage: Regime Change in Post-Soviet Central Asia*. Princeton, N.J.: Princeton University Press, 2003.

Medvedev, Roy Aleksandrovich. *Chubais i vaucher: Iz istorii rossiĭskoĭ privatizatsii*. Moscow: Izd-vo "Impëto," 1997.

Menon, Anand, and Martin Schain. *Comparative Federalism: The European Union and the United States in Comparative Perspective*. Oxford: Oxford University Press, 2006.

Messner, Steven, and Richard Rosenfeld. *Crimes and the American Dream*. Belmont, CA: Wadsworth, 1997.

Mezhuev, V. M. "Traditsiia samovlastiia v sovremennoi Rossii." In Zaslavskaia, *Kuda idet Rossiia.Vlast'*, pp. 81–92.

Michener, Andrew, John D. DeLamater, and Shalom H. Schwartz. Under the general editorship of Robert K. Merton. *Social Psychology*. San Diego, Calif.: Harcourt Brace Jovanovich, 1986.

Milekhin, A., and N. Popov. *Obshchestvennoe mnenie Rossii*. Moscow: ARPI, 2000.

Milhaupt, Curtis J., and Mark D. West. "The Dark Side of Private Ordering:

An Institutional and Empirical Analysis of Organized Crime." *The University of Chicago Law Review* 67, no. 1 (2000): 41–98.

Mills, C. Wright. *The Power Elite*. New York: Oxford University Press, 1956.

Mitchell, William, and Michael Munger. "Economic Models of Interests Groups: An Introductory Survey." *American Journal of Political Science* 35, no. 2 (1991): 512–46.

Morgan, Lewis Henry. *Systems of Consanguinity and Affinity of the Human Family*. Washington, D.C.: Smithsonian Institution, 1870.

Morozov, Sergei. *Zagovor protiv narodov Rossii segodnia*. Moscow: Algoritm, 1999.

Mukhin, Aleksei. *Kto est' mister Putin i kto s nim prishel? Dos'e na prezidenta Rossii i ego spetssluzhby*. Moscow: Izd-vo "Gnom i D," 2002.

———. *Putin: Blizhnii krug prezidenta*. Moscow: Algoritm, 2005.

Nagle, John. *Introduction to Comparative Politics*. Chicago: Nelson-Hall, 1985.

Nee, Victor. "A Theory of Market Transition: From Redistribution to Markets in State Socialism." *American Sociological Review* 54, no. 1 (1989): 663–81.

Nee, Victor, and Rebecca Mathews. "Market Transition and Societal Transformation in Reforming State Socialism." *Annual Review of Sociology* 22 (1996): 401–35.

Newton, Arthur. *Travel and Travelers in the Middle Ages*. Freeport, N.Y.: Books for Libraries Press, 1967.

Nikolaevich Semanov, Sergei. *Brezhnev: Pravitel' "zolotogo veka."* Moscow: Veche, 2004.

Oakes, G. *Introduction to G. Simmel, Essays on Interpretation in Social Science*. Totowa, N.J.: Rowman and Littlefield, 1980.

Ober, Josiah. *Political Dissent in Democratic Athens: Intellectual Critic of Popular Rule*. Princeton, N.J.: Princeton University Press, 1998.

Oleinki, Anton. *Organized Crime, Prison, and Post-Soviet Societies*. Burlington, Vt.: Ashgate, 2003.

Orbe, Mark P. *Constructing Co-cultural Theory: An Explication of Culture, Power, and Communication*. Thousand Oaks, Calif.: Sage Publications, 1998.

Parkin, R. *Kinship: An Introduction to Basic Concepts*. Oxford: Blackwell, 1997.

Parsons, Talcott. "Evolutionary Universals in Society." *American Sociological Review* 29, no. 3 (1964): 339–57.

———. *The Social System*. Glencoe, Ill.: Free Press, 1951.

———. *Societies: Evolutionary and Comparative Perspectives*. Englewood Cliffs, N.J.: Prentice Hall, 1966.

———. *The System of Modern Society*. Englewood Cliffs, N.J.: Prentice Hall, 1971.

Pavlov-Sylvanskii, N. P. *Feodalizm v drevnei Rusi*. St. Petersburg: Brokgauz-Efron, 1907.

Peregudov, S. P. "Korporativnyi kapital v bor'be za izbiratelia." In Zaslavskaia, *Kuda idet Rossiia.Vlast'*, pp. 200–207.

Piers, G., and M. Singer. *Shame and Guilt: A Psychoanalytical and Cultural Study*. New York: Norton, 1971.

Piiasheva, Larisa. "Kontury radikal'noi sotsial'noi reformy." In *Postizhenie,* edited by Fridrikh Borodkin, L. Kosals, and P. Ryvkina. Moscow: Progress, 1989.

Pipes, Richard. *Struve, Liberal on the Left, 1870–1905.* Cambridge, Mass.: Harvard University Press, 1970.

Pirenne, Henri. *Economic and Social History of Medieval Europe.* New York: Harcourt, Brace, 1937.

Platonov, Sergei. *Lektsii po Russkoi istorii.* Moscow: Vysshaia shkola, 1993.

Poliakov, L. V. "Rossiiskii avtoritarnyi sindrom: Anamnez i epikriz." In Zaslavskaia, *Kuda idet Rossiia.Vlast',* pp. 173–82.

Pollock, F., and F. W. Maitland. *The History of English Law before the Time of Edward I,* 2nd ed. Cambridge: Cambridge University Press, 1968.

Postan, M. "The Rise of the Money Economy." *The Economic History Review* 14, no. 2 (1944): 123–34.

Primoratz, Igor', and Aleksandar Pavkovi, eds. *Identity, Self-Determination and Secession.* Aldershot, England: Ashgate, 2006.

Przeworski, Adam. *Democracy and Market.* Cambridge: Cambridge University Press, 1991.

Punch, Maurice. "Suite Violence: Why Managers Murder and Corporations Kill." *Crime and Social Change* 33, no. 3 (2000): 243–80.

Putnam, Robert. *Bowling Alone: The Collapse and Revival of American Community.* New York: Simon and Schuster, 2000.

Radygin, A. *Rossiiskaia privatizatsiia kak protsess formirovaniia institutsional'noi bazy ekonomicheskikh reform.* Moscow: Institut ekonomicheskikh problem perekhodnogo perioda, 1998.

Reddaway, Peter, and Dmitri Glinski. *The Tragedy of Russia's Reforms.* Washington, D.C.: United States Institute of Peace Press, 2000.

Remington, Thomas. "Putin, the Duma, and Political Parties." In Herspring, *Putin's Russia,* pp. 56–57.

Reuter, Peter. *Disorganized Crimes: The Economics of Visible Hand.* Cambridge: MIT Press, 1983.

Reynolds, Susan. *Fiefs and Vassals: The Medieval Evidence Reinterpreted.* Oxford: Oxford University Press, 1994.

Riasanovsky, Nicholas V., and Mark D. Steinberg. *A History of Russia,* 7th ed. Oxford: Oxford University Press, 2004.

Richardson, H. G., and G. O. Sayles. "The Governance of Mediaeval England from the Conquest to Magna Carta." *Speculum* 39, no. 3 (1964): 561–65.

Rosenwine, Barbara. *A Short History of the Middle Age.* Orchard Park, N.Y.: Broadview, 2005.

Ross, Cameron. "Putin's Federal Reforms." In Ross, *Russian Politics under Putin,* pp. 170–71.

———, ed. *Russian Politics under Putin.* Manchester: Manchester University Press, 2004.

Roy, Olivier. *New Central Asia: The Creation of Nations.* New York: New York University Press, 2000.

Rumer, Boris, ed. *Central Asia in Transition: Dilemmas of Political and Economic Development.* Armonk, N.Y.: M. E. Sharpe, 1996.

———. *Soviet Central Asia: "A Tragic Experiment."* Boston: Unwin Hyman, 1989.

Rye, Thomas. *Who Is Running America? The Bush Restoration.* Upper Saddle River, N.J.: Prentice Hall, 2002.

Sakwa, Richard. *Putin: Russia's Choice.* London: Routledge, 2004.

Samuelson, Paul. *Economics,* 9th ed. New York: McGraw-Hill, 1973.

Satarov, Georgii, ed. *Diagnostika: Rossiiskaia korruptsia.* Moscow: INDEM, 2002.

Satter, David. *Darkness at Dawn: The Rise of the Russian Criminal State.* New Haven, Conn.: Yale University Press, 2003.

Schatz, Edward. *Modern Clan Politics: The Power of "Blood" in Kazakhstan and Beyond.* Seattle: University of Washington Press, 2004.

Schnitzer, Martin. *Comparative Economic Systems.* Cincinnati, Ohio: South-Western Publishing, 1994.

Shcherbinin, A. I. "Chelovek vo vlasti (regional'nye politicheskie elity v sovremennom izbiratel'nom protsesse)." In Zaslavskaia, *Kuda idet Rossiia.Vlast',* pp. 209–17.

Shcherbinina, N. G. "Mifologicheskii Komponent Regional'nogo Izbiratel'nogo Prozessa," in Zaslavskaia, *Kuda idet Rossiia. Vlast',* p. 217.

Shelokhaev, V. V. "Osobennosti otnoshenii vlasti i obshchestva v Rossii: Istoriia i sovremennost." In Zaslavskaia, *Kuda idet Rossiia.Vlast',* pp. 10–21.

Shevtsova, Liliia. "From Yeltsin to Putin: The Evolution of Presidential Power." In Brown and Shevtsova, *Gorbachev, Yeltsin, and Putin,* pp. 67–70.

———. *Putin's Russia.* Washington, D.C.: Carnegie Endowment for International Peace, 2005.

———, ed. *Rossia politicheskaia.* Moscow: Moscow Carnegie Center, 1988.

———. *Yeltsin's Russia: Myths and Reality.* Washington, D.C.: Carnegie Endowment for International Peace, 1999.

Shlapentokh, Vladimir. "Early Feudalism—the Best Parallel for Contemporary Russia." *Europe-Asia Studies* 48, no. 3 (1996): 393–411.

———. *Fear in Contemporary Society: Its Positive and Negative Effects.* New York: Palgrave, 2006.

———. "Foreign Countries in the Russian Mind." *Communist and Post-Communist Studies* 31, no. 3 (1998): 119–216.

———. "The Four Faces of Mother Russia." *Transition* 4, no. 5 (1997): 60–61.

———. "Four Russias." *The Tocqueville Review* 19, no. 1 (1998): 9–34.

———. "Hobbes and Locke at Odds in Putin's Russia." *Europe-Asia Studies* 55, no. 7 (2003): 981–1007.

———. *Love, Marriage, and Friendship in the Soviet Union: Ideals and Practice.* New York: Praeger, 1984.

———. "Moscow's Values: Masses and the Elite." In *Nation Building and*

Common Values in Russia, edited by P. Kolst, pp. 217–39. Lanham, Md.: Rowman and Littlefield, 2003.

———. " 'Normal' Russia." *Current History* 212, no. 606 (1997): 331–36.

———. *A Normal Totalitarian Society*. Armonk, N.Y.: M. E. Sharpe, 2001.

———. "Privatization Debates in Russia: 1989–1922." *Comparative Economic Studies* 35, no. 2 (1993): 19–32.

———. *Public and Private Life of the Soviet People*. New York: Oxford University Press, 1989.

———. "Russian Patience: A Reasonable Behavior and a Social Strategy." *Archives Europeene de Sociologie* 36, no. 2 (1995): 247–80.

———. "Russia: Privatization and Illegalization of Social and Political Life." *Washington Quarterly* 19, no. 1 (1996): 65–85.

———. "Social Inequality in Post Communist Russia: The Attitudes of the Political Elite and the Masses (1991–1998)." *Europe-Asia Studies* 51, no. 7 (1999): 1167–81.

———. *Soviet Ideologies in the Period of Glasnost: Responses to Brezhnev's Stagnation*. New York: Praeger, 1988.

———. *Soviet Public Opinion and Ideology: The Interaction between Mythology and Pragmatism*. New York: Praeger, 1986.

———. "Two Pictures of Putin's Russia: Both Wrong." *World Policy Journal* 22, no. 1 (Spring 2005): 61–72.

———. "Wealth versus Political Power: The Russian Case." *Communist and Post-Communist Studies* 37, no. 2 (2004): 135–60.

Shlapentokh, Vladimir, Roman Levita, and Mikhail Loiberg. *From Submission to Rebellion: The Provinces versus the Center in Russia*. Boulder, Colo.: Westview, 1997.

Shlapentokh, Vladimir, and Eric Shiraev, eds. *Fears in Post-Communist Societies: A Comparative Perspective*. New York: Palgrave, 2002.

Shleifer, Andrei, and Daniel Treisman. "A Normal Country." *Foreign Affairs*, March/April 2004.

Shleifer, Andrei, and Robert W. Vishny. "Corruption." *Quarterly Journal of Economics* 108, no. 3 (1993): 599–617.

Simis, Konstantin. *USSR: The Corrupt Society*. New York: Simon and Schuster, 1990.

Simmel, Georg. *On Individuality and Social Forms: Selected Writings*. Edited by Donald N. Levine. Chicago: University of Chicago Press, 1971.

———. *Problems in Philosophy of History*. New York: Free Press, 1977.

Smelser, Neil. *Sociology*. Cambridge, Mass.: Blackwell, 1994.

Smyth, Regina. *Candidate Strategies and Electoral Competition in the Russian Federation: Democracy without Foundation*. Cambridge: Cambridge University Press, 2006.

Solo, Robert. *Economic Organizations and Social Systems*. Ann Arbor: University of Michigan Press, 2005.

Solov'ev, Sergei. *Istoriia Rossii s drevneishikh vremen*. St. Petersburg: Tovarishchestvo "Obshchestvennaia Pol'za," 1902.

Solovyov, Vladimir, and Elena Klepikova. *Boris Yeltsin: A Political Biography.* New York: Putnam, 1992.

Southworth, Caleb. "The Dacha Debate: Household Agriculture and Labor Markets in Post-Socialist Russia." *Rural Sociology* 71, no. 3 (2006): 451–78.

Spufford, Peter. *Money and Its Use in Medieval Europe.* New York: Cambridge University Press, 1988.

Stalin, Iosif. *Vorposy Leninizma.* Moscow: Gospolitizdat, 1952.

Stavrakis, Peter J. *Shadow Politics: The Russian State in the 21st Century.* Carlisle Barracks, Pa.: Strategic Studies Institute, U.S. Army War College, 1997.

Stowell, William A. "Personal Relationships in Medieval France." *PMLA* 28, no. 3 (1913): 388–416.

Sundstrom, Lisa McIntosh. *Funding Civil Society: Foreign Assistance and NGO Development in Russia.* Stanford, Calif.: Stanford University Press, 2006.

Swenden, Wilfried. *Federalism and Regionalism in Western Europe: A Comparative and Thematic Analysis.* New York: Palgrave Macmillan, 2006.

Tadmor, Naomi. *Family & Friends in Eighteenth-Century England: Household, Kinship, Patronage.* New York: Cambridge University Press, 2001.

Tarr, G. Alan, Robert F. Williams, and Josef Marko, eds. *Federalism, Subnational Constitutions, and Minority Rights.* Westport, Conn.: Praeger, 2004.

Taylor, Charles. *Multiculturalism and the Politics of Recognitiia.* Princeton, N.J.: Princeton University Press, 1992.

Théis, Laurent. *Histoire du Moyen Age français: Chronologie commentée de Clovis à Louis XI, 486–1483.* Paris: Perrin, 1992.

Tikhmirov, Vladimir, ed. *Russia after Yeltsin.* Aldershot, England: Ashgate, 2001.

Tilly, Charles. "War-Making and State-Making as Organized Crime." In *Bringing the State Back,* edited by Peter Evans, Trich Reuschmeyer, and Theda Skocpol, pp. 170–71. Cambridge: Cambridge University Press, 1985.

Tompson, William. "The Russian Economy under Vladimir Putin." In Ross, *Russian Politics under Putin,* pp. 114–32.

Triandis, Harry C. *Individualism and Collectivism.* Boulder, Colo.: Westview, 1995.

Tullock, Gordon. "The Welfare Costs of Tariffs, Monopolies, and Theft." *Western Economic Journal* (now *Economic Enquiry*) 5, no. 3 (1967): 224–32.

Turner, Jonathan. *Sociology: The Science of Human Organization.* Chicago: Nelson-Hall, 1985.

Tyler, J. E. *The Alpine Passes: The Middle Ages (962–1250).* Oxford: B. Blackwell, 1930.

United States Senate Committee on Foreign Relations. *Democracy in Retreat in Russia: Hearing before the Committee on Foreign Relations,* 109th Cong., 1st sess., February 17, 2005. Washington, D.C.: GPO, 2005.

Vardomskii, L. "Problemy i protivorechiia regional'nogo razvitiia Rossii." In

Rossiia i SNG: Dezintegratsionnye i integratsionnye protsessy, edited by G. Kostinskii. Moscow: Institut Geografii, 1995.

Varese, Federico. *The Russian Mafia: Private Protection in a New Market Economy*. Oxford: Oxford University Press, 2001.

Vinogradoff, Paul. "Feudalism." In *The Cambridge Medieval History*, vol. 3, edited by H. M. Gwatkin et al., pp. 458–84. Cambridge: Cambridge University Press, 1957.

Vishnevskaia, Galina. *Galina: A Russian Story*. Translated from Russian by Guy Daniels. San Diego, Calif.: Harcourt Brace Jovanovich, 1984.

Volckart, Oliver. *Wettbewerb und Wettbewerbsbeschränkung im vormodernen Deutschland, 1000–1800*. Tübingen, Germany: Mohr Siebeck, 2002.

Volkov, Vadim. "Violent Entrepreneurship in Post-Communist Russia." *Europe-Asia Studies* 51, no. 5 (1999): 751–54.

———. *Violent Entrepreneurs: The Use of Force in the Making of Russian Capitalism*. Ithaca, N.Y.: Cornell University Press, 2002.

Waltz, Kenneth. *The Theory of International Politics*. New York: Random House, 1979.

Waquet, J. C. *Corruption: Ethics and Power in Florence, 1660–1770*. University Park: Pennsylvania State University Press, 1991.

Webber, Carolyn, and Aaron Wyldavsky. "Feudalism Nothing." In *The Blackwell Dictionary of Twentieth-Century Social Thought*, edited by William Outhwait and Tom Bottomore. Oxford: Blackwell, 1994.

Weber, Max. *Economy and Society: An Outline of Interpretive Sociology*. Vol. 1. Berkeley: University of California Press, 1978.

———. *Essays in Economic Sociology*. Edited by Richard Swedberg. Princeton, N.J.: Princeton University Press, 1999.

———. *Theory of Social Organization*. New York: Free Press, 1964.

Webster, William, ed. *Russian Organized Crime and Corruption*. Washington, D.C.: The CSIS Press, 2000.

White, Stephen. "Russia's Disempowered Electorate." In Ross, *Russian Politics under Putin*, pp. 76–92.

———. "The Settlement of Dispute by Compromise in Eleventh Century Western France." *The American Journal of Legal History* 22, no. 4 (1978): 281–308.

Wolfe, Martin. "French Views on Wealth and Taxes in the Middle Ages to the Old Regime." *The Journal of Economic History* 26, no. 4 (1966): 466–83.

Wolfe, Tom. *The Bonfire of the Vanities*. New York: Farrar, Straus, 1987.

———. *A Man in Full*. New York: Farrar, Straus and Giroux, 1998.

Yadov, V. A. "Rossiia kak transformiruiushcheesia obshchestvo: Reziume mnogoletnei diskussii sotsiologov." In Zaslavskaia, *Kuda idet Rossiia.Vlast'*, pp. 383–91.

Yakovlev, A. *Gor'kaia chasha*. Yaroslavl': Verkhnevolzhskoe Knizhnoe Izdatel'stvo, 1994.

Yeltsin, Boris. *Zapiski prezidenta*. Moscow: Ogonek, 1994.

Yourcenar, Marguerite. *Memoirs of Hadrian*. Translated from the French by

Grace Frick in collaboration with the author. New York: Farrar, Straus and Young, 1954.

Zaslavskaia, T. I., ed. *Kuda idet Rossiia.Vlast': Obshchestvo; Lichnost'*. Moscow: Vysshaia shkola sotsial'nykh i ekonomicheskikh nauk, 2000.

————. "O roli sotsial'noi struktury v transformatsii rossiskogo obshchestva." In Zaslavskaia, *Kuda idet Rossiia.Vlast'*, pp. 222–35.

Zdravomyslov, A. G. "Vlast' i obshchestvo: Krizis 90-x godov." In Zaslavskaia, *Kuda idet Rossiia.Vlast'*, pp. 135–47.

Zorkaia, Nataliia, ed. *Obshchestvennoe Mnenie, Ezhegodnik, 2003*. Moscow: VTSIOM, 2003.

NAME INDEX

Abramov, Yan 83
Abramovich, Roman 67, 70, 71, 72, 91, 123, 126, 220
Ackoff, Russel 194
Adzhubei, Aleksandr 229
Afanas'ev, Mikhail 153, 223
Afanas'eva, Elena 217
Akayev, Askar 93
Akhiezer, Aleksandr 12
Alekseev, Sergei 106
Aliev, Geidar 93, 163
Aliev, Ilham 164
Alliluyeva, Svetlana 159
Alsou 83
Ambartsumian, Mkhitara 59
Anderson, Perry 23
Andropov, Yurii 11, 59, 161
Antonius Pius, emperor 164
Aristotle 29, 66
Audretsch, David B 199

Babich, Denis 212
Backman, Clifford 25
Barinov, Aleksei 124
Barry, Donald 37, 165
Barsukov, Mikhail 90
Baturina, Elena 168
Beaumarchais, Pierre 158
Beck, Ulrich 200
Beliaeva, L 9
Belkovskii, Stanislav 92
Bellow, Adam 151, 157
Benedict, Ruth 16
Benjamin, Walter 21

Berezovskii, Boris 15, 42, 63, 66, 68, 69, 70, 71, 72, 118, 162, 163, 209, 212, 219, 233
Blank, Stephen 31
Bloch, Marc 26, 29, 38, 173, 184, 214
Blockmans, Wim 43
Blondel, Jean 195
Blumer, Herbert 155
Bonser, Charles F 199
Boos, Georgii 126
Borejsza, Jerzy W 201
Borisov, Yurii 142, 144
Borodin, Pavel 48, 90, 163, 214
Borovoi, Konstantin 15
Bourdieu, Pierre 156, 228
Braudel, Fernand 88
Breslauer, George 37
Brezhnev, Leonid 32, 59, 86, 88, 128, 134, 159, 161, 229
Brodskii, Vitalii 216
Brooks, Stephen 23
Brown, Archie 10
Burbulis, Gennadii 71
Bykov, Anatolii 67, 68

Cantor, Norman 136
Cardoso, Fernando 20
Carnoy, Martin 202
Catherine the Great 214
Chaika, Yurii 45
Charlemagne 117, 119, 135
Charles the Bold, Duke of Burgundy 201
Charles the Great 36, 37
Chavez, Hugo 171

Chernenko, Konstantin　59, 161
Chernomyrdin, Andrei　169
Chernomyrdin, Viktor　47, 61, 68, 169
Chernomyrdin, Vitalii　169
Chernov, Evgenii　15
Cheyette, Frederic　136
Chinball, Marjorie　26
Chubais, Anatolii　12, 47, 61, 66, 68, 71, 72, 73, 77, 80, 177, 209, 213, 219
Chugaev, Sergei　194
Churbanov, Yurii　229
Cocherham, William　10
Coleman, James　156
Colton, Timothy　10, 203
Corneille, Pierre　158
Coulloudon, Virginie　14
Crick, Bernard　195

Dahl, Robert　28, 78
Dakhin, V. N　11
Danilov, Viktor　11
Darkin, Sergei　67, 120, 127, 129
Davies, R. W　10
Davis, Natalie Zemon　38, 44
Dawkins, Richard　155
Dawson, Christopher　136
de Coulanges, Fustel　25, 26, 38, 184, 201
Dean, Trevor　43, 45, 49, 50
Dedikova, Tatiana　169
Deripaska, Oleg　71, 72, 77, 162
Dewey, John　29
Diachenko, Leonid　162, 163
Diachenko, Tatiana　89, 162, 163
Dmitrieva, Elena　169
Domhoffiam, William　214
Dorenko, Sergei　124
Dostoevsky, Fyodor　80
Douglas, David　38
Dovgal, Vladimir　145
Dreiser, Theodore　76, 157
Dubin, Boris　79
Dubinin, Sergei　177
Dubov, Yulii　76, 233

Dubuis, Pierre　26
Duby, Georges　38
Dudaev, Dzhokhar　113
Dugin, Aleksandr　12
Durkheim, Emile　22
Duus, Peter　29
Dyskin, Il'ia　144
Dzhaparidze, Zurab　147

Ericson, Richard　31

Fedorov, Nikolai　118, 124, 130
Fedorov, Valentin　104
Fedotova, V　12
Finckenauer, James　38
Fischer, Marcus　23, 136
Fisher, Bobby　128
Fitzgerald, F. Scott　76
Fossier, Robert　201
Fotianov, Dmitrii　127
Fradkov, Mikhail　169
Fradkov, Pavel　169
Fradkov, Piotr　169
Friedman, Mikhail　15, 71
Friedman, Milton　157
Fry, Timothy　175
Fukuyama, Francis　17, 156
Furet, François　22
Furtseva, Ekaterina　59

Gaidar, Yegor　9, 73, 77, 80, 141, 214, 215, 224
Galbraith, John　56, 207
Gaman-Golutvina, O. V　13
Ganshof, François-Lois　26, 38
Gates, Bill　210
Gauvard, Claude　38
Gefter, Valentin　153
Gerasimova, Oksana　217
Giddens, Anthony　9
Goffman, Erving　155
Gogol, Nikolai　80
Goldman, Marshall　167
Golubev, Valerii　166
Gorbachev, Mikhail　37, 86, 98, 108, 141, 159, 210, 217, 225

Gorbacheva, Raisa 161
Goriukhina, El'vira 144
Gorky, Maxim 80, 157, 214
Govorukhin, Stanislav 13
Gozman, Leonid 12
Granovetter, Marc 156
Gray, John 195
Grinberg, Ruslan 31
Gromov, Boris 166
Grushin, Boris 110, 163
Gryzlov, Boris 233
Gudkov, Lev 78, 79
Guizot, François 89
Gureev, Sergei 147
Gurevich, Aron 30
Guriev, Sergei 31
Gusev, Pavel 130
Gusinskii, Vladimir 42, 66, 68, 71,
    72, 107, 118, 212, 235

Hadrian, emperor 164
Hall, John 29
Hamilton, W. D 155
Hanawalt, Barbara 38
Hayek, Friedrich 81
Hedlund, Stephen 11
Henry II Plantagenet, king of
    England 136, 205
Henry V, king of England 44
Heraclites of Ephesus 21
Hitler 24, 153
Hollander, Paul 203
Holsti, Ole 22
Horgan, John 16
Huas, Magdalena 201
Hugh Capet, king of France 87
Huskey, Eugene 10

Il'in, V. I 13
Iliumzhinov, Kirsan 63, 128
Illarionov, Andrei 92, 93, 144
Ishchenko, Evgenii 124, 126
Iskhakov, Rishat 170
Ivan the Terrible 27, 159
Ivanov, Sergei 2, 127, 169
Ivanov, Viktor 92

Jack, Andrew 13
Janin, Hunt 38, 44, 205

Kadyrov, Akhmet 122
Kadyrov, Ramzan 120, 122, 188
Kaganovich, Aron 228
Kaganovich, Lazar 159, 228
Kaganovich, Mariia 228
Kaganovich, Mikhail 228
Kaganovich, Yulii 228
Kalita, Ivan 87, 88
Karstedt, Susanne 29, 200
Kasianov, Mikhail 47
Kasparov, Garry 91
Katlinskii, Anton 169
Kautsky, Karl 22
Kazantsev, Viktor 62
Kazenin, Vladislav 146
Khakhulina, L. A 9
Khapsirokov, Nazir 48
Khasbulatov, Ruslan 108
Khloponin, Aleksandr 67, 125,
    220
Khodorkovsky, Mikhail 64, 65, 66,
    69, 70, 71, 72, 73, 77, 89,
    118, 209, 210, 211
Khrushchev, Nikita 86, 134, 159,
    161, 229
Kim Il-sung 164
Kim Jong-il 164
Kingston, William 135, 136
Kivelidi, Ivan 177
Kliuchevskii, Vasilii 87, 159
Kobzon, Iosif 180, 216
Koch, Alfred 47, 80, 215
Konchalovskii, Andrei 12, 31, 152
Kopylov, Yurii 127
Korolev, Vladimir 130
Korzhakov, Aleksandr 42, 71, 90,
    204, 218, 235
Kostikov, Viacheslav 215
Kostin, Evgenii 179
Kovalev, Nikolai 179, 236
Kovalev, Sergei 70
Kozak, Dmitrii 120
Kozlov, Andrei 177

Krasnoger, Liudmila 177
Krizhnich, Yurii 11
Krueger, Anne 56
Krupskaia, Nadezhda 161
Kryshtanovskaia, Ol'ga 166, 212, 225
Kulakov, Vladimir 166
Kundera, Milan 153
Kuznetsov, Valentin 225
Kvashnin, Anatolii 52

Lane, David 10
Lane, Frederick 234
Latynina, Yuliia 31, 63, 76, 91, 93, 122, 125, 145, 209
Le Goff, Jacques 26
Lebed, Aleksandr 67, 72
Lebedev, Platon 71
Ledentsov, Oleg 49
Leiven, Anatolii 31
Lemon, Alaina 208
Lenin, Vladimir 23, 59, 161
Levada, Yurii 11, 78, 79
Levashov, Leonid 52
Liubimov, Aleksandr 214
Loshak, Viktor 215
Louis I the Pious, king of France 117, 174
Louis VI, king of France 87
Louis VIII, king of France 87
Louis IX, king of France 36
Louis Philippe, king of France 89
Lucius Ceionius Commodus 164
Luzhkov, Yurii 47, 83, 107, 118, 129, 165, 168, 219, 231, 235

Machiavelli 20
Madrich, Jeffrey 207
Maiminas, E 13
Maitland, Frederic 44
Makarov, Aleksei 77
Mamut, Aleksandr 71
Mann, Michael 23
Mann, Thomas 157
March, Luke 10
Marcus Aurelius, emperor 164

Markov, Sergei 2
Martel, Carl 135
Martynov, A 24
Marx 25, 183
Maslov, Viktor 166
Matlin, Aleksandr 213
Mauss, Marcel 22
Mayakovsky, Vladimir 214
Mbabane, Loyiso 157
McFaul, Michael 10, 37, 165
Medvedev, Dmitrii 1, 15, 92
Medvedev, Roy 72, 232
Merton, Robert 22
Mezhuev, Vadim 11
Michael, George 83
Migranian, Andranik 2, 8, 110
Millar, James 10
Miller, Aleksei 12
Mills, C. Wright 155
Minkin, Aleksandr 1, 215
Mironov, Sergei 83, 119
Moiseev, Vladimir 145
Molière 158
Montesquieu 28
Morgan, Lewis Henry 228
Morozov, Oleg 2
Mousnier, Roland 22
Mukha, Vitalii 125
Mukhin, Aleksei 166

Nazarbayev, Nursultan 93
Nazdratenko, Evgenii 48, 113, 118, 120
Nemirovich-Danchenko, Vladimir 147
Nemtsov, Boris 68, 71, 81, 109
Nevzlin, Leonid 70
Niazov, Saparmurat 93
Nurgaliev, Rashid 39

Odinartsev, Sergei 145
Okulov, Valerii 162
Orbe, Mark 23
Orekhovskii, Petr 31
Ostrow, Joel 165

Pain, Emil   236
Parsons   16, 153, 155, 183
Pavlovskii, Gleb   8
Pavlov-Sylvanskii, Nikolai   27
Pepin the Short, king of Franks
      201
Peregudov, S   13
Perekrest, Vladimir   77
Perov, Boris   105
Pertakov, Nikolai   210
Peter the Great   12
Petrov, Nikolai   11
Philip II, king of France   87, 201
Piiasheva, Larisa   76, 215, 216
Platonov, Sergei   88
Pleshakov, Vladimir   39, 50
Poliakov, L   11
Pollock, Frederick   44
Polterovich, Viktor   77
Popov, Gavriil   77
Postan, Michael   57
Potanin, Vladimir   66, 68, 71, 72,
      83, 212
Prikhodko, Sergei   92
Primakov, Evgenii   165, 231
Primoratz, Igor'   199
Privalov, Kirill   8
Prokhorov, Mikhail   83
Pugachev, Sergei   67
Putnam, Robert   156

Quine, Willard   25

Rabelais, François   144
Racine, Jean   158
Radishchev, Aleksandr   80, 214
Radyshevskii, Dmitrii   216
Rakhimov, Murtaza   122, 170
Rakhimov, Ural   170
Remington, Tom   10
Robert le Pious, king of France   40
Rodionov, Igor'   52
Rokkan, Stein   28
Rosenwine, Barbara   26
Ross, Cameron   10
Rossel, Eduard   104, 129, 138

Rostovtzeff, Michael   22
Rutland, Peter   13, 225
Rutskoi, Aleksandr   108, 118
Rye, Thomas   214

Sakharov, Andrei   70
Sakwa, Richard   24
Samuelson, Paul   195
Satarov, Georgii   47, 205, 206
Savchenko, Evgenii   126
Sarnov, Benedict   214
Schnittke, Alfred   215
Schwartz, Shalom   17
Schwarzenegger, Arnold   198
Sechin, Igor'   92
Semichastnyi, Vladimir   235
Sevast'ianov, Aleksandr   13, 36,
      202
Shabunin, Ivan   104
Shaimiev, Mintimer   121, 122,
      130, 170
Shakespeare   158
Shchekochikhin, Yurii   47, 162
Shcherbinina, N. G   11
Shcherbinin, A. I   11
Shebarshin, Leonid   110
Shelokhaev, V   11
Sheremet, Viacheslav   169
Shevardnadze, Eduard   93
Shevtsova, Liliia   10, 202
Shkolov, Evgenii   92
Shleifer, Andrei   8, 14
Shmakov, Viktor   130
Shpak, Georgii   166
Shpanagel, Sergei   49
Shuvalov, Igor'   92
Silaiev, Ivan   64
Simmel, Georg   20, 22, 184
Sinclair, Upton   157
Skokov, Yurii   220
Skuratov, Yurii   162
Slider, Darrell   11
Sliska, Liubov'   233
Smelser, Neil   28
Smolenskii, Nikolai   71, 212
Sobchak, Anatolii   109

Sobianin, Sergei 139
Sokolov, Maxim 2
Solo, Robert 17
Soloviev, Eric 31
Sovmen, Khazret 120
Spencer, Herbert 183
Stalin 11, 23, 58, 59, 69, 70, 86, 96, 97, 153, 159, 160, 161, 217, 218, 227, 228
Stanislavsky, Konstantin 147
Starovoitov, Aleksandr 61
Stavrakis, Peter 31
Stepanov, Viktor 108
Stroev, Yegor 125, 223
Struve, Piotr 12
Sundiev, Igor' 236
Surkov, Vladislav 1, 8, 92
Svanidze, Nikolai 130
Swift, Jonathan 1, 2

Tabakov, Oleg 214
Tarasov, Artem 15
Taylor, Charles 23
Théis, Laurent 26
Thucydides 20
Tikhomirov, Vladimir 165
Tilly, Charles 174
Timofeev, Lev 47
Titov, Konstantin 109
Tkachev, Aleksandr 222
Tokugawa 24
Tolokonskii, Viktor 125
Tolstoy, Lev 80
Tompson, William 13
Travin, Aleksandr 144
Travin, Dmitrii 71, 212
Travkin, Nikolai 109
Treisman, Daniel 8
Tretiakov, Vitalii 91, 212
Triandis, Harry 17
Trojan, emperor 164
Tucker, Robert 203
Tuleev, Aman 218, 219, 223
Tullock, Gordon 56
Turgenev, Ivan 80

Uglanov, Andrei 63, 209
Uliukaev, Aleksei 80, 215
Uskov, Nikolai 81

Vavilov, Andrei 61, 177
Viakhirev, Rem 169
Vinogradoff, Paul 27, 135, 158, 175
Vinogradov, Vladimir 71, 212
Vishnevsky, Boris 62
Vlasik, Nikolai 218
Volchek, Galina 214
Volkov, Aleksandr 130
Volkov, Evgenii 46
Volkov, Vadim 14, 43, 176, 179
Volodin, Viacheslav 2
Voltaire 28
Voronin, Yuri 38
Voznesenskii, Andrei 214

Waltz, Kenneth 23
Waquet, JC 43
Weber, Max 21, 22, 25, 29, 153, 155, 156, 183, 184, 200
Webber, Carolyn 29
Webster, William 14, 43
White, Stephen 11, 136
Wiebel, Jane 200
Wolfe, Martin 87
Wolfe, Tom 76
Wyldavsky, Aaron 29

Yadov, Vladimir 9, 12
Yakovlev, Aleksandr M 81, 82
Yakovlev, Aleksandr N 80, 215
Yakovlev, Vladimir 118
Yakubovskii, Dmitrii 181
Yavlinsky, Grigorii 14, 118, 149, 202
Yeltsina, Elena 162
Yeltsina, Naina 163
Yeltsina, Tatiana 89, 162, 163
Yumashev, Valentin 162

Zaslavskaia, Tatiana 9
Zdravomyslov, Andrei 11

Zhdanov, Andrei 159
Zhdanov, Yurii 159
Zhuravlev, V. V 11
Ziemer, Klaus 201

Ziuganov, Gennadii 118, 124
Zorkin, Valerii 2, 191
Zurabov, Mikhail 169, 233

SUBJECT INDEX

Absolute monarchies 35, 173

Africa 16, 21, 93, 157, 171, 175, 186

Ancient Greece 22, 75

Annales School 26, 184

Antidemocratic trends in Russia 10, 15

Anti-Semitism or the Jewish factor 66, 70–71

Army, post-Soviet Russian 48–49, 52, 97, 101, 161, 166

Athens 75

Attitudes of the public 7, 50, 113, 129, 139–41, 165, 171

Authoritarianism or authoritarian model 2–4, 7, 10–11, 14–15, 17–20, 24, 31–32, 77, 79, 81, 84, 86, 130, 153–54, 173, 183–84, 187–88
  bureaucratic form of 11
  oligarchic form of 4, 11

Babylon 21

Bailiffs 44

Bashkortostan 99, 101, 112, 122, 123, 128, 130, 138

Bolsheviks 23, 81, 96, 161, 210, 215

Bureaucracy or bureaucrats 4, 13, 15, 17–18, 21, 35, 45, 47, 55, 60–62, 68, 77, 84, 98, 100–101, 124–26, 128, 136, 141, 143, 147, 168, 184, 187–88, 190, 225

Byzantine civilization 12

Capitalism
  bureaucratic form of 8, 13
  criminal form of 7, 13
  crony form of 8, 13, 157, 166, 189
  Kremlin form of 13
  oligarchic form of 7, 13
  predatory form of 7, 11
  in the West 17–18, 25

Caroling Empire 37, 65, 95, 117, 136, 174

Chechnya 27, 71, 99, 102, 113–14, 121–23, 139, 146

China 2, 17, 21, 86, 156

Church, monasteries and clergy 25, 32, 38, 43, 49–50, 55, 57, 87–88, 108, 119, 128, 135–36, 153, 161, 173, 181, 184, 229

Commendation 30, 174

Communism 2, 17–18, 76, 82, 140

Corporations 4, 17, 25, 29, 31, 39, 41–43, 46, 52, 55–56, 58, 61, 65, 67, 71, 75–77, 92–93, 121, 126, 142, 145, 148, 184–86, 188, 236

Corruption
  bribes 44–46, 48, 51, 58–60, 62, 125, 143–44, 152, 224
  extortion 48–49, 53, 152, 177, 184
  gifts 43, 44, 56, 59, 64, 73, 162, 186
  immunity of elites and 45, 127
  inefficiency of state and 39, 43, 51, 120, 184

Corruption—*continued*
justice system and   44–46, 49–50
in the Middle Ages   4, 35, 37,
43–45, 53, 64, 73, 181,
184–85, 205
in Post-Soviet Russia   3, 9, 14,
35, 45, 49, 56, 60, 77, 177,
185, 187
in Putin's regime   1, 10, 45,
49, 52, 93, 120, 122, 127,
214
in Russian regions   67, 100, 120,
122, 124–25
in the Soviet Union   39, 58–60,
208, 227
in Yeltsin's regime   37, 42, 47,
64, 162, 205, 214
Crime
business and   42–43
capitalism and   7, 13, 30, 158,
166, 179, 189
dangerous roads and   40
drug related   39
fear of   35, 40–42
gang   41, 43, 178, 205, 236
local barons and   63, 120, 124,
127
in the Middle Ages   4, 40,
43–44
murder as   39, 40, 42, 44, 46,
122, 127–28, 130, 164, 177
organized   17, 39, 42–43, 120,
145, 185, 235
violent   13, 43, 179
Culture
in America   16
in Japan   16
and models of society   23, 31,
153
in Russia   79, 96, 97, 121, 140,
164, 170

Dictatorship   10
Domain, presidential or royal
in the Middle Ages   4, 57, 85,
87–88

Putin's   91–93
as a source of physical security
90
struggle for power and   90
in totalitarian societies   88
Yeltsin's   37, 89–91
Empire
Carolingian   37, 65, 95, 136,
174
Roman   22, 26, 63, 87, 99, 113,
119, 139, 141, 143, 164,
173
Russian   11–12, 114
Soviet   12, 160
England   21, 44, 136, 180
Enron   71
Ethnic discrimination   122
Eurasian ideology   12, 71

Far East   48, 52, 67, 96, 103–4,
106, 110, 118, 125, 127, 169
Federal Council   83, 187
Federalism   27, 198, 199
Feudalism
conflicts among elites and
36–37, 108
definitions of   7–8, 25–26, 33
economic school of   28
in Europe   28–29
federalism and   27
in Japan   25, 29
legal aspects of   26, 38
in the Middle Ages   28, 31, 57,
134
military aspects of   26, 38, 57,
175
as a model of society   12, 24–26,
28–29
political school of   28–29,
184
in Russia   27, 31, 86
universalism and   29
France   21–22, 26, 38, 40, 44–45,
83, 87, 90, 107, 136, 162,
173–74, 201, 205

Gazprom   61, 68, 91–92, 166,
     168–69, 179, 235–36
Germany   21, 24, 44, 52, 89
Globalization   18
Greece   22, 28, 75

Historical approach   20
Holistic vision of the world   16
Holy Roman Empire   119
Humanists   40

Ideal types   21–22
Ideology
     anti-Communist   59
     authoritarian   79
     democratic   99
     Eurasian   12, 71
     liberal   76, 79, 82, 99
     of local barons   95
     nationalist   112, 121
     oligarchic (or feudal)   4, 75–79,
        82, 84, 187
     regional   96, 99–101, 113–14
     social   160
     Soviet   23
India   21, 45, 57, 60
Individualism   17, 114
Institute of Transitional Economy
     9, 215
Integrative-system or holistic
     approach   7, 15–18, 23, 183
Israel(i)   15, 66, 70
Italy   45, 51, 72, 78, 162, 171

Japan   16, 24–25, 29, 51
Judicial system
     the General Prosecutor and   46,
        69, 143
     in the Middle Ages   35, 43–45,
        124, 135, 158
     in post-Soviet Russia   32, 35, 45,
        47, 107, 126, 144–45, 185

KGB and FSB   62, 69, 90–91, 97,
     110, 149, 160, 165–66,
     178–80, 189–90, 235–36

Khodorkovsky, the case of
     conflict with Putin and   65,
        69–73, 77, 118, 187
     lack of oligarchs' support for
        71–73

Law and order
     disrespect of   38–39, 50, 142,
        170, 185, 188
     law enforcement agencies and
        47–52, 66, 145, 147, 231
     in the Middle ages   142, 184
     in regions   47
     in Russia   33, 47–51, 66
Liberalism, liberal capitalism, liberal
     model   10, 12, 14, 18–19,
        24–25, 32, 77, 80–81, 84, 131,
        184
Lithuania   45
Local barons
     alliances of   103
     calls for separatism of   104
     conflict with state (Moscow) and
        99–101
     cult of   130
     democracy and   128–29
     during early Yeltsin period
        101–2, 105–6
     Federal Council and   187
     ideology of   99–101
     during late Yeltsin period
        111–13
     in the Middle Ages   4, 102–3,
        188
     during perestroika   98
     presidential emissaries and
        119–20
     public attitudes toward   113–15
     during Putin's period   63, 67,
        117–18, 120, 127
     in Soviet times   96–97
     taxes and   102–3
London   15, 81–82, 106
Loyalty   20, 48, 71, 109, 120,
     122–24, 136, 153–54, 157–59,
     188, 227

Mafia   28, 30, 52, 110, 125, 127, 159, 176–77, 216
Magyars   26
Market relations and economy   7, 9, 10, 15–18, 22, 141, 148, 154, 170, 176, 195, 216, 232
Marx, Marxists, and Marxism   21–23, 25, 30, 84, 152, 155–56, 183, 189, 196
McCarthyism   70
Mercenaries   48, 175
Merovingians   36
Ministry of Internal Affairs   39, 43, 97, 144, 149, 179–80, 236
Monarchism, monarchic principle, and the choice of leaders   7, 11, 163–64, 189
Money
  in the Middle Ages   40, 57–58
  in Russia   43, 49, 56, 58, 61, 66, 70, 80, 82, 88, 99, 124, 128, 186
  social role of   55–58, 66
  in the Soviet Union   58–59
  in Western society   44
Multiculturalism   23
Muslims   26, 59, 121

Nazism   17
Neoclassical economic model or economists   17, 28, 30, 77, 157, 183, 195
Neopositivists   25
New liberals   81
Nomenklatura   8, 59–60, 63, 97, 141, 153, 176, 225
Nominalists   25
Non-Russian republics   99–102, 107, 111–12, 114, 118–19, 121–23, 130, 137, 169, 187
Normal society   7, 8, 9, 14, 78
North Caucasus   103, 114, 127

Oligarchic ideology
  attitudes toward the masses   78–79

  corruption and   77–78
  democracy and   78
  origins   75–76
  social equality and   79–82
  the state and   76–77
Oligarchs, oligarchy, and big business
  antistate attitudes of   76–77
  attitudes toward public of   78–79, 82–83
  autonomy of   67–68
  conflicts between   71–72
  conflicts between state and   69–71
  conspicuous consumption (high style of life) of   83–84
  democracy and   78
  disregard and justification of corruption of   77
  fortunes and wealth of   63–65
  greed of   82–84
  the group of   13, 66
  hostility toward social equality of   79–82
  Kremlin and   12–13, 63–64, 67–68
  Moscow, the regions, and   67
  as political actors   36, 65–66
  rent-seeking and   55–57
  solidarity between   72–73

Peloponnesian war   20, 75
Perestroika   37, 39, 61, 76, 98, 101, 115, 134, 136–37, 141, 161, 187, 224, 225
Personal relations
  children of leaders and   162–63, 169
  after the collapse of the Soviet system   153, 160
  crony capitalism and   166–68
  kinship and   151–52, 155, 157–59, 166, 168–69
  in the Middle Ages   90, 151–53, 155, 158–60

Personal relations—*continued*
  nepotism as a type of   151–52, 159
  in non-Russian republics 159–60, 169–70
  public institutions and   154
  Putin's   165–66
  in the Russian mind   170–71
  selection of people for jobs and positions in society and 152–53
  in the social sciences   154
  in the Soviet Union   153–54, 159–60
  trust and   153–54, 156, 158, 161, 163, 165
  Yeltsin's   161–63
Petersburg   42, 46, 53, 92–93, 103, 106, 109, 115, 118, 145–46, 179–80, 186, 204
Pluralism   11, 25
Poland   177
Police and law enforcement   36, 47–52, 143–45, 175
Politburo   37, 86, 96, 159, 176, 228, 235
Private property
  confiscation of   146–47
  in the Middle Ages   85–87, 134–36
  national republics and   137–38
  public attitudes toward   140–42
  raiding and   142–47
  redistribution of   149
  relations between the center and provinces and   136–37, 145–46
  renationalization of   147–48
  in the Russian regions   138–39
  in Soviet Union   88, 133–34
  struggle for land   143–44
  weakness and precariousness of rights to   142
Private security
  criminals and   177
  FSB and   179–80

gated communities and   181
  legal   179–80
  in the Middle Ages   30, 173–75, 179, 190
  in modern society   175–76
  people in media, science, the arts and   180
  in post-Soviet Russia   176–77
  private detectives and   180
  private protection organizations as a type of   176–80
  roof (or krysha) and   174, 176–77, 180
  semilegal   178
  weakness of the state and   30, 175, 181
Privatization   18, 39, 42, 63–64, 73, 76, 80–81, 113, 139–42, 148, 157, 166–70, 176–77, 189, 224–25, 232, 236

Rent-seeking activity
  buying offices and   56
  in the Middle Ages   65
  in Russia   60–61, 65, 125, 186–87
  theory of   56
Rome   21, 22
Rosneft   61, 92, 148
Russian democracy
  antidemocratic trends of   10, 15
  Communist Party and   120
  as directed   7, 11
  elections and   123–24, 128–29
  as independent   1, 7
  justifications for violating principles of   78
  as managed   1, 7
  media and press freedoms and 129–30
  as middle income   9, 14
  political parties and   128–29
  as sovereign   1–3, 7–8, 14
  transition or transformation of 9, 11
  United Russia and   128–29

Segmented approach   19, 20–24, 33, 183
Siberia   67, 96–97, 103–6, 108–9, 125, 145
Social organizations and institutions   20–22, 28, 56, 153, 160–61, 171, 173, 183, 189
Sociology, social psychology, and social sciences in general   16, 21–22, 28, 154, 156, 183–84
Soviet Union
    collapse of   37–38, 41, 60, 63, 76, 96, 99, 101, 113, 136
    color markets in   58
    ideologues in   8, 24, 99–100
    money in   58
    private plots and houses in   58
    Supreme Council of   32
State Duma   14, 49, 56, 62, 66, 107, 147, 161, 165, 170, 179, 229, 233
Switzerland   162, 175, 214
System analysis   16

Tatarstan   99, 101–2, 112, 121, 123, 128, 130, 138, 170
Terrorism   28, 70
Totalitarianism   8, 18, 22, 99, 167, 227

Transition   7, 9–11, 14, 17–18, 164–65, 183, 215, 225
Transparency International   45, 60
Tuva   67, 102, 138

Union (Alliance) of Right Forces   12
United States
    Civil War in   21
    personal relations in   154, 157
    Revolution in   2, 21
    textbooks in   21, 28, 154, 157, 183
Universalism   9, 10, 16, 22, 29, 155, 184
Ural   103, 106, 115

Vassal relations   26, 29, 151, 153, 159, 165, 184
Vikings   26

Weakness of the state
    causes of   36–37
    inefficiency and   184
    types of   36
World War II   16, 78

Yeltsin regime   4, 12, 37, 100, 162
Yukos   64, 70–71, 89, 91, 148, 211